LETHAL FORCE, THE RIGHT TO LIFE AND THE ECHR

In its case law on the use of lethal and potentially lethal force, the European Court of Human Rights declares a fundamental connection between the right to life in Article 2 of the European Convention on Human Rights and democratic society. This book discusses how that connection can be understood by using narrative theory to explore Article 2 law's specificities and its deeper historical, social and political significance. Focusing on the domestic policing and law enforcement context, the book draws on an extensive analysis of case law from 1995 to 2017. It shows how the connection with democratic society in Article 2's substantive and procedural dimensions underlines the right to life's problematic duality, as an expression of a basic value demanding a high level of protection and a contextually limited provision allowing states leeway in the use of force. Emphasising the need to identify clear standards in the interpretation and application of the right to life, the book argues that Article 2 law's narrative dimensions bring to light its core purposes and values. These are to extract meaning from pain and death, ground democratic society's foundational distinction between acceptable force and unacceptable violence, and indicate democratic society's essential attributes as a restrained, responsible and reflective system.

Lethal Force, the Right to Life and the ECHR

Narratives of Death and Democracy

Stephen Skinner

•HART•
OXFORD • LONDON • NEW YORK • NEW DELHI • SYDNEY

HART PUBLISHING
Bloomsbury Publishing Plc
Kemp House, Chawley Park, Cumnor Hill, Oxford, OX2 9PH, UK
1385 Broadway, New York, NY 10018, USA
29 Earlsfort Terrace, Dublin 2, Ireland

HART PUBLISHING, the Hart/Stag logo, BLOOMSBURY and the Diana logo
are trademarks of Bloomsbury Publishing Plc
First published in Great Britain 2019
First published in hardback, 2019
Paperback edition, 2021

A catalogue record for this book is available from the British Library.

Library of Congress Cataloging-in-Publication data

Names: Skinner, Stephen (Law teacher), author.
Title: Lethal force, the right to life and the ECHR: narratives of death
and democracy / Stephen Skinner.
Description: Oxford, UK; Chicago, Illinois: Hart Publishing, 2019. |
Includes bibliographical references and index.
Identifiers: LCCN 2019007724 (print) | LCCN 2019009139 (ebook) |
ISBN 9781509929542 (ePub) | ISBN 9781849464062 (hardback)
Subjects: LCSH: Law enforcement–Europe. | Police–Complaints against–Europe. |
Right to life–Europe. | European Court of Human Rights. |
Convention for the Protection of Human Rights and Fundamental
Freedoms (1950 November 5). Article 2. | BISAC: LAW / Civil Rights. |
POLITICAL SCIENCE / Political Freedom & Security / Law Enforcement.
Classification: LCC KJC5977 (ebook) | LCC KJC5977.S55 2019 (print) |
DDC 345.24/052–dc23
LC record available at https://lccn.loc.gov/2019007724

ISBN: HB: 978-1-84946-406-2
PB: 978-1-50994-669-3
ePDF: 978-1-50992-953-5
ePub: 978-1-50992-954-2

Typeset by Compuscript Ltd, Shannon

To find out more about our authors and books visit www.hartpublishing.co.uk.
Here you will find extracts, author information, details of forthcoming events
and the option to sign up for our newsletters.

To Catherine

ACKNOWLEDGEMENTS

Several people provided support and advice while I was researching and completing work on this book, and I offer my thanks to them here in a roughly chronological order. Richard Ireland, Ann Sherlock and Michele Papa gave me essential advice and guidance at foundational moments. I am grateful to Richard Hart for believing in my project at the book proposal stage and the anonymous reviewers for their comments on the initial outline. Representatives of Inquest, Justice, and the Council of Europe, as well as Michael O'Boyle and Judge Paul Mahoney at the European Court of Human Rights, kindly fitted me into their busy schedules and provided informative perspectives on police uses of force, the right to life and the ECHR. I thank the firearms officers with the Metropolitan Police Service and Devon and Cornwall Constabulary who made time to talk to me, invited me to observe training, and provided valuable insights into operational realities. The participants in the workshop on 'Lethal Force, Policing and the ECHR: *McCann and Others v UK* at Twenty' that I convened at Doughty Street Chambers in March 2015 provided stimulating discussions of many of the issues addressed in this book, and I am especially grateful to Jonathan Cooper for his support. Toby Fisher of the South African Human Rights Commission kindly kept me informed about the Marikana report and Daniel Machover of Hickman and Rose Solicitors provided a copy of the Third-Party Intervention in the *McCann* case. For giving generously of their time and providing helpful feedback on draft chapters of this book, I wish to thank Brice Dickson, Liz Wicks, Hans Petter Graver and Catherine Dupré. Of course, the usual caveat applies, and any errors are entirely my own. I would also like to thank David Fraser and Cosmin Cercel for their interest in 'the killing book' and their encouragement at pivotal points along the way. My penultimate thanks go to the team at Hart and then Bloomsbury for their work in piloting the manuscript to publication. Lastly and once again I offer my thanks, and dedicate this book, to Catherine for discussing the initial ideas that became a proposal, for bearing with me while the proposal turned into this book and, more precisely, for everything.

BRIEF CONTENTS

TABLE OF CONTENTS

LIST OF ABBREVIATIONS

ECHR	European Convention on Human Rights
ECtHR	European Court of Human Rights
ICCPR	International Covenant on Civil and Political Rights
UDHR	Universal Declaration of Human Rights

TABLE OF CASES

The table lists all cases referred to in the book in alphabetical order for ease of reference. All ECHR cases can be found on the Council of Europe's HUDOC database. Case names are given here with the date of judgment and application number, while in footnotes they are referred to by name and year only. Where a judgment is only available in French, the citation is given in that language. Admissibility decisions and pre-1998 Plenary judgments are indicated as such and Grand Chamber judgments are indicated with the initials [GC].

European Commission of Human Rights

European Court of Human Rights

Other Courts

TABLE OF LEGISLATION

National Provisions

International Treaties and Other Provisions

1

Introduction: From Death to Democracy

On 6 March 1988 soldiers from a British military special forces unit were deployed to support the civil police in Gibraltar as part of an operation to apprehend a group of terrorists, who were thought to have planted a remote-controlled car bomb. When the suspects were located, the police called for military support to carry out the arrest. During the ensuing confrontation, the soldiers shot the suspects dead. Seven years later, and 45 years after the European Convention on Human Rights (ECHR) was signed, the incident resulted in the first judgment by the European Court of Human Rights (ECtHR) in a case about the right to life under Article 2 of the ECHR and the use of lethal force by a Member State of the Council of Europe.[1] This was the landmark ruling in *McCann and Others v The United Kingdom* (27 September 1995).

Article 2 establishes legal protection for the right to life, but that protection is not absolute, as the article makes allowances for the use of lethal force by the state in narrowly defined circumstances of absolute necessity. In *McCann*, the ECtHR faced the task of interpreting and applying this provision, not only for the first time but also in the context of a sensitive case involving one of the Council of Europe's founding members and its response to terrorism. In the introduction to the main legal analysis stage of the *McCann* judgment, the ECtHR began by declaring the importance of the right to life and the scope of the legal protection it can provide, stating that Article 2 'ranks as one of the most fundamental provisions in the Convention' and that (together with Article 3[2]) it 'enshrines one of the basic values of the democratic societies making up the Council of Europe'.[3] The ECtHR also declared that 'in keeping with the importance of this provision

[1] The term 'lethal force' is used to mean force that results in death. Although the terms lethal, deadly and fatal are synonymous, albeit with different roots, the first of these is the predominant term in ECHR law and commentary and is used here for reasons of consistency. The term 'deadly force' appears to be favoured in US legal commentary, while the term 'fatal force' generally seems to be used less frequently. As indicated later in this chapter and discussed in Ch 4, Article 2 law also covers potentially lethal force.

[2] Article 3 ECHR covers the prohibition of torture, and of inhuman and degrading treatment or punishment. Although Article 2 and Article 3 are closely related, and both concern the control of state power and coercive force, this book only discusses Article 2.

[3] *McCann and Others v United Kingdom* (27 September 1995) para 147, echoing on Article 3 *Soering v United Kingdom* (7 July 1989) para 88.

in a democratic society, the Court must, in making its assessment, subject deprivations of life to the most careful scrutiny, particularly where deliberate lethal force is used'.[4] That connection between Article 2 and democratic society was a foundational aspect of the ECtHR's analysis in *McCann* and has been repeated in all subsequent judgments on the right to life and the state's use of force. These have rapidly grown into an extensive body of case law, in which the ECtHR has enlarged Article 2's protective scope to include not only a use of lethal but also potentially lethal force by state agents, as well as the state's legal framework, its planning and control of operations and a duty to investigate deaths. Each of these aspects of the expanded interpretation of Article 2 sets criteria for assessing state compliance with the right to life, but the ECtHR has also interpreted Article 2 to allow a degree of flexibility for state action. As a result, despite the large number of judgments on Article 2 and the array of detail in decisions about what states can and cannot do when using force, the fundamental purpose of the right to life and of its conceptual connection with democratic society has not been evident in terms of core values or rigorous rationales. Rather, the law on the right to life seems to have become more a matter of deducing the technical consequences of proportionate compromise than a driving set of normative standards.

This book examines how the connections between the right to life and democratic society, as declared by the ECtHR, can be understood in Article 2 case law on uses of force in the context of situations like that in *McCann*, namely domestic policing and law enforcement operations involving civil and military agents of the state.[5] This involves exploring why the right to life is said to be a fundamental provision in the ECHR and a basic value of the democratic societies in the Council of Europe, what the ECtHR means when it refers to 'democratic societies', and how the ECtHR uses the connection between the right to life and democratic societies when interpreting and applying Article 2. On that basis, the book considers what Article 2 and the case law on it can tell us about the nature of democratic society in relation to the deprivation and endangerment of life by the state, so as to identify fundamental values that can, it is hoped, be used to reinvigorate and strengthen the development of clear standards in this area of ECHR law.

The book addresses these issues through a combined theoretical and doctrinal analysis. Theoretically, the book draws on narrative theory to provide a

[4] *McCann* para 150.

[5] These terms are used to indicate internal crime prevention, public order, public assistance and security activities by civil police officers and members of military forces acting for the state, as discussed further in Part I.B below. In international law terms, most of these policing activities fall into the category of 'law enforcement': United Nations Code of Conduct for Law Enforcement Officials, adopted by UN General Assembly resolution 34/169 of 17 December 1979 and the United Nations Basic Principles on the Use of Force and Firearms by Law Enforcement Officials, adopted on 7 September 1990 by the Eighth United Nations Congress on the Prevention of Crime and the Treatment of Offenders. On the meanings of police (encompassing a range of state law-enforcement institutions) and policing (encompassing the broad range of their duties and activities) see Ralph Crawshaw, Barry Devlin and Tom Williamson, *Human Rights and Policing: Standards for Good Behaviour and a Strategy for Change* (The Hague, Kluwer Law International, 1998) 18 and Stuart Casey-Maslen and Sean Connolly, *Police Use of Force under International Law* (Cambridge, Cambridge University Press, 2017) 51–52.

conceptual framework for its discussion of Article 2 and related case law. Narrative theory focuses on the ways in which human activity and experience can be represented in an account that is intended to make sense of them by organising their interpretation around a structuring theme in order to convey a particular meaning. Discussed further in Chapter 2, theories of interpretation in ECHR law have addressed the ECtHR's analytical processes and the justification of its judgments in terms of fundamental principles and functional objectives, including democracy,[6] and the concept of narrative itself has already received some attention in human rights scholarship.[7] The aim here though is to complement and enhance these approaches to ECHR law by focusing in detail on a specific right and its interpretation and application by the ECtHR, developing and applying a method of analysis that goes further than those existing interpretive studies by adopting a broader, external and socially situated perspective on ECHR law that engages more closely with its construction and function as a form of narrative.[8] This is undertaken in the context of what is perhaps the greatest challenge to legal reasoning in the human rights field, namely the deprivation of human life by the state in a democratic system.

The book bases its narrative analysis primarily on the work of Robert Cover and Paul Ricoeur. Cover's influential jurisprudential argument was that law needs to be understood in relation to the narratives that locate it in a particular context and value matrix and so give it meaning.[9] This is used here to bring to light the ways in which ECtHR judgments on Article 2 involve narratives about core values and competing interests in terms of democratic society, including both the wider socio-political narratives to which those judgments are connected and the narratives that those judgments constitute. Ricoeur's hermeneutic theory of narrative as a human response to experience examined the layers of representation encompassed within fictional and historical narratives and how they support the production of meaning, as well as the shaping of identity.[10] Ricoeur's work is referred to here in

[6] Such as Steven Greer, *The European Convention on Human Rights: Achievements, Problems and Prospects* (Cambridge, Cambridge University Press, 2006) and George Letsas, *A Theory of Interpretation of the European Convention on Human Rights* (Oxford, Oxford University Press, 2007), considered in Ch 2. Other commentary has to some extent identified the presence of teleological themes or leitmotivs in the ECHR and related case law, such as Jens Meyer-Ladewig, 'The Rule of Law in the Case Law of the Strasbourg Court' in Hermann-Josef Blanke and Stelio Mangiameli (eds), *The European Union After Lisbon: Constitutional Basis, Economic Order and External Action* (Berlin, Springer, 2012) 235 and 248.

[7] Note especially Günter Frankenberg, *Comparative Law as Critique* (Cheltenham, Edward Elgar, 2016).

[8] Note the argument for a culturally aware, 'socially situated' and critical approach to jurisprudence in JM Balkin, 'Understanding Legal Understanding: The Legal Subject and the Problem of Legal Coherence' (1993) 103 *Yale Law Journal* 105, 108–110, 134 and the distinction between external (social theory-oriented) and internal (law-centric) analyses of law and legal interpretation in Ronald Dworkin, *Law's Empire* (London, Fontana, 1986) 12–13.

[9] Robert M Cover, 'Foreword: Nomos and Narrative' (1983) 97 *Harvard Law Review* 4.

[10] Paul Ricoeur (Kathleen McLaughlin and David Pellauer, trans), *Time and Narrative, Volume 1* (Chicago, University of Chicago Press, 1984), first published as *Temps et Récit* (Paris, Editions du Seuil, 1983).

order to deepen engagement with the explicit and implicit narrative components of ECtHR judgments, as well as their processes of configuration and communication of meaning, by using his primarily philosophical theory to develop a fresh (extra-legal) reflective perspective on the ECtHR's decision-making processes. The book is inspired by elements of both theories, which it draws on in tandem to guide the discussion, rather than adhering strictly to the terms of each or seeking to bend ECHR law into either theorist's specific theoretical framework. The main aims here are rather to explore the narrative dimensions of judgments on the right to life and state uses of lethal or potentially lethal force, and the overall significance of Article 2 law, in order to focus on the deeper values and meanings that can be derived from those judgments, and their significance for human rights law and democracy in contemporary Europe.

This turn to narrative theory is not intended to trivialise ECHR law by appearing to suggest that it is a mere linguistic fabrication or literary construction, abstracted to a remote conceptual dimension, and so the book's theoretical reflection is rooted in an in-depth doctrinal analysis of Article 2 and state uses of lethal and potentially lethal force. As ECHR law constitutes the highest human rights system in Europe that responds to and influences concrete experience and practice, it reflects and shapes a reality beyond the text,[11] mediated through the interpretation and judgment of the ECtHR. The book therefore critically discusses the scope of Article 2, including its political, philosophical, historical and legal origins, its connections with other provisions of international law, and its application by the ECtHR. Through an extensive analysis of case law, the book examines how the ECtHR's narratives have supported its extended interpretation of Article 2 to include substantive and procedural dimensions, which have been constructed around the inherent tension in that provision between protecting the right to life and allowing state action in the interests of society, as well as the ECHR requirements of effectiveness, proportionality and respect for subsidiarity. This analysis shows the importance of the ECtHR's connection between Article 2 and democratic society in developing strong protection for the right to life, whilst making practical – and not unproblematic – provision for state conduct in the policing and law enforcement context.

Overall, the book argues that the connections among lethal force, the right to life and democratic society that are identified through its combined theoretical and doctrinal analysis of ECtHR decisions on Article 2 can and should be understood to form the core of this branch of ECHR law.[12] This core encompasses the

[11] 'Human rights are a living force' for Christian Tomuschat, 'Democracy and the Rule of Law' in Dinah Shelton (ed), *The Oxford Handbook of International Human Rights Law* (Oxford, Oxford University Press, 2013) 469.

[12] Note also the brief outline of some doctrinal aspects of this discussion in Stephen Skinner, 'The Core of *McCann*: Lethal Force and Democracy under the European Convention on Human Rights' in Lawrence Early, Anna Austin, Clare Ovey and Olga Chernishova (eds), *The Right to Life under Article 2 of the European Convention on Human Rights: Twenty Years of Legal Developments since McCann v The United Kingdom* (Oisterwijk, Wolf Legal Publishers, 2016) 67–73.

objectives of fostering control of the state, seeking to prevent arbitrary killing, ensuring accountability under the rule of law, and supporting essential qualitative dimensions of state conduct in relation to state agents' behaviour and the intangible implications of state practices. Addressing Article 2 law's experiential bases in the loss of life and serious harm, the book shows how this body of law reflects and expresses democratic society's (self-)defining distinction between acceptable force and unacceptable violence, and how Article 2 law's core objectives can be used to articulate its underlying ethos, in terms of democratic society's distinguishing attributes. Through a cumulative and inductive reading of the case law in narrative terms, the book argues that Article 2 law can ground a normative understanding of democratic society as a system that should be restrained, responsible and reflective. These attributes, it is suggested, can support the establishment of essential guiding principles in this area of ECHR law, to offset the emphasis on pragmatic compromise with a greater clarity of standards. The book thus analyses the role of the right to life in the relationship between death and democracy in the context of state law enforcement, and provides a new critical perspective on the content and contribution of Article 2 law through the lens of its narrative dimensions. To introduce this analysis, Part I of this chapter offers a preliminary outline of the main issues arising under Article 2 and the scope of the discussion, and Part II provides an overview of how the book is developed, chapter by chapter.

I. The Right to Life, Policing and State Power

Although Article 2 ECHR protects the right to life, in its textual formulation it appears to be predominantly about the state's power to kill. The origins, application and significance of Article 2 are explored in depth in Chapters 3–6, but some key introductory points are necessary here to orient the discussion. This section sets out the scope of Article 2 in terms of deprivation of life by the state, the range of cases examined, and the importance of these matters in broader conceptual terms of state power and society.

A. The Right to Life in the ECHR in Outline

The right to life is the most fundamental right. It reflects belief in the paramount value of human life and its protection is the precondition for all other rights. As formulated in Article 2, it is the first substantive right established in the ECHR and, under Article 15, no derogations from it are permitted in peacetime.[13]

[13] Article 15 ECHR on Derogation in Time of Emergency states: '1. In time of war or other public emergency threatening the life of the nation any High Contracting Party may take measures derogating from its obligations under this Convention to the extent strictly required by the exigencies of the

Textually the same today as it was when finalised in 1949, Article 2 ECHR has two parts:

> 1. Everyone's right to life shall be protected by law. No one shall be deprived of his life intentionally save in the execution of a sentence of a court following his conviction of a crime for which this penalty is provided by law.
>
> 2. Deprivation of life shall not be regarded as inflicted in contravention of this Article when it results from the use of force which is no more than absolutely necessary:
>
> (a) in defence of any person from unlawful violence;
> (b) in order to effect a lawful arrest or to prevent the escape of a person lawfully detained;
> (c) in action lawfully taken for the purpose of quelling a riot or insurrection.

Article 2(1) declares that the right to life must be protected by law. This aspect locks the right into the ECHR's fundamental focus and dependence on the rule of law. The wording of Article 2(1) also contains an allowance for the death penalty, which originally reflected ongoing support for capital punishment in the post-war era when it came into force. Under that provision, the only permitted circumstance in which an intentional deprivation of life by the state could be permitted was as a punishment following a criminal trial resulting in the application of a lawful penalty. Article 2(2) establishes that a deprivation of life will not breach the right to life if it is due to an absolutely necessary use of force in a limited range of narrowly defined circumstances. The terms of Article 2 thus involve both protection of the right to life and provision for killing, through capital punishment and law enforcement operations.

By the time of the *McCann* judgment the scope of Article 2(1) had evolved but the meaning of Article 2 was still unclear in the context of lethal force. With regard to Article 2(1), by 1995 most states in the Council of Europe had committed themselves under ECHR Protocol 6 to abolishing the death penalty, although states could still make provision for it in time of war.[14] Consequently, at that stage for most states Article 2(2) indicated the only permissible grounds on which state agents could take life in peacetime. However, despite a number of Commission decisions, the effect of Article 2(2) on state powers to resort to lethal force had yet to be tested before the ECtHR, so the right to life was still an open question in this context in terms of its actual meaning and impact. This is why the judgment was so important.

situation, provided that such measures are not inconsistent with its other obligations under international law; 2. No derogation from Article 2, except in respect of deaths resulting from lawful acts of war, or from Articles 3, 4 (paragraph 1) and 7 shall be made under this provision; 3. Any High Contracting Party availing itself of this right of derogation shall keep the Secretary General of the Council of Europe fully informed of the measures which it has taken and the reasons therefor. It shall also inform the Secretary General of the Council of Europe when such measures have ceased to operate and the provisions of the Convention are again being fully executed'.

[14] Protocol 6 (1983) has been in force since 1985. At the time of writing Russia is the only member to have signed but not ratified it, although it has a moratorium on use of the death penalty.

In *McCann* and the extensive body of case law on the right to life and state uses of force that has been developed subsequently, the ECtHR has refined the meaning of Article 2's terms and expanded its scope beyond its original wording, to include serious life-threatening but non-lethal force, the planning and control of operations and a duty to investigate incidents engaging state responsibility under this provision. Also, since 1995 the importance of these judgments has been further emphasised by an implicit revision of Article 2(1). This is due to the abolition of the death penalty in all circumstances by the majority of Council of Europe members under Protocol 13.[15] Reading that Protocol together with Article 2's non-derogable status in time of peace, the ECtHR has held in its case law on Article 3 (on the prohibition of inhuman and degrading treatment and punishment) that Article 2(1) has in effect been amended so as to entail a total prohibition of the death penalty and an absolute injunction to protect the right to life by law.[16] Given that the deprivation of life as a penalty following a judicial process is no longer allowed in the Council of Europe, Article 2(2) therefore now covers the only ways in which deprivation and grave endangerment of life may be permissible following action by a Member State, not in circumstances involving a court process, trial or conviction, but in the context of state agents' conduct (including actions and reactions) in the largely unpredictable and circumstantially contingent field of law enforcement activities.

Furthermore, it is important to note that the development of Article 2 law has taken place since 1995 in a shifting political landscape in the Council of Europe. In the early years of the ECHR the signatory states (High Contracting Parties) were fewer in number and generally similar in terms of the quality of their democracy and internal conditions, even though they included both established democracies and countries that had previously been dictatorships. As membership of the Council of Europe has increased, especially since the admission of former Communist states in the early 1990s, the increasingly wide range of internal conditions in High Contracting Parties has brought significant challenges. Article 2 law has thus been developed in response to uses of force in very different policing and security contexts. These have included generally pacific states with long-standing democracies, newer democracies with varying degrees of stability, and states with more contestable political credentials at the Eastern and South-Eastern fringes of the Council of Europe as well as large-scale internal problems of political turmoil and insurrection. Consequently, the ECtHR has had to develop a body of European human rights law in the name of democratic society and the rule of law for radically diverse national systems and conditions. Applying Article 2 in

[15] Protocol 13 (2002) has been in force since 2003. At the time of writing Russia and Azerbaijan have not signed Protocol 13; Armenia has signed but not ratified it.

[16] See *Al-Saadoon and Mufdhi v United Kingdom* (2010) para 120 and Bernadette Rainey, Elizabeth Wicks and Clare Ovey (eds), *Jacobs, White & Ovey: The European Convention on Human Rights* (Oxford, Oxford University Press, 2017) 151. In the EU context, this prohibition is echoed in Article 2.2 of the Charter of Fundamental Rights of the European Union (2012/C 326/02).

these divergent circumstances means that the ECtHR has to decide whether or not democratic (and in some cases what might diplomatically be called 'less than democratic') states have taken life or endangered it in a way that is compatible with ECHR standards that are supposed to support democracy. For these legal and contextual reasons, therefore, the ECtHR's development of its interpretation and application of Article 2 in relation to state uses of force, and in terms of the narrative theme of a connection between the right to life and the concept of democratic society, demands close attention.

B. Domestic Policing and Law Enforcement Operations under Article 2 ECHR

In December 1993 a disturbed young man and his girlfriend, whom he had been holding hostage in their flat, were shot dead in Paphos by a police special operations team armed with automatic weapons. In an attempt to end the siege, the officers burst into the flat and opened fire in the belief that the man was about to use a weapon against them or his captive.[17] In September 1995, police in Athens tried to stop a man who had driven his car through a security road block, resulting in a chaotic chase during which firearms were discharged, injuring him and endangering his life.[18] In July 1996 in Londonderry during a 'major disturbance', involving clashes between protesters and the police, an armoured personnel carrier was used to clear barricades, crushing a man who fell underneath it.[19] In March 2000 in Thessalonica, a police officer inadvertently discharged his weapon during an arrest, killing the young man he was trying to restrain.[20] In July 2001 in Genoa a police officer fired his gun to warn off a group of people attacking the vehicle in which he was sheltering, but the bullet apparently ricocheted and killed one of them.[21] In July 2005 in London, police officers acting in the belief that they were dealing with a terrorist suicide bomber shot a man dead in a case of mistaken identity.[22] In each of these incidents, as in the *McCann* case, state agents involved in domestic policing and law enforcement activities in a European country killed a person, or seriously endangered life. The examples highlight the challenges of policing in circumstances of differing degrees of difficulty, including the strains of facing armed crime and terrorism, especially the acute fear and danger of a suspected suicide bomber. As such they illustrate the conflicting interests at stake in this sort of case – those of the victim, the state agent and wider society – and the range of complex incidents to which the ECtHR has to apply Article 2.

[17] *Andronicou and Constantinou v Cyprus* (1998).
[18] *Makaratzis v Greece* (2004).
[19] *McShane v United Kingdom* (2002).
[20] *Leonidis v Greece* (2009).
[21] *Giuliani and Gaggio v Italy* (2011).
[22] *Armani da Silva v United Kingdom* (2016).

The cases addressed here can be further specified as follows. In terms of the period covered, the book discusses several ECtHR judgments from September 1995 to December 2017 on Article 2 and uses of force in domestic law enforcement operations, focusing on Grand Chamber rulings and taking into account numerous other decisions, but does not purport to engage with every case on these issues.[23] All of the cases involve operations within a High Contracting Party to the ECHR, carried out primarily by officers of the civil or military police,[24] or by soldiers, in order to prevent or suppress a crime, stop or arrest a suspect, protect themselves or others, maintain public order, or tackle an apparent threat to security.[25] In other words, the focus is on cases involving uses of force in the state's exercise of its domestic policing functions. While some cases involving military force are considered in the discussion, judgments relating to large-scale military interventions and counter-insurgency operations in Turkey and Russia are not addressed.[26]

As noted above and as subsequent chapters explore in more detail, the cases discussed include both lethal force and life-threatening force, which ECHR law addresses under the same set of Article 2 standards, so even though the principal focus is on the deprivation of life, some examples include near-fatal injury, or a use of force that otherwise caused a risk of death. The cases involve persons killed, harmed or endangered – the victim in human rights law terms – in various ways, including persons correctly identified as a threat, persons against whom force is used by mistake (involving mistaken identity or misapprehension of circumstances), and persons unexpectedly affected by a use of force (such as bystanders or other third parties). These cases also encompass planned operations and spontaneous incidents, and almost all of them involve a range of unexpected elements at different stages, affecting both the use of force and its outcomes.

In addition to these cases involving a use of lethal or potentially lethal force by a state agent in the policing context, other Article 2 decisions on positive obligations and investigations relevant to that context have been included.[27] However,

[23] See the table of cases and explanatory note about references. Some pre-1995 Commission decisions are also referred to.

[24] In English the term 'military police' often refers to the internal police body of a branch of the armed forces. Here though it is used to mean the military or paramilitary 'third forces' common in continental Europe, including the French *gendarmerie* and Italian *carabinieri*, which are part of the army.

[25] See n 5 above and note also Paul Tavernier, 'Le recours à la force par la police' in Christian Tomuschat, Evelyne Lagrange, and Stefan Oeter (eds), *The Right to Life* (Leiden, Martinus Nijhoff Publishers, 2010) 41, 43–52 and Casey-Maslen and Connolly, *Police Use of Force under International Law* 51–52, 81.

[26] For discussion of these cases and contexts see Hannah Russell, *The Use of Force and Article 2 of the ECHR in Light of European Conflicts* (Oxford, Hart, 2017) and Onder Bakircioglu and Brice Dickson, 'The European Convention in Conflicted Societies: The Experience of Northern Ireland and Turkey' (2017) 66 *International and Comparative Law Quarterly* 263.

[27] These other cases are discussed in Chs 4 and 5. Cases that have not been included here concern the responsibilities of state agents in relation to fatal road traffic accidents, such as *Voiculescu c Roumanie* (2009) involving a military driver or *Zavoloka c Lettonie* (2009) and *Dâmbean c Roumanie* (2013)

the study excludes cases involving disappearances and deaths following uses of force in custody (or in other forms of state care and control, such as psychiatric hospitals). The issue of disappearances is not included because it is – fortunately – not a general feature of policing and law enforcement activities across the Council of Europe and raises distinct issues that require separate treatment. Similarly, whereas deaths in custody are a significant and all too frequent occurrence across Europe, the legal and theoretical dimensions of cases involving deaths in the care of the state in the context of democratic society are also deemed to require a separate study.[28] Although an analysis of the use of force, human rights and narratives of democratic society in Europe would ideally cover all of these matters, this book has a more specific focus.

Lastly, while this book concentrates on one specific area of ECHR law and is contextually and conceptually focused on European systems within the Council of Europe, it is important to note that Article 2 law has wider international connections and relevance. This is partly because of the global influence of ECHR law, which as the most successful and developed system of human rights law is referred to internationally, including by the UN Human Rights Committee and the Inter-American Court of Human Rights.[29] Moreover, as noted in Chapters 3–5, the ECtHR itself draws on international law, including other international provisions on the right to life, such as the 1948 Universal Declaration of Human Rights and the 1966 International Covenant on Civil and Political Rights, United Nations provisions on the use of force in law enforcement and the prevention and investigation of extra-legal executions,[30] and occasionally key decisions of other international courts. ECtHR judgments are also drawn on at the national level outside Europe, with a notable recent example occurring in South Africa, where the report on the 2012 Marikana mine incident[31] relied on aspects of the law developed under Article 2 ECHR.[32] Consequently, the use of force, ECHR law on the

involving accident investigations by the police. Other cases excluded relate to police investigations of deaths caused by third parties, such as *Velcea et Mazăre c Roumanie* (2009), about the investigation of an off-duty police officer's presence during a homicide, and *Abdullah Yilmaz c Turquie* (2008), about army officers' responsibilities for a conscript who committed suicide during military service.

[28] On disappearances and deaths in custody see Rainey, Wicks and Ovey, *Jacobs, White & Ovey: The European Convention on Human Rights* 158–161.

[29] See Tavernier, 'Le recours à la force par la police' 61–63.

[30] United Nations Code of Conduct for Law Enforcement Officials, United Nations Basic Principles on the Use of Force and Firearms by Law Enforcement Officials, and United Nations Principles on the Effective Prevention and Investigation of Extra-Legal, Arbitrary and Summary Executions, adopted on 24 May 1989 by Economic and Social Council Resolution 1989/65. Note also Tavernier, 'Le recours à la force par la police' 47–48, 55–56.

[31] IG Farlam, PD Hemraj and BR Tokota, *Marikana Commission of Inquiry: Report on Matters of Public, National and International Concern Arising out of the Tragic Incidents at the Lonmin Mine in Marikana, in the Northwest Province* (Pretoria, 31 March 2015). Note Casey-Maslen and Connolly, *Police Use of Force under International Law* 396–398.

[32] The report was the result of an investigation into the events of August 2012 at the Lonmin platinum mine in Marikana where during industrial action the police opened fire and killed around 44 striking miners and injured around 70 others. In its discussion of the relevant law, the report refers to the

right to life and the question of democratic society in the European context as discussed here are interconnected with similar issues arising around the world.[33] In more general theoretical terms, these commonalities in discussions of the right to life and the use of lethal force are due to a shared concern with deprivation of life through the state's exercise of its monopoly of force and the extent to which it is, and can remain, lawful and legitimate.

C. Lethal and Potentially Lethal Force, Policing and State Power

At the risk of stating the obvious, it is essential not to lose sight of the fact that by definition, the use of lethal force by a state agent against another human being results in death, the negation of human life. As such it is the most serious and irreparable action a state can take, for which there can be no adequate or effective remedy.[34] Even when a state agent uses potentially lethal force, it can result in severe life-changing injury, or at least a risk of death even if no physical harm is caused. The right to life and its protection thus involve situations in which the deployment of state power risks not merely interfering with an individual's enjoyment of a right but ending her or his very existence. In addition, it is important to recall that causing a death or near-deadly harm or danger can result in severe emotional and psychological harm to others, including relatives, witnesses and bystanders, possibly also the state agents themselves, and in some cases the wider public. Very simply therefore, the impact and effect of this specific exercise of state power are what make it, and the law and legal processes relating to it, so problematic and so significant.

In addition to its impact, the state's use of lethal and potentially lethal force in exercising domestic policing and law enforcement powers involves a defining feature of the state itself, which Max Weber famously expressed as its monopoly of

decision of the Transkei High Court in the case of *Ntamo and Others v Minister of Safety and Security* (2001 (1) SA 830 (Tk HC); *Marikana Commission of Inquiry*, paras 5.7–5.19) in which it was held that in determining the proportionality of police lethal force in relation to the right to life under the South African Constitution, the principles established by the ECtHR provided 'informative and useful' guidance (2001 (1) SA 830 paras 36–38; *Marikana Commission of Inquiry*, para 5.10). This was based on the 1996 South African Constitution, s 39(1), which states that when interpreting the Bill of Rights, a court must consider international law and may consider foreign law, and s 233 states that when interpreting legislation, a court must prefer any reasonable interpretation consistent with international law: note John Dugard, 'International Law and the South African Constitution' (1997) *European Journal of International Law* 77, 84–85. The High Court in *Ntamo* referred to the planning and control responsibility of state authorities as established in *McCann* and confirmed in *Andronicou and Constantinou*, applying it to the case in hand and so adopting it as part of South African law, which was then relied on by the Commission in the Marikana report (*Marikana Commission of Inquiry*, para 5.19).

[33] Other examples are noted in the discussion in Ch 7.

[34] See also Stuart Casey-Maslen, 'The Use of Firearms in Law Enforcement' in Stuart Casey-Maslen (ed), *Weapons Under International Human Rights Law* (Cambridge, Cambridge University Press, 2014) 3.

the legitimate use of force.[35] The exercise of that monopoly is inherently related to the value system that underpins the social, political and legal order.[36] Policing and law enforcement powers lie at the centre of liberal-democratic social contract assumptions, involving the supposed formation of political community to protect liberty and order by ceding protection thereof to the state within limits.[37] In that sense a key theoretical basis of modern democratic societies is that civilised social order requires the individual right to use force – except for self-defence or the defence of others in extremis[38] – to be replaced by the state's monopoly, which in Weber's interpretation would be legitimate if based in legality, that is, reliance on law. The state's monopoly over the use of force will only be legitimate in a broader socio-political sense though if perceived to be exercised for good reasons, in accordance with the rule of law and not arbitrarily.[39] The legitimacy of state uses of force in the democratic context therefore depend, in theory, on both law and a correlation between state practice and socio-political expectations of good government. Yet it has to be noted that, as Mark Neocleous has argued, social order is not universally or naturally civilised and pacific and can be seen to be largely dependent on the state's police power to guarantee the conditions in which some sort of a social contract can even exist.[40]

In the democratic context, given both the theoretical role of the state as a means for protecting the socio-political community it structures, and arguably

[35] Max Weber, 'Politics as a Vocation' in HH Gerth and C Wright Mills (eds), *From Max Weber: Essays in Sociology* (London, Routledge, 1991) 77, 78. Note also PAJ Waddington, *Policing Citizens: Authority and Rights* (London, UCL Press, 1999) 30; Maurice Punch, *Shoot to Kill: Police Accountability, Firearms and Fatal Force* (Bristol, The Policy Press, 2011) 2–3 and Casey-Maslen and Connolly, *Police Use of Force under International Law* 4–5.

[36] Note also the introductory discussion in Maurice Punch, Ralph Crawshaw and Geoffrey Markham, 'Democratic Principles and Police Fatal Force: Avoidance of Debate, Unresolved Accountability and Human Rights' (2016) 46 *International Journal of Law, Crime and Justice* 2, 2–4. On the state as a reflection of values see Kenneth Dyson, *The State Tradition in Western Europe: A Study of an Idea and Institution* (Martin Robertson, Oxford, 1980) 206. For a comparative historical perspective on these questions note also Stephen Skinner, 'Criminal Law and the Use of Force: Ideology and State Power in Fascist Italy and England in the Interwar Period' in Stephen Skinner (ed), *Ideology and Criminal Law: Fascist, National Socialist and Authoritarian Regimes* (Oxford, Hart, forthcoming) Ch 14.

[37] More concretely, for a brief historical outline of aspects of modern policing see Casey-Maslen and Connolly, *Police Use of Force under International Law* 10–50.

[38] As well as, in some systems such as England and Wales, the entitlement to use reasonable force in the prevention of crime.

[39] For a critical reflection on Weber's interpretation in this regard see Anthony E Bottoms and Justice Tankebe, 'Police Legitimacy and the Authority of the State' in Antje du Bois-Pedain, Magnus Ulväng and Petter Asp (eds), *Criminal Law and the Authority of the State* (Oxford, Hart, 2017) 47.

[40] Mark Neocleous, *War Power, Police Power* (Edinburgh, Edinburgh University Press, 2014) 127–32, 136–37. Compare Norbert Elias, who suggested in more general terms that the impetus of societies towards centralised states with monopolies of internal force engendered a civilizing process and a reduction in violence: *The Civilizing Process: Volume 2 – State Formation and Civilization* (Oxford, Basil Blackwell, 1982) 235–39. Experience shows though that civilization and an absence of violence are not coterminous, even in democracies: John Scott and Gordon Marshall, *The Oxford Dictionary of Sociology* (Oxford, Oxford University Press, 2009) 209; Samy Cohen, 'Introduction: Dilemmas in the War against Terrorism' in Samy Cohen (ed), *Democracies at War against Terrorism: A Comparative Perspective* (Basingstoke, Palgrave Macmillan, 2008) 1, 3–5.

implicit (although not absolute) ideological connections among democracy, consensual government, equality before the law and the goal of (predominantly) peaceful co-existence within society,[41] the use of force in policing illustrates inherent tensions. According to Egon Bittner in his influential study of the police (albeit from an American perspective), that institution is 'a corps of specially deputized officials endowed with the exclusive monopoly of using force contingently'.[42] In that sense, as highlighted by other studies of police and policing, the agent charged with exercising that monopoly on behalf of the state is given discretionary powers to compel and coerce compliance, or to act to eliminate a threat. That is, the agent is empowered to use force in ways that would otherwise generally be forbidden for ordinary members of society,[43] subject to the law and his or her individual judgement, with a consequent impact on the scope of others' rights and freedoms,[44] or even their existence. The state agent's ability to use force thus highlights the power of the state and the imbalance between it and those against whom it is deployed. Consequently, the state's monopoly of force can ultimately override other apparent values in the democratic context. This leads to a problematic question, as asked by Bittner: 'How can we arrive at a favourable or even accepting judgement about an activity which is, in its very conception, opposed to the ethos of the polity that authorizes it?', and '… on what terms can a society dedicated to peace institutionalize the exercise of force?'[45] Although it would be more accurate to refer to 'a society supposedly and in principle dedicated to peace', and cultures of policing vary across the societies that make up the Council of Europe, the fundamental issue raised by Bittner goes to the heart of the democratic social contract and the challenge of managing the conceptual and practical tension between the idea of democracy as an association of right-bearers, and the need for organised force in the hands of the state.

[41] Much discussion of the link between democracy and peace is focused on external relations and war: see for example Alison Duxbury, *The Participation of States in International Organisations: The Role of Human Rights and Democracy* (Cambridge, Cambridge University Press, 2011) 60–61; James Crawford, 'Democracy and International Law' (1993) 64 *British Yearbook of International Law* 113; and Todd Landman, *Human Rights and Democracy: The Precarious Triumph of Ideals* (London, Bloomsbury, 2013) 136–37.

[42] Egon Bittner, *The Functions of the Police in Modern Society – A Review of Background Factors, Current Practices, and Possible Role Models* (New York, Jason Aronson, 1975) 46. Bittner's approach has though been challenged: for example, Jean-Paul Brodeur, 'Police et coercition' (1994) 35 *Revue française de sociologie* 457.

[43] For example, PAJ Waddington, 'Public Order Policing: Citizenship and Moral Ambiguity' in Frank Leishman, Barry Loveday and Stephen P Savage (eds), *Core Issues in Policing* (London, Longman, 1996) 114.

[44] Waddington, *Policing Citizens* 20–30; Quirine Eijkman, 'A Socio-Legal Perspective on Human Rights and Policing' (2007) 25.1 *Netherlands Quarterly of Human Rights* 5; Trevor Jones, Tim Newburn and David J Smith, *Democracy and Policing* (London, Policy Studies Institute, 1994) 1; Crawshaw, Devlin and Williamson, *Human Rights and Policing*, 35–36.

[45] Bittner, *The Functions of the Police in Modern Society*, 46–47. As addressed in F Jobard, 'Comprendre l'Habilitation à l'Usage de la Force Policière' (2001) 25.3 *Déviance et Société* 325, the dilemma identified by Bittner may be lessened to the extent that the use of force is only a potential attribute of policing.

In that light, a further key point here involves the role of law in circumscribing state power and supporting the legitimacy of its deployment. As discussed in Chapters 3 and 6, the rule of law in the democratic context is the principal mechanism for grounding, limiting and legitimating the exercise of state power. Human rights norms under the ECHR and their application are a vital part of that mechanism. As a legal expression of fundamental values, and a trans-national framework for holding the state to account for conduct interfering with those values to the detriment of individuals, ECHR law is a crucial element and expression of the hypothetical social contract, and the rule of law over arbitrary power. Combining legal permissibility with evaluation of the correspondence between state conduct and socio-political values, human rights law addresses elements of both legality and legitimacy, which are essential to democracy. This is nowhere more important than in the state's use of lethal or potentially lethal force in policing and law enforcement activities, which in the absence of robust accountability mechanisms can raise concerns about covert execution and the abuse of power.[46]

At the same time, human rights law and its effect on legality and legitimacy can affect the operational capacity of state agents in democratic societies.[47] The application of human rights law to state policing and law enforcement operations may confirm, expand and curtail the parameters for the use of force, thus shaping the state's capability to prepare for, respond to and manage situations in which force may be needed.[48] Human rights – specifically Article 2 ECHR – are therefore a fundamental determinant of the state's domestic policing powers and its ability to perform some of its core functions.[49] In short, this area of human rights law has numerous implications in the democratic context, involving questions of life and death, the legitimacy and limits of state power, and the nature of society's politico-legal values and priorities.

II. Outline by Chapter

As the first substantive chapter, Chapter 2 lays the foundations for the rest of the book by establishing its approach to narrative analysis and showing why this is relevant in the study of human rights law. The chapter introduces the concept of narrative by outlining how it has been discussed in historiographical and legal theory, including semiotic and interdisciplinary approaches to law. It then turns

[46] For example, this point is highlighted in a reflection on the *McCann* case in 'The Observer Files – This week in 1988', *The Observer*, 11 March 2018, 60.

[47] Note also Punch, Crawshaw and Markham, 'Democratic Principles and Police Fatal Force' 2–4.

[48] Compare Peter Squires and Peter Kennison, *Shooting to Kill? Policing, Firearms and Armed Response* (Chichester, Wiley-Blackwell, 2010) 193–94.

[49] Juliet Chevalier-Watts, 'A Rock and a Hard Place: Has the European Court of Human Rights Permitted Discrepancies to Evolve in their Scrutiny of Right to Life Cases?' (2010) 14.2 *The International Journal of Human Rights* 300.

to the book's two main theoretical points of reference, which as noted above are the jurisprudential work of Robert Cover on how law needs to be understood in relation to wider networks of meaning, and the hermeneutic theory of Paul Ricoeur on the narrative structure of fiction and historiography. In its second part, Chapter 2 underlines the relevance of narrative analysis to human rights law by considering the layers of meaning that are embodied in human rights norms; the reasoning, adjudication and accountability processes through which rights are interpreted and applied; and the framework of principles and requirements in ECHR law, which are used to indicate how legal narrative plays a distinct role in its development.

Turning to the specifics of the book's subject matter, Chapter 3 discusses the ECtHR's foundational statement in *McCann* about the right to life as a fundamental provision of the ECHR and an expression of a basic value of the democratic societies making up the Council of Europe. Chapter 3's first part discusses key elements of the genesis of the right to life in the ECHR, focusing on the significance of the idea of a right to life and of legal protection for rights in relation to state power, and the development of the ECHR as a foundational instrument in post-war European democracy building. In its second part Chapter 3 addresses the concept of democratic society as the narrative theme in Article 2 case law, arguing that it has three overlapping meanings: a partially descriptive and legitimating representation of democracy and democratic standards in Europe, an interpretive principle in ECHR law involving proportionate balance in determining the scope of human rights, and a normative concept for developing the meaning of rights.

On that basis, Chapters 4–5 demonstrate how through the interpretation and application of Article 2, narratively configured in terms of democratic society, the ECtHR has produced a set of substantive and procedural standards for the state's resort to lethal and potentially lethal force that reflect the inherent tension in the right to life. Chapter 4 focuses on the substantive dimensions of Article 2 and examines how the ECtHR has relied on that right's nexus with democratic society both to refine and extend its scope, and to allow a significant degree of flexibility in its application. Chapter 5 continues this analysis by examining how and why the ECtHR has extended the meaning of Article 2 to include a procedural dimension, namely a duty to investigate deaths. The chapter explores the components of this duty, again underlining how the nexus with democratic society serves both to support standards for state accountability, whilst allowing flexibility in the democratic context.

Chapter 6 reflects on the degree of apparent flexibility in the substantive and procedural dimensions of Article 2 law discussed in Chapters 4–5, and on that basis turns to look more closely at the deeper purposes and values that can be identified in the ECtHR's case law on the right to life in relation to democratic society. The chapter focuses on two sets of issues: the importance of the rule of law and the qualitative aspects of democracy. The first encompasses core concerns with controls over state power under the rule of law and the prevention of arbitrariness that underpin leading Article 2 judgments, and the second includes the ECtHR's concerns with the behavioural preconditions for rights protection, issues of public confidence, and values of humanity and sensitivity in right to life cases.

Chapter 7 discusses how the principal points from the analysis in Chapters 2–6 can be combined to form an overarching interpretation of the ECtHR's narratives of the relationship between the right to life and democratic society in the context of state uses of force. The chapter considers the significance of the physical and emotional impact of state uses of force in relation to the possibility of meaning-making through law, and the function of human rights law in distinguishing between acceptable and unacceptable force by constructing a justificatory narrative that seeks to confirm democracy's self-understanding. The chapter then argues that taken together, the Article 2 narratives indicate the essential attributes of democratic societies, as systems that must be restrained, responsible and reflective. These attributes, it is suggested, can usefully ground a sense of Article 2 law's fundamental ethos and strengthen the purposive thrust of protecting the right to life by law.

Chapter 8, the Conclusion, outlines the key contributions of the book's dual theoretical and doctrinal analysis, reflects on its potentially wider relevance with regard to other aspects of Article 2 and ECHR law, and points to some areas of discussion that are touched on in the book but which need further exploration. The Conclusion ends by noting the current period of uncertainty in Europe, including major challenges to democratic society and its core values, including adherence to the foundational nature of universal human rights that have been at the heart of the post-war goals to achieve and maintain peace and justice. In this volatile context, reflecting on the narrative function of human rights law, the protection of the right to life by law, and what both of them reveal about democratic identity has never been more relevant or urgent.

2

Narrative and Human Rights Law

This chapter establishes the theoretical bases and rationales for the book's analysis of the connections among lethal and potentially lethal force, the right to life and democratic society under Article 2 ECHR in terms of narrative theory. As indicated in Chapter 1, the book's conceptual framework for exploring Article 2 law is based primarily on Robert Cover's reflection on the location of legal meaning in narrative,[1] together with Paul Ricoeur's philosophical study of the components and functions of narrative.[2] This approach is intended to begin to develop a socio-politically and culturally 'thick'[3] critical analysis of Article 2 law's layers of meaning, and its meaning-making processes and purposes. As Paul Kahn argued, '[i]f we approach law's rule as the imaginative construction of a complete worldview, we need to bring to its study those techniques that take as their object the experience of meaning',[4] and it is suggested here by extension techniques for addressing the development of meaning, especially legal and therefore by implication authoritative meaning, from experience. Examining Article 2 law through the critical lens of narrative theory thus serves to bring to light how the ECtHR shapes and justifies its judgments by reference to the narrative theme of the right to life's connection with democratic society, the meanings encapsulated within that theme and communicated through it, and their implications.

This discussion of Article 2 law is intended to be complementary to, but 'thicker' than, existing interpretive theories of ECHR law. For example, in his important study of the ECHR system and the ECtHR, Steven Greer noted that '[s]ince the Convention's provisions are abstract and sparse, the key to resolving individual complaints ultimately lies in how the text is interpreted'.[5] He analysed how the ECtHR's interpretive practice draws on the ECHR and related principles to resolve disputes and justify its rulings, based on a 'formal and hierarchical structure' of

[1] Robert M Cover, 'Foreword: Nomos and Narrative' (1983) 97 *Harvard Law Review* 4.

[2] Paul Ricoeur (Kathleen McLaughlin and David Pellauer, trans), *Time and Narrative, Volume 1* (Chicago, University of Chicago Press, 1984).

[3] In the sense established by Clifford Geertz, *The Interpretation of Cultures* (London, Fontana Press, 1993 [1973]). See further fn 51 and related text.

[4] Paul W Kahn, *The Cultural Study of Law: Reconstructing Legal Scholarship* (Chicago, The University of Chicago Press, 1999) 2.

[5] Steven Greer, *The European Convention on Human Rights: Achievements, Problems and Prospects* (Cambridge, Cambridge University Press, 2006) 193–94.

what he terms primary and secondary constitutional principles.[6] Greer presents this structure as a form of reading grid through which ECtHR decisions about the interpretation and application of the ECHR can be understood. That is, his analysis focuses on the internal working of the ECHR legal order and how judicial choices are made in selecting and relying on competing principles. Similarly addressing the ECtHR's interpretive practices, George Letsas developed a theory of ECHR law that concentrated on the need for ECtHR decisions to be justifiable in a way that respects that system's normative foundations.[7] This was based on the view that the essence of human rights under the ECHR is their legal and liberal nature, such that 'they entail liberal egalitarian principles that impose conditions on the legitimate use of coercion by Member States against persons within their jurisdiction'.[8] Discussing coercion in a more general sense of the state's exercise of power (rather than in relation to law enforcement specifically), Letsas's analysis thus focuses on a (primarily Dworkinian) jurisprudential concern with how the ECtHR exercises its discretion in determining and justifying how a right in the ECHR should be applied to a case, and which principles should shape that application.[9]

While this book's approach in terms of narrative theory similarly addresses the ECtHR's interpretation of the ECHR and related principles to resolve disputes, and is embedded in a close study of Article 2 law, it has been developed with a view to achieving (to paraphrase Kahn again) an 'imaginative act of separation' and thus a critical distance[10] from that body of law. The intention is not to consider ECHR law solely as a self-contained normative order, but to explore its layers of signification in the context of the subject matter of Article 2, and to reflect on its deeper purposive sense as a process of constructing meaning from traumatic, life-and-death conflicts between individual and state in order to establish boundaries and develop guidelines for state conduct and public life. In other words, it seeks to consider the function and mode of functioning of human rights law under Article 2 ECHR, as well as what meaning that law can be understood to bear and to produce in this specific context. To introduce this approach in terms of narrative theory in more detail this chapter begins by tracing the lineage of narrative analysis from its roots in historiography and its development in jurisprudence, before focusing on the theories of Cover and Ricoeur. The chapter turns in its second part to reflect on and underline the relevance of a narrative approach to human rights law by identifying its main narrative aspects in general terms, as well as in the ECHR system specifically.

[6] Greer, *The European Convention on Human Rights* 194–230.

[7] George Letsas, *A Theory of Interpretation of the European Convention on Human Rights* (Oxford, Oxford University Press, 2007).

[8] Letsas, *A Theory of Interpretation of the European Convention on Human Rights* 5, also 38–40.

[9] Letsas, *A Theory of Interpretation* 100–102; see also Ronald Dworkin, *Taking Rights Seriously* (London, Bloomsbury, 2011 [1977]).

[10] Kahn, *The Cultural Study of Law* 3.

I. Narrative Analysis and its Theoretical Foundations

Across the human and social sciences, narratives are understood to be a fundamental feature of human culture and efforts to comprehend experience. As Donald Polkinghorne put it in his study of 'narrative knowing':

> Our encounter with reality produces a meaningful and understandable flow of experience. What we experience is a consequence of the action of our organizing schemes on the components of our involvement with the world. Narrative is the fundamental scheme for linking human actions into interrelated aspects of an understandable composite … Narrative displays the significance that events have for one another.[11]

Narrative can in this way be understood as an essential aspect of humanity, and the individual and social ways in which meaning is made about life. When applied to forms of human expression and science, the concept of narrative encompasses a number of possible meanings, which as Greta Olson has recently emphasised need to be understood as inter-related but separate.[12] As she explains, in its specific sense 'narrative' indicates an account of human activity and experience, told by a narrator for a purpose, but it can also be used to indicate specific aspects of that concept and related processes, including 'narration', which indicates the telling of that narrative and 'narrativity', which indicates the 'degree to which a text or object possesses qualities … that lead people to treat and engage with it as narrative'.[13] It is also important to note that a narrative involves both the 'story' of facts and their sequence,[14] as well as aspects of form, or how the story is told.[15]

[11] Donald E Polkinghorne, *Narrative Knowing and the Human Sciences* (Albany, State University of New York Press, 1988) 13. See also Günter Frankenberg, *Comparative Law as Critique* (Cheltenham, Edward Elgar, 2016) 168 on the psychological assumption that 'human beings give their life sense and meaning by rendering their experience in the form of a story'.

[12] Greta Olson, 'On Narrating and Troping the Law: The Conjoined Use of Narrative and Metaphor in Legal Discourse' in Michael Hanne and Robert Weisberg (eds), *Narrative and Metaphor in the Law* (Cambridge, Cambridge University Press, 2018) 19, 23–25.

[13] Olson, 'On Narrating and Troping the Law' 25.

[14] Jane B Baron and Julia Epstein, 'Is Law Narrative?' (1997) 45 *Buffalo Law Review* 141, 147 also note that 'narrative' is a broader term for conveying the interpretation and meaning-making process that can be identified on a smaller scale in an individual 'story'.

[15] In narratology the form of a narrative can be referred to as discourse, although usage of the two terms is not always clear cut. In linguistic theory narrative and discourse do not appear to have generally recognised or determined meanings and have been both differentiated and interlinked. While discourse is generally considered to indicate use of language involving more than a sentence, it has also been interpreted as a more speaker- and context-specific language-use that can be distinguished from narrative in grammatical terms: Émile Benveniste, (Mary E Meek, trans), *Problems in General Linguistics* (Coral Gables, University of Miami Press, 1971). Other approaches consider that narrative and discourse are different parts of the same process of representing reality through language, with narrative indicating the story and its content, and discourse indicating how the story is told or narrated: Gérard Genette, (Jane E Lewin, trans) *Narrative Discourse Revisited* (Ithaca, Cornell University Press, 1988) 13–15; Alun Munslow, *Narrative and History* (Basingstoke, Palgrave Macmillan, 2007) 20; and Olson, 'On Narrating and Troping the Law' 25. In relation to law see Peter Goodrich, *Legal Discourse: Studies in Linguistics, Rhetoric and Legal Analysis* (Basingstoke, Macmillan, 1987) who uses the concept of discourse to explore, inter alia, the linguistic and semiotic production of legal meaning. In social and

In this book, the discussion of narrative is based on the idea that it reveals something fundamental about human understanding of the world, and the need to make sense of events and experience by interpreting them in ways that reflect multiple layers of signification, construct connections among them and give them an overall meaning. In its analysis of Article 2 law, the book uses the concept of narrative in this way, in line with the first specific sense noted above, as a purposive account for producing meaning. However, this requires an important caveat in that in the legal sphere meaning is not freely constructed on the basis of perceptions of experience or facts alone but also in terms of a given set of interpretive parameters, the law itself. A legal narrative's production of meaning is therefore a process of interpretation, largely but not always entirely bounded by the applicable norm, related rules of procedure and evidence, and conventions of legal argumentation, which is authoritative due to the socio-political status of law and related institutions.[16] In other words, experience must be filtered through the terms of the law, including human rights norms, which influence the resulting interpretive narrative. This is not to say that the norm and legal mode of reasoning completely determine the narrative, but they are boundaries within which it is constructed.[17] This is, of course, well known to critical lawyers and to critics of the law,[18] but it is useful to recall that it is both law's strength as a specialised mode of analysis and conflict resolution, and its contestable restriction.[19] Analysing the narrative dimensions of law underlines the ways in which meaning is produced in relation to these boundaries and the extent of their permeability.

legal theory, the concept of discourse has also been used in other ways, ranging from synonymy with the whole social system to a specific manifestation of economic relations: note for example the overview in David Howarth, *Discourse* (Buckingham, Open University Press, 2000) 2–8, 49–60. Discourse is perhaps especially associated with the work of Michel Foucault, which grounds David Baker's analysis of lethal force in policing and accountability processes in the UK context in *Deaths After Police Contact: Constructing Accountability in the 21st Century* (London, Palgrave Macmillan, 2016).

[16] Frankenberg, *Comparative Law as Critique* 176–77; Peter Brooks and Paul Gewirtz (eds), *Law's Stories: Narrative and Rhetoric in the Law*, (New Haven, Yale University Press, 1996) 3–6.

[17] Peter Brooks, 'Narrative Transactions – Does the Law Need a Narratology?' (2006) 18.1 *Yale Journal of Law and the Humanities* 1, 20 underlines the controlled nature of legal narrative: 'The law tends to limit and formalize conditions of telling and listening, as if from a suspicion of the force of narratives … The fragmented, contradictious, murky unfolding of narrative in the courtroom is subject to formulae by which the law attempts to impose rule on story, to limit its free play and extent'. Note also David Kennedy, 'The International Human Rights Movement: Part of the Problem?' (2001) 3 *European Human Rights Law Review* 245, 258–60 who argues that a focus on human rights law as a source and reflection of certain knowledge about socio-political ideals and justice has inherent limits, in that it rigidly reduces the range of possible developmental paths for different communities and shuts down the potential for discursive growth through other means.

[18] See for example Scott Veitch, *Law and Irresponsibility: On the Legitimation of Human Suffering* (Oxford, Routledge-Cavendish, 2007) 76–77; Michael Freeman, *Human Rights: An Interdisciplinary Approach* (Cambridge, Polity Press, 2011) 8 and Amartya Sen, 'Human Rights and the Limits of Law' (2006) 27.6 *Cardozo Law Review* 2913, 2914 and 2927.

[19] Susan Marks, 'False Contingency' (2009) 62.1 *Current Legal Problems* 1, 10 and 'Human Rights and Root Causes' (2011) 74.1 *Modern Law Review*, 57, 74–75.

A. Antecedent Approaches to Narrative and Law

Narratives in human experience have multiple manifestations[20] and they have been explored through numerous theoretical approaches in the humanities and social sciences, including jurisprudence.[21] In general terms, the work of the historian and historiographer, Hayden White, is often considered to be a key point of origin in the development of narrative studies.[22] His reflections on narrative in the writing of history have been influential on subsequent studies of narrative because of how he underlined the need to consider narrative as both form and an influence on content. For White, 'narrative discourse' involves the representation of reality in ways that supposedly allow its sense to be revealed.[23] As a method of explanation that is embedded in culturally-specific forms of expression and ways of understanding,[24] narrative form shapes narrative content by imposing meaning while purporting to allow it to emerge.[25] White also argued that narratives can convey meaning in terms of their representation of events in a certain order, reaching a particular outcome (the idea of plot), and in terms of the way they focus on a theme, or way of sustaining an argument indicating an overall point.[26]

In similar ways in the legal sphere, narrative has been recognised as central to argumentation (in substantive terms) and rhetoric (in stylistic terms) in advocacy and judgment, and as such has attracted attention from theoretical and interdisciplinary perspectives. For example, Bernard Jackson's landmark study of the semiotics of law discussed the importance of narrative in the representation of facts, the persuasiveness of legal argument and justification, as well as the deep structures of signification in legal analysis.[27] Drawing on White's historiographical work, Jackson also underlined how legal narrative both produces a layer

[20] Roland Barthes (Lionel Duisit, trans), 'An Introduction to the Structural Analysis of Narrative' (1975) 6.2 *New Literary History* 237: 'There are countless forms of narrative in the world'.

[21] A survey of the various approaches in linguistics, literature and social sciences more generally unfortunately falls beyond the scope of this study. However, for an informative annotated bibliography of works on narrative see Corinne Squire et al, *What is Narrative Research?* (London, Bloomsbury, 2014) 115–32. From different disciplinary perspectives see also Polkinghorne, *Narrative Knowing and the Human Sciences* 13–36; Rick Altman, *A Theory of Narrative* (New York, Columbia University Press, 2008) 1–27; and Michael Hanne and Robert Weisberg, 'Introduction: Narrative and Metaphor in the Law' in Hanne and Weisberg (eds), *Narrative and Metaphor in the Law* 1.

[22] Hayden White, *The Content of the Form: Narrative Discourse and Historical Representation* (Baltimore, The Johns Hopkins University Press, 1987).

[23] White, *The Content of the Form* x.

[24] Hayden White (Robert Doran (ed)), *The Fiction of Narrative: Essays on History, Literature, and Theory 1957–2007* (Baltimore, The Johns Hopkins University Press, 2010) xvii–xviii.

[25] White, *The Content of the Form* xi.

[26] Hayden White, 'The Structure of Historical Narrative' in White, *The Fiction of Narrative* 112, 115–20; see also Hayden White, 'Storytelling – Historical and Ideological' in White, *The Fiction of Narrative* 273, 274.

[27] Bernard Jackson, *Law, Fact and Narrative Coherence* (Liverpool, Deborah Charles Publications, 1988), for example 11–12, 18, 92, 155–56.

of meaning that corresponds to objective facts, making them intelligible, and produces another layer of meaning through the creation of a story that is intended to achieve a distinct and additional aim, such as a (substantively and rhetorically) persuasive argument towards a particular interpretation of a norm or outcome of its application.[28]

Furthermore, interdisciplinary legal studies have focused on law's narrative dimensions, following the critical and literary turn in legal analysis, particularly in the United States from the 1970s–80s onwards, that saw the exploration of lawyers' and especially judges' construction of stories come to the fore.[29] Including critical engagement with the language and culture of law as a way of examining how legal meaning is produced,[30] these interdisciplinary studies have focused on the literary, aesthetic and rhetorical dimensions of law as structured storytelling that shapes meaning within particular conceptual and socio- or politico-linguistic frameworks,[31] or in terms of 'narrativity'.[32] A prominent example of this sort of narrative approach to law is an influential study of US Supreme Court decisions by Anthony Amsterdam and Jerome Bruner.[33] In it they offered a synthetic definition of narrative as a socio-cultural concept, closely linked to the way that the human mind and language function, which focuses on human protagonists, the centrality of will and choice, and a particular form of plot.[34] In their view, narrative serves to produce a (legal) meaning that is of relevance both within the story of an

[28] Jackson, *Law, Fact and Narrative Coherence* 157–61. Similarly, on the construction of coherent legal narratives ordering the representation of facts and activities over time, see Neil MacCormick, *Rhetoric and the Rule of Law* (Oxford, Oxford University Press, 2005) 214–36. Ronald Dworkin reflected on law's narrative role in *Law's Empire* (London, Fontana, 1986): note the first page of the 'Preface', vii where he argues 'that legal reasoning is an exercise in constructive interpretation, that our law consists in the best justification of our legal practices as a whole, that it consists in the narrative story that makes of these practices the best they can be'. On the rhetorical (persuasive) aspect of legal narrative see Hans Petter Graver, 'Sense and Sensibility: Classic Rhetoric as a Model for Modern Legal Thinking' (2008) 53 *Scandinavian Studies in Law* 231, 234, 236 and generally Goodrich, *Legal Discourse*.

[29] For useful overviews of this process and key works note Hanne and Weisberg, 'Introduction'; Olson, 'On Narrating and Troping the Law' 19–36; and Shulamit Almog, 'As I Read, I Weep – In Praise of Judicial Narrative' (2001) 26.2 *Oklahoma City University Law Review* 471.

[30] For example, James Boyd White, *Heracles' Bow: Essays on the Rhetoric and Poetics of Law* (Madison, University of Wisconsin Press, 1985) 168, on law's roots in story-telling, or narrative.

[31] Including Cover, 'Foreword: Nomos and Narrative' (discussed in depth in the next subsection); Robin West, 'Jurisprudence as Narrative: An Aesthetic Analysis of Modern Legal Theory' (1985) 60 *New York University Law Review* 145; Richard Delgado, 'Storytelling for Oppositionists and Others: A Plea for Narrative' (1989) 87.8 *Michigan Law Review* 2411; Richard H Weisberg, *Poethics* (New York, Columbia University Press, 1992); Brooks and Gewirtz (eds), *Law's Stories*; Baron and Epstein, 'Is Law Narrative?' 141; Guyora Binder and Robert Weisberg, *Literary Criticisms of Law* (Princeton, Princeton University Press, 2000).

[32] Peter Brooks, 'Narrativity of the Law' (2002) 14.1 *Law and Literature* 1 and 'Narrative Transactions – Does the Law Need a Narratology?' (2006) 18.1 *Yale Journal of Law and the Humanities* 1; compare David Rudrum, 'From Narrative Representation to Narrative Use: Towards the Limits of Definition' (2005) 13.2 *Narrative* 195.

[33] Anthony G Amsterdam and Jerome Bruner, *Minding the Law* (Cambridge, Mass, Harvard University Press, 2000).

[34] Amsterdam and Bruner, *Minding the Law* 115–17.

individual judgment and as a 'moral of the story' that is more widely applicable.[35] In particular, Amsterdam and Bruner highlight the significance of narrative for law in terms of meaning-making in relation to the passage of time, the importance of protagonists' agency, and the need to find a resolution for some sort of disruption or problem,[36] as well as narrative's value in constructing an interpretive story due to its inherent flexibility when compared with purely logical construction and deduction.[37] Consequently, for Amsterdam and Bruner the main point about narrative in the legal context is its usefulness in coping with uncertainty, both in terms of problematic facts requiring adjudication and the inherent need for flexibility and universality in the application of law.

More recently, the significance of narrative has been discussed in relation to human rights law. Focusing on their processes and purposes, Günter Frankenberg has interpreted human rights as narratives 'for exposing the scandals of abuse of power and miserable living conditions'.[38] Using a definition of narrative as 'a story created in a constructive format … joining description, explanation, and argumentation as a further rhetorical mode of discourse', he has considered how legal and judicial narratives involve setting out 'a coherent or plausible story about a series of disparate past events', requiring 'a coherent, or at least plausible, structure provided by reasoned doctrinal elaboration', and above all in relation to human rights, involving 'justificatory arguments' about issues of entitlement and responsibility.[39] Discussing how rights arguments seek to make 'actions or decisions, standards or beliefs' appear to be right or acceptable to others, Frankenberg has underlined how they involve processes of 'ordering the world, by communicating a normative point of view'.[40] Yet, he has observed, such narratives are only ever partial and incomplete, providing a selective, state-centric perspective and not the 'whole story' of the situation in question.[41] Noting the ideological and even (obscure) mythical content and effect of rights narratives, Frankenberg has pointed to their legitimating and educative functions, through which the communication of an interpretation seeks to transmit a worldview and shape understanding.[42] He has thus considered narrative to be an essential concept for capturing what human rights law involves.

[35] Amsterdam and Bruner, *Minding the Law* 113–14, 127.
[36] Amsterdam and Bruner, *Minding the Law* 139–40.
[37] Amsterdam and Bruner, *Minding the Law*, 141.
[38] Frankenberg, *Comparative Law as Critique* 167–72, 167. Note also Catherine Dupré, *The Age of Dignity: Human Rights and Constitutionalism in Europe* (Oxford, Hart, 2015) 13–15, who presented her mapping of key stages in the development of human dignity in the context of European human rights and constitutionalism as a narrative intended 'to reconstruct the connections among these events and bring to light their deeper and more complex significance, and ultimately to make sense of human dignity by telling a fuller story from its origin to its current uses'. In other words, the study of human dignity was itself presented as a narrative, rather than an analysis of narrative in human dignity law.
[39] Frankenberg, *Comparative Law as Critique* 168, 170–72.
[40] Frankenberg, *Comparative Law as Critique* 172–73.
[41] Frankenberg, *Comparative Law as Critique* 176–77.
[42] Frankenberg, *Comparative Law as Critique* 186–89, 195, 197, 199–201.

For all of these approaches, narrative in the legal sphere is fundamentally about the construction of meaning by a narrator from uncertain facts and events, through argumentation and justification, in order to present an interpretation as a certain, persuasive, and thus authoritative representation of reality (in the case in question) with an additional layer of meaning, the point of law that is of more general application.[43] While these approaches inform this book's analysis of Article 2 law, in order to explore more closely the relationship between legal prescriptions and narratives of value, as well as what narrative involves as an interpretive process, the book draws more specifically on two major points of reference in the field of narrative theory, namely the work of Cover and Ricoeur.

B. Robert Cover's Theory of Law and Narrative

Cover's influential work on nomos and narrative[44] is a landmark jurisprudential reflection that offered an original perspective on the ways in which law (in all its forms) needs to be understood in terms of its basis in and connections with narrative. As he argued:

> No set of legal institutions or prescriptions exists apart from the narratives that locate it and give it meaning … Once understood in the context of the narratives that give it meaning, law becomes not merely a system of rules to be observed, but a world in which we live.
>
> In this normative world, law and narrative are inseparably related. Every prescription is insistent in its demand to be located in discourse – to be supplied with history and destiny, beginning and end, explanation and purpose. And every narrative is insistent in its demand for its prescriptive point, its moral. History and literature cannot escape their location in a normative universe, nor can prescription, even when embodied in a legal text, escape its origin and its end in experience, in the narratives that are the trajectories plotted upon material reality by our imaginations.[45]

In Cover's interpretation, understanding law needs to be approached by considering it as a form of narrative and by situating it within a web of narratives about the world, which give law a place, a significance and a force, not only by supporting the meaning of a particular instance of law, but also by supporting acceptance of and reliance on law more generally.[46] Cover referred to the normative world being

[43] Note Jackson, *Law, Fact and Narrative Coherence* 157–61; Amsterdam and Bruner, *Minding the Law* 113–41 and Graver, 'Sense and Sensibility' 234.

[44] Cover's work is described as 'seminal' by Olson, 'On Narrating and Troping the Law' 21 and has inspired numerous narrative studies of law. The focus here is on the introductory theoretical part of Cover's paper, rather than his subsequent examples, which draw on biblical texts and US cases.

[45] Cover, 'Foreword: Nomos and Narrative' 4–5.

[46] Cover, 'Nomos and Narrative' 7–10. Similar approaches can be identified in other studies: for example, JM Balkin, 'Understanding Legal Understanding: The Legal Subject and the Problem of Legal Coherence' (1993) 103 *Yale Law Journal* 105 argued for a culturally and sociologically informed critical jurisprudence; also, Jürgen Habermas argued that law in society needs to be understood in terms

shaped by the 'interpretive commitments' of those determining law's meaning and application, which are in turn shaped by wider narratives of social life, and he argued that '[n]arratives are models through which we study and experience transformations that result' when facts are filtered through an application of rules.[47] Essentially here, law as narrative 'gives reality a shape' and models it in line with the 'world of value' that is implied within that narrative.[48]

Moreover, Cover underlined how legal narrative enables a conceptual movement between a situation in the world of fact and an ideal or teleological aim towards which human conduct may be guided by legal value and principle. Whereas in some contexts, such as in literature or cinema, the concept of narrative can involve an entirely imaginary construction, Cover reminds us that legal and specifically judicial narrative involves a combination of the real and the imagined. Although legal narratives are predominantly based on an assumption that the narrative account corresponds to an objectively discoverable reality, that is, facts and rules in the real world, and that experience can be consequentially interpretable by ordering and evaluating facts and events in the process of retelling, they also contain dimensions shaped by the imagination.[49] This can involve interpretations and representations of past, present and future experience, and the construction of normative interpretations against which reality may be evaluated. For Cover:

> A legal tradition is … part and parcel of a complex normative world. The tradition includes not only a corpus juris, but also a language and a mythos – narratives in which the corpus juris is located by those whose wills act upon it. These myths establish the paradigms for behaviour. They build relations between the normative and the material universe, between the constraints of reality and the demands of an ethic …
>
> Law may be viewed as a system of tension or a bridge linking a concept of a reality to an imagined alternative – that is, as a connective between two states of affairs, both of which can be represented in their normative significance only through the devices of narrative …
>
> The codes that relate our normative system to our social constructions of reality and to our visions of what the world might be are narrative. The very imposition of a normative force upon a state of affairs, real or imagined, is the act of creating narrative.[50]

of its embeddedness in layers of socio-political meaning, which he referred to as discourse: see Jürgen Habermas (William Rehg, trans), *Between Facts and Norms: Contributions to a Discourse Theory of Law and Democracy* (Cambridge, Polity Press, 1996).

[47] Cover, 'Nomos and Narrative' 7, 10.

[48] Julen Etxabe, 'The Legal Universe after Robert Cover' (2010) 4.1 *Law and Humanities* 115, 121. According to Etxabe at 116, 'Robert Cover's metaphor of the legal universe [is] a viable *paradigm of law*, which includes an *ontology* (an understanding of the basic units and organisational structure of law), an *epistemology* (an account of legal knowledge, reasoning and interpretation), an *axiology* (how legal value is created, assessed and maintained), and a *sociology* (how law relates to and fits in the larger non-legal environment)'. Aspects of this article subsequently informed Etxabe's *The Experience of Tragic Judgement* (London, Routledge, 2013), but for present purposes it is the article that is more relevant.

[49] This nexus of law and imagination was also subsequently addressed by Jackson, *Law, Fact and Narrative Coherence* 157–61 and Frankenberg, *Comparative Law as Critique* 195–99.

[50] Cover, 'Nomos and Narrative' 9–10; at 45 Cover states '[c]reation of legal meaning entails, then, subjective commitment to an objectified understanding of a demand … This objectification of the

In this regard, Cover acknowledged the significance of Clifford Geertz's discussion (drawing on the work of Gilbert Ryle) of the method of 'thick description', for exploring how and why forms of human conduct in a social context have specific and stratified cultural meanings, and how they come to be adopted and integrated in a systemic form by human agents.[51] Cover's principal contribution was to argue that law is situated in a narrative matrix which supports its meaning-making processes, stating that 'the creation of legal meaning – "jurisgenesis" – takes place always through an essentially cultural medium'.[52] By pointing to the narratives that ground normative world views and interpretation, Cover underlined how legal narrative can link a perception of what is to a vision of what ought to be, and what might be.[53]

The connection between the normative world and narrative in Cover's theory can be seen to raise not only the question of narratives within law, which locate legal prescription, but also the relationship between legal and non-legal narratives in the wider social context. That is, law's production of meaning, the ways in which it is understood, and its externally perceived validity and legitimacy, also depend on how law is situated in relation to other narratives and layers of signification.[54] As Frankenberg subsequently observed, legal narrative is only ever partial, incomplete and selective,[55] so a key lesson from Cover's theory is the need to consider law in its broader narrative context as well:

> The rules and principles of justice, the formal institutions of the law, and the conventions of a social order are, indeed important to that world [of right and wrong, of lawful

norms to which one is committed frequently, perhaps always, entails a narrative – a story of how the law, now object, came to be, and more importantly, how it came to be one's own'. On Cover's bridge metaphor note also Aviam Soifer, 'Covered Bridges' (2005) 17.1 *Yale Journal of Law and the Humanities* 55.

[51] Cover, 'Nomos and Narrative' 5 fn 7 referring to Geertz, *The Interpretation of Cultures* – note in particular 6–10, 18. See also Frankenberg, *Comparative Law as Critique* 168 on narrative and the influence of Geertzian thick description in comparative law.

[52] Cover, 'Nomos and Narrative' 11. Cover's argument about jurisgenesis and its narrative construction has been drawn on to support an analysis of 'cosmopolitan legal narrative' in supranational European constitutionalism, in which the idea of wider narrative foundations motivates citizens' commitment and fosters law's creativity and 'transformation through time': Paul P Linden-Retek, 'Cosmopolitan Law and Time: Toward a Theory of Constitutionalism and Solidarity in Transition' (2015) 4.2 *Global Constitutionalism* 157, 178–85.

[53] Cover, 'Nomos and Narrative' 7–10. Etxabe, 'The Legal Universe after Robert Cover' 122 suggests that the 'might be' addressed by Cover is a third category of legal possibility beyond the binary categories of 'is' and 'ought'. Cover's examples in developing his analysis partly involved the Bible and religious law, on which see Howard J Vogel, 'In the Cause of Justice: Reflections on Robert Cover's Turn Toward Narrative' (1989) 7 *Journal of Law & Religion* 173.

[54] Kahn, *The Cultural Study of Law* 44 refers to Cover in his discussion of law's authority 'within an historical narrative of the community of which we are a part'. Cover's interpretation has though been criticised for its apparently unrealistic relativism in some respects: see John Alder, 'Robert Cover's "Nomos and Narrative": The Court as Philosopher King or Pontius Pilate?' (2006) 6 *Issues in Legal Scholarship* (article 4; no page numbers – see nn 4–5 and related text); other criticisms of imprecision in Cover's concept of nomos are set out in Thom Brooks, 'Let a Thousand Nomoi Bloom? Four Problems with Robert Cover's "Nomos and Narrative"' (2006) 6 *Issues in Legal Scholarship* (article 5; no page numbers).

[55] Frankenberg, *Comparative Law as Critique* 176–77.

and unlawful]; they are, however, but a small part of the normative universe that ought to claim our attention.[56]

Cover's engagement with 'nomos and narrative' thus demonstrates the need to question and explore how law is based on a relationship between prescription and the rationales, beliefs and values that ground and direct the law's meanings. This involves an interplay between perception of the real and the imaginary and, as Cover underlined, requires law to be considered through a wide contextual lens. Yet the core concept of narrative in Cover's analysis was not fully outlined in his paper, which raises the need for an additional layer of theoretical reflection.

C. Paul Ricoeur's Theory of Narrative

Partly responding to Hayden White's discussion of historiographical narrative and focusing on how meaning is produced in history and fiction, Ricoeur's hermeneutic analysis of narrative is perhaps the most detailed engagement with what it involves. For Ricoeur, narrative is a process for giving meaning to occurrences over time, primarily as a way of making sense of them in relation to their temporality and how this relates to memory and understanding.[57] Linking the mode of historical reflection with the poetics of fiction in order to expose the processes of 'readerly narrative understanding' at stake, Ricoeur's theory of *récit* (meaning story, account or as it is usually translated, narrative) shows how a narrative rooted in human experience is constructed so as to configure a particular meaning and thereby authorise a way of understanding, thus (indirectly echoing Hayden White) blending and supporting what is represented with the way of doing so.[58] It is this aspect of Ricoeur's theory, rather than his focus on temporality, that is drawn on

[56] Cover, 'Nomos and Narrative' 4. See also Michael Ryan, 'Meaning and Alternity' in Martha Minow, Michael Ryan and Austin Sarat (eds), *Narrative, Violence and the Law: The Essays of Robert Cover* (Ann Arbor, The University of Michigan Press, 1995) 267, 271: 'Our narratives, epics, and stories embody our norms, while locating and giving meaning to our legal institutions, but narratives, especially alternative narratives developed by communities and movements, contest the unity of law. They are the open doors at the other end of the hallway, pointing in their trajectories toward other meanings, other possible worlds'.

[57] Ricoeur, *Time and Narrative, Volume 1*, 3 and 52. For a useful supplemental outline see David Pellauer, 'Foreword: Recounting Narrative' in Morny Joy (ed), *Paul Ricoeur and Narrative: Context and Contestation* (Alberta, University of Calgary Press, 1997) ix–xxiii. On time in narrative see also Mario J Valdés, *A Ricoeur Reader: Reflection and Imagination* (Toronto, University of Toronto Press, 1991) 99–116. The potential of Ricoeur's theory for jurisprudence is discussed at a more abstract theoretical level in Marcin Pieniążek, 'The Application of Paul Ricoeur's Theory in Interpretation of Legal Texts and Legally Relevant Human Action' (2015) 28 *International Journal for the Semiotics of Law* 627.

[58] Hans Kellner, '"As Real as it Gets" – Ricoeur and Narrativity' in David E Klemm and William Schweiker (eds), *Meanings in Texts and Actions: Questioning Paul Ricoeur* (Charlottesville, University Press of Virginia, 1993) 49–50, 59.

here, especially his insightful exposition of the interlocking layers of representation through which a narrative is constructed.

In Ricoeur's analysis, the construction of narrative involves three levels of representation, which he referred to as *mimesis* (a concept with Aristotelian origins)[59] and subdivided into $mimesis_1$, $mimesis_2$ and $mimesis_3$.[60] It is essential to note though that these levels are not envisaged as distinct stages of narrative, but as overlapping layers, with the third the product of the first through the pivotal mediating process of the second.[61] The first level, $mimesis_1$, encompasses a narrative's grounding in the real world, or the 'world of action'[62] and itself involves three dimensions. These are its structural dimension, which involves understanding action in terms of human agents, their reasons or motives, and their interaction with others; its symbolic dimension, involving the contextually-defined cultural significance of actions and their perceived underlying values; and its temporal dimension, involving understanding actions and events through a process of ordering their occurrence in time.[63] What is particularly interesting in this level of *mimesis* is the way the theory seeks to capture the complexity of events through a focus on human agency and experience, including the understanding that human conduct is not only a matter of fact with causal effects, but also charged with symbolic significance due to the cultural, historical, social and political matrix within which human conduct occurs.

The second level, $mimesis_2$, is the dynamic level of narrative at which diverse actions and events, as well as their temporal character, are configured or organised into 'an intelligible whole', giving them a plot and transforming them into a story.[64] As Polkinghorne observes:

> The plot functions to transform a chronicle or listing of events into a schematic whole by highlighting and recognizing the contribution that certain events make to the development and outcome of the story. Without the recognition of significance given by the plot, each event would appear as discontinuous and separate, and its meaning would be limited to its categorical identification or its spatiotemporal location.[65]

[59] *Mimesis* is Greek for 'imitation' or 'representation'; in Ricoeur's work it echoes the Platonic concern with artifice in artistic, especially poetic, representations of reality and human behaviour but is used more specifically as part of an engagement with Aristotle's *Poetics*: Ricoeur, *Time and Narrative Volume 1*, xi and 31–52. Note also Ted Honderich (ed), *The Oxford Companion to Philosophy*, 2nd edn (Oxford, Oxford University Press, 2005) 603.

[60] Note Mara Rainwater, 'Refiguring Ricoeur: Narrative Force and Communicative Ethics' in Richard Kearney (ed), *Paul Ricoeur: The Hermeneutics of Action* (London, Sage Publications, 1996) 103–104.

[61] Ricoeur, *Time and Narrative Volume 1*, 53.

[62] Ricoeur, *Time and Narrative Volume 1*, 54.

[63] Ricoeur, *Time and Narrative Volume 1*, 54.

[64] Ricoeur, *Time and Narrative Volume 1*, 64–65. Valdés, *A Ricoeur Reader* 99, 106 explains that '... a plot is a way of connecting event and story. A story is made out of events, to the extent that plot makes events into a story' – it is the configurational dimension, Valdés explains, that 'construes significant wholes out of scattered events'.

[65] Polkinghorne, *Narrative Knowing and the Human Sciences* 18–19 and see also 64–69.

In this sense, what is of interest is the way in which an *a posteriori* narrative is an active, directed and selective process of meaning-making about past experience.[66] Ricoeur's engagement with this level of representation highlights how the sense, connectivity and effects of the events and actions in question are interpreted and evaluated through narrative, and given meaning through the construction of its plot or theme.[67]

The third level, *mimesis*$_3$, involves the process whereby the events and actions that are configured in the narrative through emplotment (the making of the narrative) in terms of a particular theme result in the communication of the narrative's point, or overarching meaning, through its transmission to and reception by another or others.[68] This can involve communication of a narrative meaning intended by the narrator, but may also involve a meaning that is discernible in the narrative, and received and understood by an audience, in a way that can be independent from the original narrative purpose. This potentially open-textured character of narrative meaning is relied on here to interpret and evaluate Article 2 law as a source of meaning that is not necessarily restricted to an apparent narrative intention on the part of the ECtHR.

Although selectively extracted from the longer hermeneutical analysis of temporality and narrative meaning that Ricoeur developed, these three levels of representation provide a useful way of 'unpacking' the components of a narrative. In particular, as they do not derive from a purposively legal theory, they can be understood as providing an external and critically informative perspective for reflecting on the deeper processes and functions of narrative construction. As such, Ricoeur's analysis is drawn on here as a source of inspiration, rather than a restrictive framework, to extend and enhance Cover's outline of the nomos and narrative relationship, in order to examine and evaluate Article 2 law.[69] In essence, this study seeks to apply narrative theory to what Cheryl Hughes, in an analysis based on other aspects of Ricoeur's theory, has called 'the concrete realizations of human rights' and their contextual implementation.[70]

[66] Note on this point Kellner, '"As Real as it Gets"' 65.

[67] Ricoeur, *Time and Narrative Volume 1* 66–67. See also Paul Ricoeur, 'Between Hermeneutics and Semiotics' (1990) 3.8 *International Journal for the Semiotics of Law* 115, 122.

[68] Ricoeur, *Time and Narrative Volume 1* 70–71; compare Mark Van Hoecke, *Law as Communication* (Oxford, Hart, 2002) 7–8.

[69] Note Paul Ricoeur, 'A Response by Paul Ricoeur' (David Pellauer, trans) in Joy (ed) *Paul Ricoeur and Narrative*, xxxix–xliv, xliv: 'It is the passage from the norm to a concrete decision, taken within situations of uncertainty at the very heart of the tragic dimension of all action, that constitutes the critical moment par excellence of a morally intelligible action. Imagination and memory – metaphor and narrative – only provide handholds, at best incitement, for our making sense of this. But neither function includes as such within itself the dimension of evaluation'.

[70] Cheryl L Hughes, 'Reconstructing the Subject of Human Rights' (1999) 25.2 *Philosophy and Social Criticism* 47, 58. On the question of the subject of rights as addressed by Hughes see Paul Ricoeur (Kathleen Blamey, trans), *Oneself as Another* (Chicago, University of Chicago Press, 1992) and 'Who Is the Subject of Rights?' in Paul Ricoeur (David Pellauer, trans), *The Just* (Chicago, University of Chicago Press, 2000) 3.

II. Narrative and Human Rights: Sources, Processes and the ECHR

Having considered some theoretical dimensions of narrative and its potential application to law, and especially this book's two main theoretical foundations, this section concentrates on the relevance of narrative to human rights law, with regard to its sources, processes and functions. The issues addressed here are the multiple layers of meaning encapsulated in human rights norms; the role of practical reasoning in the application of rights, the processes of adjudication and justification, and the nature of accountability through rights; as well as the body of principles, requirements and purposes that are particular to the ECHR system. The first two parts of this discussion are predominantly abstract, in that they are intended to outline some fundamental aspects of human rights law in general terms so as to underline the place of narrative in addressing them, rather than focusing on concrete instances and examples. The third part turns to ECHR law in more specific terms. Overall this section provides a general conceptual overview of the matters addressed in depth in relation to Article 2 ECHR in Chapters 3–6.

A. Human Rights Norms

One of the main aims of the narrative analysis of human rights law developed here is to address its socio-cultural thickness, or its layers of meaning. The first step is to consider the source norm itself: the human right in question and its legal expression. This is because human rights norms are in themselves a form of story, with a distinct nature that raises a need for story-telling, or narrative interpretation, both in analyses of their content and scope, and in their application.

The distinct nature of human rights in legal terms is partly due to their status as a form of international law that is considered to be special, due to the ways it treats both individuals and states. It is primarily concerned with the protection and enforcement of fundamental values, claims and liberties appertaining to individuals, through the construction of negative and positive obligations for states[71] and the determination of whether or not state action that is claimed to breach

[71] Commentators generally agree that human rights in international law can be understood as claims, or as positive and negative liberties: for example, Michael Haas, *International Human Rights: A Comprehensive Introduction* (London, Routledge, 2014) 4–5. Importantly, whereas some rights are expressed as 'rights to' and others as 'freedoms from', that is 'positive rights' and 'negative rights', some commentators emphasise how such rights contain a range of forms of duties of avoidance, protection and assistance: see Henry Shue, *Basic Rights: Subsistence, Affluence and US Foreign Policy* (Princeton, Princeton University Press, 1996) 52–53, as discussed in Alastair R Mowbray, *The Development of Positive Obligations under the European Convention on Human Rights by the European Court of Human Rights* (Oxford, Hart, 2004) 222–24.

such obligations is justifiable (as discussed further in the next section). It extends beyond state actors to make individuals the subject of international norms and, by setting standards and limits with which states are required to comply, it makes a signatory state's internal affairs and domestic conduct the object of such norms and related scrutiny or challenge, rather than just that state's own concern.[72] As such, human rights norms have distinctly complex dimensions when compared with ordinary national legal provisions, due to their politically-charged nature and their particular recasting of, and effect on, power relations (among states, and between states and individuals). While all forms of law, as noted in the first part of this chapter, arguably require the construction of narratives to situate and justify their interpretation and application, the nature of human rights norms makes this process especially important and contestable.

The special nature of human rights norms can also be noted with regard to their content. Human rights norms are generally agreed to involve a core in the form of a prior attribute (involving identification of a state of being or condition to which a person is compellingly entitled), which might be expressed as a fundamental value (an imperative or 'ought' factor deemed to require respect), or as a claim, both of which may be absolute or expressed in a way that includes permissible limitations.[73] Both the core and the form of its expression as a legal norm reflect their origins and production, including the range of influences on their selection, development and formulation. The core value or claim can reflect religious or philosophical ideas, and historical conditions, and the form of legal expression reflects contextual influences on the drafting process and the determination of a right's absolute or qualified status.[74] Furthermore, the nature of rights norms as expressions of fundamental values of, or claims about humanity mean that they are often emotive and at times contentious, depending on the context. Consequently, human rights provisions have a thick significance encompassing the conditions that gave rise to them, their perceived importance, and their

[72] Andrew Moravcsik, 'The Origins of Human Rights Regimes: Democratic Delegation in Postwar Europe' (2000) 54.2 *International Organization* 217; Fionnuala Ní Aoláin, *The Politics of Force: Conflict Management and State Violence in Northern Ireland* (Belfast, The Blackstaff Press, 2000) 182.

[73] On the defining features of human rights norms see James W Nickel, *Making Sense of Human Rights*, 2nd edn (Oxford, Blackwell Publishing, 2007 [1987]) 9–10, 23–24, 28–33, and on critical opposition to the relevance of claim-based justifications for human rights see 26–28. On the problematic relationship between prior moral claims as the foundation of human rights and their legal expression see Samantha Besson, 'Human Rights: Ethical, Political … or Legal? First Steps in a Legal Theory of Human Rights' in Donald Earl Childress, III (ed), *The Role of Ethics in International Law* (Cambridge, Cambridge University Press, 2011) 211 and Allen Buchanan, *The Heart of Human Rights* (Oxford, Oxford University Press, 2013) 12–21, 50–84. On the primacy of a moral conception and grounding of human rights see James Griffin, *On Human Rights* (Oxford, Oxford University Press, 2008).

[74] Almost all (monographic) studies of human rights in law begin by noting their roots and historical development, theoretically and legally: on the European context see Greer, *The European Convention on Human Rights*; on the more general United Nations and international law context note Charles Beitz, *The Idea of Human Rights* (Oxford, Oxford University Press, 2009) 14–27. For a discussion of the reliance on and predominance of law in the development of practical and enforceable formulations of human rights see Buchanan, *The Heart of Human Rights* 38–42.

historical, socio-political and cultural resonance.[75] Although a right's core and origins are not always necessary or sufficient factors in establishing its meaning, its genesis and the story constructed about that genesis are often key aspects of legal and judicial interpretive narratives. In this regard, the combination of real and imaginary dimensions of law noted in the previous section are apparent in the foundational narratives used to ground the interpretation and application of rights, by expressing how they can be understood to be rooted in, and legitimated by, actual or narratively reconstructed historical experience.[76]

Furthermore, like other laws, the technical textual expressions of human rights provisions in conventions or declarations do not exist in isolation, but in an intertextual interpretive relationship with other provisions. This can include parts and aspects of the source documents (such as a preamble, overall structure and the order of provisions that indicate a specific right's relative importance in relation to other rights) as well as other legal instruments at the national or international level. The special nature and thickness of human rights norms arguably mean that such interpretive relationships can in turn also take on multiple layers of significance. Human rights norms can thus be seen to be multi-dimensional and to encapsulate a range of contributory factors and influences. Critical engagement with human rights norms therefore needs to involve both their technical elements as provisions of law with a particular importance – especially where the right to life and the state's use of force are involved – and their wider connections and significations, that is, the stories within them and around them. All of these factors, it is argued here, indicate the need to consider the interpretation and application of human rights in narrative terms.

B. Reasoning, Adjudication and Accountability in Human Rights Law

In addition to human rights norms' special nature and thickness, their interpretation and application also point to the relevance of narrative, due to the processes by which their meaning is constructed through legal reasoning and adjudication, and their fundamental purpose as a means for achieving accountability. With regard to reasoning, in the pragmatic or political understanding of human rights law, the moral or ethical core of a right – the prior philosophical or moral position that grounds the value or claim that the right encompasses – is insufficient to explain or support its application.[77] Instead, its validity as a functioning norm is achieved

[75] Compare Allison Tait and Luke Norris, 'Narrative and the Origins of Law' (2011) 5.1 *Law and Humanities* 11.

[76] Note Cover, 'Foreword: Nomos and Narrative' 7–10 and Frankenberg, *Comparative Law as Critique* 195–99.

[77] Allen Buchanan, 'Human Rights and the Legitimacy of the International Order' (2008) 14.1 *Legal Theory* 39 and Buchanan, *The Heart of Human Rights* 12–21, 50–84. See also Beitz, *The Idea of Human*

through processes of practical reasoning. It is through these 'complex modes of practical reasoning in which both moral values and responsible fact-finding play a prominent role' that rights' meaning and scope are developed and justified.[78] In other words, '[s]ince human rights are irremediably thick and abstract, judicial organs play a crucial role in specifying their normative content'.[79] In this sense, the meaning of a norm can only ever be a result of a process of configuration, based on the source text interpreted and applied in context.

This practical reasoning by judicial organs about the meaning of rights is a core part of their adjudication function, namely finding appropriate outcomes in disputes and justifying the interpretation and application of rights in relation to facts.[80] The adjudication of human rights disputes involves determining whether or not an individual's right has been breached and a state has acted in a permissible way, based on an interpretation of the right that is both consistent and generally applicable to all such cases.[81] In so doing, adjudication as a process is meant to make sense of facts through the filter of a norm, to make sense of the norm in the context of the facts, and to provide an overall meaning or purpose that justifies the decision reached and supports it through persuasive argumentation.[82] This is especially important where a ruling is binding and without further possibility of appeal. While in a positive light this process of reasoning and justification is intended to support justice and the fair protection of a right, rights-based justifications can though also serve to legitimate, normalise or mask state activity that might otherwise be contested and to explain away forms of injustice, especially in systemic or structural forms.[83]

Rights 1–3, 102–17 and 126–41; and Alain Zysset, *The ECHR and Human Rights Theory: Reconciling the Moral and the Political Conceptions* (London, Routledge, 2017) 8, 11, 13.

[78] Buchanan, 'Human Rights and the Legitimacy of the International Order' 63.

[79] Zysset, *The ECHR and Human Rights Theory* 13.

[80] Note Aharon Barak, 'On Judging' in Martin Scheinin, Helle Krunke and Marina Aksenova (eds), *Judges as Guardians of Constitutionalism and Human Rights* (Cheltenham, Edward Elgar, 2016) 27 and *The Judge in a Democracy* (Princeton, Princeton University Press, 2006) 205–206. Here the idea of justification concerns decisions on the basis of norms, rather than the (philosophical) justification of the norm itself: see Nickel, *Making Sense of Human Rights* 53 and Buchanan, *The Heart of Human Rights* 11–21.

[81] See further Dworkin, *Taking Rights Seriously* 86–88. According to Paul Ricoeur, 'The Act of Judging' in Ricoeur, *The Just* 127, 132, adjudication processes seek 'to put an end to uncertainty' and 'to make each party recognize the share the other has in the same society' through the construction of persuasive interpretations.

[82] For Rainer Forst (Jeffrey Flynn, trans), *The Right to Justification* (New York, Columbia University Press, 2007) 1–2, 15–16, 18–21, 205, 214, 264–65 and Forst (Ciaran Cronin, trans) *Justification and Critique: Towards a Critical Theory of Politics* (Cambridge, Polity Press, 2014) 38–39, the element of justifiability, or the demand for justification, is the root and essence of justice and of human rights. In *Justification and Critique*, 39 he states '... if it is true that human rights are meant to ensure that no human being is treated in a way that could not be justified to him or her as a person equal to others, then this implies – reflexively speaking – that one claim underlies all human rights, namely, human beings' claim to be respected as autonomous agents who have the right not to be subjected to certain actions or institutional norms that cannot be adequately justified to them'.

[83] On this critical perspective on rights and justification see Frankenberg, *Comparative Law as Critique* 167–72.

Furthermore, the role of narrative in processes of legal interpretation is especially pertinent when human rights law is considered in terms of its purpose of achieving accountability. With its origins in historical practices of financial accounting,[84] most studies agree that the concept of accountability:

> implies telling a story, based on some obligation and with some consequence in view. Accountability is anchored in the mundane yet important practice of record-keeping and gives rise to story-telling in a context of social (power) relations within which enforcement of standards and the fulfilment of obligations is a reasonable expectation. [...] Accountability thus has a relational core to it; it refers to the obligation to provide an account to, usually, a superior or at least someone with a legitimate stake.[85]

The core narrative attribute of accountability is thus its story-telling[86] function of producing an explanation of events and the role of the person or institution being held to account. This is rooted in its relationality, in that it always involves the giving of an account by one party to another or others, due to the various relationships between or among them.[87] In terms of human rights law, accountability through judicial processes involves giving those alleging interference with a right the opportunity to present their version of events and requiring the state in question to explain and justify what it has done. The role of the court is then to formulate a final interpretation of what happened in the light of both accounts. This concerns not only the immediate parties, the state in question and those affected by its conduct, but also other states and people in general, as everyone in society – nationally and internationally – arguably has a legitimate stake in the protection of rights.[88]

[84] Mark Bovens, 'Analysing and Assessing Accountability: A Conceptual Framework' (2007) 13.4 *European Law Journal* 447, 448–49.

[85] Mark Bovens, Thomas Schillemans and Robert E Goodin, 'Public Accountability' in Mark Bovens, Robert E Goodin and Thomas Schillemans (eds), *The Oxford Handbook of Public Accountability* (Oxford, Oxford University Press, 2014) 1, 1–3. See also Melvin J Dubnick, 'Accountability as a Cultural Keyword' in Bovens et al, *The Oxford Handbook of Public Accountability* 23–38; Kathryn Sikkink, 'The Age of Accountability: The Global Rise of Individual Criminal Accountability' in Francesca Lessa and Leigh A Payne (eds), *Amnesty in the Age of Human Rights Accountability* (Cambridge, Cambridge University Press, 2012) 19.

[86] Note in parallel some responses to the April 2016 verdict of the inquest into the deaths that occurred at the Hillsborough football ground in 1989. Some commentary focused on the importance of accountability, such as the editorial on 'Holding Power to Account: Count the Value, Not the Cost' (28 April 2016) *The Guardian* 30, and especially the role of narratives in expressing and coming to terms with traumatic experience, as well as remembering and establishing truth, such as the editorial entitled 'Those Who Dared to Tell the Truth are the Antigones of Our Time' (30 April 2016) *The Guardian* 38. According to the latter: 'People have always told stories. Stories are part of the human condition: they are as old as self-consciousness, as the remembering of dreams, as the sense that a life is a journey to be walked through. The ability to mould the material of life into narrative – and, into truthful narrative, in which the psyche and the story are not separated by self-deceit – is a fundamental need, as necessary to the soul as air or water is to the body'.

[87] Richard Mulgan, '"Accountability": An Ever-Expanding Concept?' (2000) 78.3 *Public Administration* 555, 571; Baker, *Deaths After Police Contact* 169–74.

[88] Note Richard Mulgan, *Holding Power to Account: Accountability in Modern Democracies* (Basingstoke, Palgrave Macmillan, 2003) 13; Bovens, 'Analysing and Assessing Accountability' 447, 463–64;

Crucially, accountability in terms of human rights law is also essentially connected with the rule of law.[89] As this is discussed further in Chapter 3, it suffices to note here that the rule of law is a foundational value and mechanism of democratic societies that in principle requires equal subordination of individuals and state to legal processes. Accountability under the rule of law in the democratic context[90] is considered to be both a virtue, or an end in itself, in that an obligation to account for and justify conduct is an inherent good and objective of democracy; and a control mechanism, or means to an end, by seeking to ensure that governmental power is exercised responsibly, transparently and in compliance with legal standards.[91] In these ways, narrative is central to human rights law in its accountability function, which through the rule of law arguably links it intrinsically with the values and processes of democracy.

C. Key Aspects of ECHR Law: Context, Interpretation and Communication

Moving from the general to the system-specific, the significance of narrative in human rights law can be further underlined with regard to ECHR law in particular. The aim here is not to summarise all of this system's features,[92] but simply to highlight three points about context, interpretation and communication. First, it is essential to note in contextual terms that the ECHR system, dating from 1950 and in force since 1953, is a unique example of an international human rights system with a strong adjudication process in which individuals play a vital role, not only as subjects, but also as protagonists. Adjudication by the ECtHR has altered over time from the ECHR system's initial primary concern with inter-state checks on compliance with human rights norms in the 1960s–70s,[93] through the emergence of the ECtHR as a strong and proactive institution, involving the

Mark H Moore, 'Accountability, Legitimacy and the Court of Public Opinion' in Bovens et al, *The Oxford Handbook of Public Accountability* 632–46.

[89] Note Mulgan, *Holding Power to Account* 75–83; Mark Philp, 'Delimiting Democratic Accountability' (2009) 57 *Political Studies* 28–53; and Carol Harlow, 'Accountability and Constitutional Law' in Bovens et al, *The Oxford Handbook of Public Accountability* 195, 198–200.

[90] Mulgan, *Holding Power to Account* 1, 8; Mark E Warren, 'Accountability and Democracy' in Bovens et al, *The Oxford Handbook of Public Accountability* 39–54.

[91] Mark Bovens, 'Two Concepts of Accountability: Accountability as a Virtue and as a Mechanism' (2010) 33.5 *West European Politics* 946–67; Bovens et al, 'Public Accountability' 6–7; Baker, *Deaths After Police Contact* 170. Note also Joseph Slaughter, 'A Question of Narration: The Voice in International Human Rights Law' (1997) 19 *Human Rights Quarterly* 406.

[92] Compare along similar lines the recent overviews in Zysset, *The ECHR and Human Rights Theory*, 120–38 and Lize R Glas, *The Theory, Potential and Practice of Procedural Dialogue in the European Convention on Human Rights System* (Cambridge, Intersentia, 2016) 17–68.

[93] Ed Bates, *The Evolution of the European Court of Human Rights: From its Inception to the Creation of a Permanent Court of Human Rights* (Oxford, Oxford University Press, 2010) 1–25, 277–359.

extension of the right of individual petition in 1998,[94] to its current status as an established and powerful 'quasi-constitutional' court for the High Contracting Parties.[95] Although Steven Greer has argued that there has been a significant shift in the ECtHR's substantive focus during this evolution, from securing last-resort justice for individuals to a more constitutional concern with state conformity with the general principles of the ECHR,[96] the role played by individual claimants is still significant. In that regard, in the context of the Council of Europe as an ensemble of politically diverse sovereign states, the resolution of individual-state disputes by the ECtHR can be particularly sensitive, especially in relation to Article 2 where state power to take life in policing and law enforcement is concerned. Considering the narrative configuration of ECtHR judgments can thus provide valuable insights into its aims and concerns, its perception of systemic context, and how it manages the competing individual and collective interests at stake in a case.

Second, the ECHR system's interpretive parameters and practices also indicate the significance of narrative analysis. The interpretation of rights under the ECHR should generally require two stages of analysis, namely determining the meaning or scope of a right and whether or not interference with it may be justified, although the extent to which the ECtHR always makes this distinction is questionable.[97] Considering the ways in which ECtHR interpretations of rights are constructed and justified, that is, how they are formulated as interpretive narratives, can elucidate the extent to which these interpretive dimensions are kept apart or interlinked. For example, as Chapters 4–5 explore, the connection made by the ECtHR between Article 2 and democratic society in cases of lethal and life-threatening force is a narrative theme that serves both to emphasise the meaning of the right to life as enshrining a fundamentally important value needing strict protection, and to provide the rationale justifying the proportionate limitation of its scope in specified circumstances.

Moreover, in interpreting and applying rights, the ECtHR is not solely concerned with the text of the ECHR, but can take into account external factors

[94] Article 33 ECHR covers applications by High Contracting Parties and Article 34 applications by 'any person, non-governmental organisation or group of individuals claiming to be the victim of a violation' of a right by a High Contracting Party. Initially dependent on acceptance by states, Article 34 was made compulsory under Protocol 11, which came into force in 1998.

[95] Bates, *The Evolution of the European Court of Human Rights* 20–23, 432–86.

[96] Greer, *The European Convention on Human Rights*; Steven Greer and Luzius Wildhaber, 'Revisiting the Debate about "Constitutionalising" the European Court of Human Rights' (2013) 12.4 *Human Rights Law Review* 655.

[97] Janneke Gerards and Hanneke Senden, 'The Structure of Fundamental Rights and the European Court of Human Rights' (2009) 7.4 *International Journal of Constitutional Law* 619, 619–20; Zysset, *The ECHR and Human Rights Theory* 121; see also Janneke Gerards and Eva Brems, 'Introduction' in Eva Brems and Janneke Gerards, *Shaping Rights in the ECHR: The Role of the European Court of Human Rights in Determining the Scope of Human Rights* (Cambridge, Cambridge University Press, 2013) 1.

including national (comparative) and – although approached selectively – other international law provisions.[98] The ECtHR also considers interpretive principles that it has recognised and developed over time, but on which it does not always rely in a coherent way.[99] Such principles include the fundamental requirement of proportionality,[100] the purposive[101] and evolutive interpretation of the ECHR as a living instrument,[102] and the interpretation of its provisions that seeks to achieve their practical and effective protection in terms of the ECHR's non-abstract object and purpose.[103] In addition there is the fundamental principle of subsidiarity, according to which the primary responsibility for securing ECHR rights rests with the signatory states, with the ECtHR playing a secondary, albeit vital, role in deciding on disputes.[104] As recognised by the ECtHR, the primacy of the High Contracting Parties is established by Article 1 (the general obligation to secure the rights in the ECHR), Article 13 (the right to an effective remedy at the domestic level for a breach of a right), Article 19 (on the establishment of the ECtHR with regard to the engagements undertaken by the High Contracting Parties) and Article 35(1) (the admissibility criteria requiring an applicant to exhaust domestic remedies).[105] On that basis, the ECtHR has used the principle of subsidiarity to demarcate its role in relation to state responsibilities, to recognise where necessary the sovereign competences of the High Contracting Parties,[106] and to give them

[98] The principal provisions relating to the use of force are the United Nations Principles on the Effective Prevention and Investigation of Extra-Legal, Arbitrary and Summary Executions, Economic and Social Council Resolution 1989/65, 24 May 1989 and the Basic Principles on the Use of Force and Firearms by Law Enforcement Officials, Eighth United Nations Congress on the Prevention of Crime and the Treatment of Offenders, Havana, 1990. See further Magdalena Forowicz, *The Reception of International Law in the European Court of Human Rights* (Oxford, Oxford University Press, 2010) 382–83 and Michael Hamilton and Antoine Buyse, 'Human Rights Courts as Norm Brokers' (2018) 18 *Human Rights Law Review* 205, 215, 219, which includes consideration of the ECtHR's reliance on Article 31(3)(c) of the Vienna Convention on the Law of Treaties 1969 regarding the use of international law in legal interpretation.

[99] Greer, *The European Convention on Human Rights* 193–94.

[100] Note *Soering v United Kingdom* (1989) para 89.

[101] The purposive or teleological approach to interpreting the ECHR is grounded in Articles 31–33 of the Vienna Convention on the Law of Treaties 1969 and is one of the ECtHR's main guiding principles: see Greer, *The European Convention on Human Rights* 195.

[102] Alastair Mowbray, 'The Creativity of the European Court of Human Rights' (2005) 5 *Human Rights Law Review* 57; Kanstantsin Dzehtsiarou, 'European Consensus and the Evolutive Interpretation of the European Convention on Human Rights' (2011) 12 *German Law Journal* 1730.

[103] Note *Soering* para 87 and *McCann* para 146; also, Mowbray, 'The Creativity of the European Court of Human Rights'. In *Artico v Italy* (1980) para 33 the ECtHR stated: 'The Court recalls that the Convention is intended to guarantee not rights that are theoretical or illusory but rights that are practical and effective'.

[104] Note Alastair Mowbray, 'Subsidiarity and the European Convention on Human Rights' (2015) 15 *Human Rights Law Review* 313.

[105] Mowbray, 'Subsidiarity and the European Convention on Human Rights' 319–20, citing a series of Grand Chamber decisions upholding these foundations.

[106] Mowbray, 'Subsidiarity and the European Convention on Human Rights' 321–37. Note also Baroness Hale of Richmond, 'Human Rights in the Age of Terrorism: The Democratic Dialogue in Action' (2008) 39 *Georgetown Journal of International Law* 383–405.

a margin of appreciation in the application of rights in the national context.[107] It suffices to note at this point that the ways in which the ECtHR charts its interpretive course through these various sources of law and principles constitute narratives that reveal how the ECtHR manages the porosity, interconnectedness and systemic contingencies of ECHR law.

Third, the components of narrative as outlined in the first part of this chapter, particularly with regard to Ricoeur's theory, draw attention to ECHR law's communicative functions.[108] These can be specified as involving cohesive, dialogic and disseminative aspects. On the first of these, it is essential to note that although reference is made to 'the' ECtHR, it has changed over time and, since the reformed ECtHR started work in 1998, its decisions have been produced by Chambers and the Grand Chamber, with shifting judicial composition. Therefore 'the ECtHR', as adjudicator and narrator, is in fact a plural and changing body, further complicated by the fact that its Grand Chamber is not required to decide unanimously and may include majority and minority (dissenting) opinions. The ECtHR also works in two languages, English and French, producing rulings in both, which at times leads to conceptual uncertainty.[109] Moreover, although the ECtHR generally follows its previous decisions, it does not have a rigid system of precedent.[110] In that context therefore the development of recurring themes and rationales, or long-running narratives with common refrains across cases and over time, is a way of achieving some cohesion and coherence in the ECtHR's case law.[111] This can be seen in the way the ECtHR adopts (or more precisely the Registry seeks to ensure that the ECtHR adopts) a more or less identical structure in all of its judgments and tends to repeat key points and maintain justificatory themes in related rulings. As such, the narrative of one judgment needs to be read in relation to, and considered as part of, the wider narrative across other judgments, in terms of both consistency and change.

[107] See the general discussion in Yutaka Arai-Takahashi, *The Margin of Appreciation Doctrine and the Principle of Proportionality in the Jurisprudence of the ECHR* (Antwerp, Intersentia, 2002) and note also Nicholas Lavender, 'The Problem of the Margin of Appreciation' (1997) *European Human Rights Law Review* 380; Michael R Hutchinson, 'The Margin of Appreciation Doctrine in the European Court of Human Rights' (1999) 48.3 *International and Comparative Law Quarterly* 638; George Letsas, 'Two Concepts of the Margin of Appreciation' (2006) 26.4 *Oxford Journal of Legal Studies* 705. Protocol 15, as and when ratified, will incorporate the margin of appreciation into the ECHR Preamble, although the effect of this is unclear: Article 1, Protocol 15, adopted 24 June 2013. In August 2018 Protocol 15 had been ratified by 43 out of 47 Member States. The significance of the margin of appreciation has though been questioned: Janneke Gerards, 'Margin of Appreciation and Incrementalism in the Case Law of the European Court of Human Rights' (2018) 18 *Human Rights Law Review* 495.

[108] Note also Van Hoecke, *Law as Communication* 7–8.

[109] Note for example James Brannan, 'Coming to Terms with the Supranational: Translating for the European Court of Human Rights' (2013) 26.4 *International Journal for the Semiotics of Law* 909, 913–17.

[110] Note Alastair Mowbray, 'An Examination of the European Court of Human Rights Approach to Overruling its Previous Case Law' (2009) 9 *Human Rights Law Review* 179.

[111] See Jens Meyer-Ladewig, 'The Rule of Law in the Case Law of the Strasbourg Court' in Hermann-Josef Blanke and Stelio Mangiameli (eds), *The European Union After Lisbon: Constitutional Basis, Economic Order and External Action* (Berlin, Springer, 2012) 235 and 248.

As for the dialogic aspect, the narratives developed in ECtHR decisions arguably play an essential role in the multi-party dialogue that can be seen to be necessary in ECHR law,[112] due to the relationship between the ECtHR and the sovereign High Contracting Parties as reflected in the principle of subsidiarity noted above. Due to the ECtHR's respect for this principle, it has sought to develop a dialogue with Member States' courts, partly to respect and foster co-operation with them and partly because it cannot force state compliance with its rulings.[113] Subsidiarity and the endeavour to develop dialogue have become increasingly significant because of political sensitivities about judicial review of state action, due to concerns about the legitimacy of courts in the context of majoritarian democracy, exacerbated by the ECtHR's international status.[114] Considering ECtHR rulings and the justificatory reasons and themes developed in them as constituting narratives is thus informative in exploring the ways in which case law is shaped to engage and persuade its audiences – including states and national courts – about the fundamental merits and teleological rationales that the ECtHR is seeking to develop.

Lastly, the dialogic aspect is part of the broader disseminative role of ECtHR rulings. It was noted above that a key element of accountability through international human rights law is its relational dimension, that is, how it supports holding power to account to applicants in a case and to the public, in line with democratic principles and the rule of law. In seeking to achieve accountability, ECtHR judgments serve to spread knowledge of case outcomes, as well as ECHR law and principles, across the Council of Europe (and beyond), which can be understood as fulfilling not only informative, but also educative goals.[115] That is, they both convey details and results of accountability processes to states, other interested parties and the public, and seek to educate them about the key aspects of ECHR law that can guide and limit state and individual conduct. As with the other factors above, these communicative aspects of ECHR law indicate its narrative characteristics, which are particularly significant in the area of Article 2 due to the potentially wide impact and socio-political sensitivity of state uses of force.

[112] Note especially Glas, *The Theory, Potential and Practice of Procedural Dialogue in the European Convention on Human Rights System* 107–53; also, Paul Mahoney, 'The Relationship between the Strasbourg Court and the National Courts' (2014) 130 *Law Quarterly Review* 568.

[113] Glas, *The Theory, Potential and Practice of Procedural Dialogue in the European Convention on Human Rights System* 3. Although under Article 46(1) ECHR, the 'High Contracting Parties undertake to abide by the final judgment of the Court in any case to which they are parties', the ECHR enforcement mechanism is generally rather limited. Note Mahoney, 'The Relationship between the Strasbourg Court and the National Courts' 5. Under Protocol 16, adopted 6 May 2013 and in force since 1 August 2018 for the ten states that have so far ratified it, the highest courts of state parties can seek an advisory opinion from the ECtHR on questions of principle relating to the interpretation and application of rights in the ECHR and related protocols. See Thomas Voland and Britta Schiebel, 'Advisory Opinions of the European Court of Human Rights: Unbalancing the System of Human Rights Protection in Europe?' (2017) 17 *Human Rights Law Review* 73.

[114] Glas, *The Theory, Potential and Practice of Procedural Dialogue in the European Convention on Human Rights System* 48–52, 70, 109–11. See also Mowbray, 'Subsidiarity and the European Convention on Human Rights' 329.

[115] Frankenberg, *Comparative Law as Critique* 199–200.

Overall, this chapter has outlined the main theoretical axes for the following chapters. Part I explored the lineage of narrative theory with regard to law before focusing on the main sources for this book's narrative approach to Article 2 ECHR, drawn from the work of Cover and Ricoeur. Part II has discussed the sources, methods and functions of human rights law, together with selected features of ECHR law, in order to outline the relevance of narrative theory in exploring the processes of meaning-making and construction of purposive themes in ECtHR judgments. These issues can now be addressed more specifically in terms of the right to life in Article 2 ECHR and its connections with democratic society in the ECtHR's interpretation.

3

Lethal Force, the Right to Life and Democratic Society: Key Connections

In its introductory statements about the right to life under Article 2 ECHR in *McCann*, with which this book began, the ECtHR underlined that right's importance (it is 'one of the most fundamental provisions in the Convention'), stressed its essential nature (it enshrines a basic value), and situated it in a foundational and interpretive context ('the democratic societies making up the Council of Europe').[1] Before considering the role and purpose of these statements in *McCann* and all the subsequent judgments which refer to them, it is necessary to 'unpack' them and explore their origins, influences and possible interpretations. In terms of the narrative theory addressed in the previous chapter, the ECtHR's statements about the right to life and democratic society can be understood as having a thick significance that encapsulates historical socio-political and theoretical factors, and as grounding and orienting Article 2 case law's underlying values and overarching purposes. In Cover's terms, these statements and connections form 'the narratives that locate' the judgments and give them meaning, by supplying them with 'history and destiny, beginning and end, explanation and purpose'.[2] In Ricoeur's terms, addressing these issues involves considering how the ECtHR's statements about the right to life and democratic society reflect and represent aspects of concrete experience ($mimesis_1$), indicate the theme around which ECtHR case narratives are configured ($mimesis_2$), and inform the meanings that those narratives communicate ($mimesis_3$).[3]

In Part I this chapter considers the foundations of the ECtHR's connection between Article 2 and democratic society by addressing its factual and symbolic bases, that is, the genesis of a right to life, what that right represents in terms of deeper concerns relating to the state and the organisation of political community, and the right's formulation in the specific context of post-war democracy and the ECHR order. As discussed in Chapter 2, human rights norms encapsulate the story of their origins and the ideas and contextual forces that shaped them. For present

[1] *McCann and Others v United Kingdom* (1995) para 147.
[2] Robert M Cover, 'Foreword: Nomos and Narrative' (1983) 97 *Harvard Law Review* 4, 4–5.
[3] Paul Ricoeur (Kathleen McLaughlin and David Pellauer, trans), *Time and Narrative, Volume 1* (Chicago, University of Chicago Press, 1984) 54–71.

purposes though, as the origins of the right to life in international law and in the ECHR are already well documented, the aim here is not to reproduce existing studies,[4] but to focus on the development of the right to life as a response to state oppression. The principal issue is the post-war formation of a politico-legal system of values through the ECHR, that recognises the need for protection against the state and state intervention in the name of society, and that links democracy and rights together, factually, legally and imaginatively. In Part II the chapter considers the ways in which these factual and imaginative dimensions feed into the concept of 'democratic societies' and how that concept is used by the ECtHR in Article 2 case law.

I. A Fundamental Provision and Basic Value: The Right to Life, State Power and Law

Discussion of Article 2's 'fundamental' and 'basic' character, and how it can be linked with democratic society in the context of state uses of force, needs to encompass its theoretical roots, historical development and the jurisprudential structure on which it is based and through which it functions.[5] While the idea that human life should be the object of a universal legal right protecting it is an essentially twentieth-century development that began with the United Nations (UN) Universal Declaration of Human Rights (UDHR) of 1948, the right to life also encapsulates a longer story that can in part be traced by considering earlier foundational ideas. In examining these factors, the section highlights three key issues: fundamental concerns with the value of life and the problem of state power, the limitation of state power through law and, in the post-war era, the development of human rights and democracy in response to totalitarianism.

A. The Value of Human Life and the Problem of State Power: Theoretical Roots

The right to life in Article 2 echoes and is partly informed by a number of older philosophical positions, which upheld human life as having a special and inherent value. Noting this partial reflection of past ideas is not to suggest though that there

[4] See primarily BG Ramcharan (ed), *The Right to Life in International Law* (Dordrecht, Martinus Nijhoff, 1985); Louis Henkin, *The Age of Rights* (New York, Columbia University Press, 1990); Johannes Morsink, *The Universal Declaration of Human Rights: Origins, Drafting and Intent* (University of Philadelphia Press, Philadelphia, 1999); Elizabeth Wicks, *The Right to Life and Conflicting Interests* (Oxford, Oxford University Press, 2010); see also Council of Europe, *Collected Edition of the Travaux Préparatoires of the European Convention on Human Rights* (The Hague, Martinus Nijhoff, 1975–1985).

[5] See also Samuel Moyn, *The Last Utopia: Human Rights in History* (Cambridge, Mass, Harvard University Press, 2010) 11–12.

is necessarily a direct link between them and the development of human rights law in the twentieth century or that origins determine present meanings.[6] Rather, grasping the significance of the right to life in the ECtHR's narrative of Article 2 as a 'fundamental provision' and 'basic value' needs to involve tracing its layers of meaning, including its conceptual history. In so doing, the key point addressed here for the purposes of the analysis of the right to life, lethal force and democratic society today is the extent to which past ideas about such a right related it to state power and so show that the right has long been grounded in concerns with the tension and even danger inherent in state-individual relations.

As other studies have indicated, the idea that human life has value and must be respected and protected can be traced to various sources, including a number of systems of religious belief.[7] For the present analysis however, more informative conceptual roots of the right to life can be identified in seventeenth- and eighteenth-century political theory and philosophy, specifically the work of John Locke and Immanuel Kant. These theorists sought to move understanding of human society and the nature of humanity beyond divine authority, and to locate ideas about rights and the value of human life in the natural order, or in relation to reason and inherent worth. It is important to recall though that whilst these ideas were influential, they were nevertheless based on limited conceptions of the value of life, due to long-standing inequalities between the sexes and amongst socio-political classes, as citizens, freemen and slaves,[8] and enduring support for the death penalty.

In the natural law theory of John Locke, human life was closely related to liberty and, as an aspect of property, was a fundamental value that should be respected.[9] This was based partly on (non-universal) grounds of 'some form of equality of human beings' (although for Locke this meant men) and mainly in negative terms, that is, as protection against deprivation of life.[10] For Locke the 'right' to one's life

[6] Mikael Rask Madsen and Gert Verschraegen, 'Making Human Rights Intelligible: An Introduction to a Sociology of Human Rights' in Mikael Rask Madsen and Gert Verschraegen (eds), *Making Human Rights Intelligible: Towards a Sociology of Human Rights* (Oxford, Hart, 2013) 1, 6.

[7] See further Micheline R Ishay, *The History of Human Rights: From Ancient Times to the Globalization Era* (Berkeley, University of California Press, 2004) 84; Christian Tomuschat, 'The Right to Life – Legal and Political Foundations' in Christian Tomuschat, Evelyne Lagrange and Stefan Oeter (eds), *The Right to Life* (Leiden, Martinus Nijhoff, 2010) 3–18; Wicks, *The Right to Life and Conflicting Interests* 22–29; Fiona Leverick, *Killing in Self-Defence* (Oxford, Oxford University Press, 2006) 55–59.

[8] For example, Alan Rosas, 'Democracy and Human Rights' in Allan Rosas, Jan Helgesen and Donna Gomien (eds), *Human Rights in a Changing East-West Perspective* (London, Pinter, 1990) 17, 19–20; Moyn, *The Last Utopia* 25–26.

[9] John Locke (Peter Laslett, ed), *Two Treatises of Government* (Cambridge, Cambridge University Press, 1988) Book II, II.6, 270–71 and IV.23, 283–84. See also Ishay, *The History of Human Rights* 85; Leverick, *Killing in Self-Defence* 56; Tomuschat, 'The Right to Life – Legal and Political Foundations' 3–4; Wicks, *The Right to Life and Conflicting Interests* 33–35; Steven Greer, *The European Convention on Human Rights: Achievements, Problems and Prospects* (Cambridge, Cambridge University Press, 2006) 2–3; and David Held, 'Central Perspectives on the Modern State' in Gregor McLennan, David Held and Stuart Hall (eds), *The Idea of the Modern State* (Milton Keynes, Open University Press, 1984) 29, 38–41.

[10] James Griffin, *On Human Rights* (Oxford, Oxford University Press, 2008) 213–14.

was a basic element of the law of nature, which men could understand and follow due to their capacity to reason. The right to life though required protection, necessitating the formation of a state bounded by (constitutional) law, which could be resisted or changed if it did not fulfil its purpose of protecting peoples' natural rights.[11] Significantly in Locke's theory of government, 'Political Power' primarily entailed 'a Right of making Laws with Penalties of Death',[12] thus situating the power to take life through capital punishment at the apex of his conceptual structure of society and government. Consequently, even though according to James Griffin '[i]t never becomes fully clear what Locke's view of the right to life is',[13] the importance of a right to life, the need for a state to protect it, the connection between government and the power to kill, and the importance of controlling government through law were fundamental aspects of Locke's theory of political community.

The other main philosophical approach to the right to life that is widely recognised as being of foundational significance for the modern version of it can be located in Enlightenment theories about the centrality of humankind in the universe and the primacy of individual life. The principal expression of this view is generally understood to be Immanuel Kant's representation of the importance of human life, with the related paramount aim for all human existence being to respect its intrinsic worth.[14] Kant's theory is a crucial part of the development of human rights and the right to life in particular, it is suggested here, for two reasons. One is that it establishes the importance of individual worth on its own terms: for Kant, an individual's life is important in and of itself, based on the human capacity to reason, and is considered to be an end in itself, never merely a means.[15] The second reason is that Kant's theory became a keystone in the development of individual (human) rights and democratic theory, which came to value the demos as a collective consisting of equally important individuals.[16] In contrast, in the early twentieth century aspects of anti-democratic totalitarian theory scorned and rejected the Kantian concept of individual worth, emphasising instead the importance of the state as the embodiment of collective interests.[17] Kantian theory is

[11] Locke, *Two Treatises of Government* Book II, IV.22, 283–84; see also Greer, *The European Convention on Human Rights* 3.

[12] Locke, *Two Treatises of Government* Book II, I.3.

[13] Griffin, *On Human Rights* 214.

[14] Immanuel Kant (M Gregor, ed and trans), *Groundwork of the Metaphysics of Morals* (Cambridge, Cambridge University Press, 1991) 38; Wicks, *The Right to Life and Conflicting Interests* 30–31; compare Ishay, *The History of Human Rights* 87–89; Katrin Flikschuh, 'Human Rights in Kantian Mode: A Sketch' in Rowan Cruft, S Matthew Liao and Massimo Renzo (eds), *Philosophical Foundations of Human Rights*, Oxford, Oxford University Press, 2015) 653–70 and Luigi Caranti, 'Kant's Theory of Human Rights' in Thomas Cushman (ed), *Handbook of Human Rights* (Abingdon, Routledge, 2014) 35.

[15] Kant, *Groundwork of the Metaphysics of Morals* 38.

[16] See further Catherine Dupré, *The Age of Dignity: Human Rights and Constitutionalism in Europe* (Oxford, Hart, 2015) 28–38.

[17] Note for example from a theoretical perspective the Fascist rejection of Kantian inherent worth and the reconceptualisation of individual life as a means to the state's ends in Alfredo Rocco, 'The Political

therefore a direct foundational influence on the right to life, as well as human rights and democracy, and is also significant for them by representing what was rejected by the totalitarian regimes in response to which universal human rights were first formulated in the post-war era, and human rights and democracy were developed in combination through the ECHR.

B. Rights, State Power and Protection through Law: Common Law and Constitutional Developments

While respect for the importance of human life has a long legal history, evidenced by long-standing prohibitions on taking life in criminal law rules on unjustified killing, the creation in the twentieth century of a right to life protected by law has a legal lineage that included two main historical influences. One was the common law development of the idea of liberty through law, and of the role of law in both grounding and limiting executive (or state) power. The other, closely connected to the common law approach, was the advent of early modern republican constitutional systems and their inclusion of legal rights so as to limit state power through law, including recognition of the need (as reflected in Locke's theory) for protection by, as well as from, the state.[18] The protection of the right to life by law in Article 2 ECHR is an indirect result of these influences, and both arguably contribute to the idea that that right is a basic value of democratic societies.

As a system that has long rejected and resisted ideas of rights and a written constitution, the British common law has nevertheless been an important influence on their development through its tradition of legal limitations on executive power.[19] Although the common law's emphasis on liberties through law was predominantly, for most of its history, restricted by social class and was not always as liberal as systemic self-representation may have claimed, the fundamental idea that law and judicial decisions focusing on facts and remedies could shape limitations on government came to be a keystone in the Western legal tradition. The ideological essence of the common law was that (at least in principle) freedoms could be protected as residual liberties once the boundaries of lawful action had been determined, and that the law could control all conduct, including – within

Doctrine of Fascism' (1926–27) 11 *International Conciliation* 393, 401–403; note also the discussion in Stephen Skinner, 'Violence in Fascist Criminal Law Discourse: War, Repression and Anti-Democracy' (2013) 26.2 *International Journal for the Semiotics of Law* 439, 450–52.

[18] Ishay, *The History of Human Rights* 87–90; Tomuschat, 'The Right to Life – Legal and Political Foundations' 4; Wicks, *The Right to Life and Conflicting Interests* 35–38; Greer, *The European Convention on Human Rights* 4–5; Charles Leben, 'Is there a European Approach to Human Rights?' in Philip Alston (ed), *The EU and Human Rights* (Oxford, Oxford University Press, 1999) 69, 73–74. See also Aryeh Neier, *The International Human Rights Movement: A History* (Princeton, Princeton University Press, 2012) 26–60.

[19] AW Brian Simpson, *Human Rights and the End of Empire: Britain and the Genesis of the European Convention* (Oxford, Oxford University Press, 2001) 20.

certain limits – the government's.[20] In the eighteenth-century age of revolutions, the common law nexus among law, liberty and the restraint of the state also informed the emergence of the first two systems of constitutionally-protected rights in North America and France, which are generally considered to be the main legal forebears of twentieth-century human rights provisions.

Contextually, the American and French formulations of constitutional law and legal rights both stemmed from revolutions against rulers who were using military force to try to impose control. Both of them, albeit with historical and ideological specificities that preclude over-generalisation, were thus based on a turn to law in the face of governmental violence and oppression.[21] The American Revolution in particular was in significant part triggered by military action against civilians, reliance on martial law rather than the due process of ordinary law, and the use of standing armies for maintaining order, which was seen as a direct attack on liberty.[22] Although in early American constitutional debates development of a right to life was in part deemed to be 'too obvious' to need justification,[23] its importance must be assessed in light of that military context.

In the American Declaration of Independence, life was linked with liberty and enshrined as the foremost inherent right:

> We hold these truths to be self-evident, that all men are created equal, that they are endowed by their Creator with certain unalienable Rights, that among these are Life, Liberty and the pursuit of Happiness. – That to secure these rights, Governments are instituted among Men, deriving their just powers from the consent of the governed, – That whenever any Form of Government becomes destructive of these ends, it is the Right of the People to alter or to abolish it, and to institute new Government, laying its foundation on such principles and organizing its powers in such form, as to them shall seem most likely to effect their Safety and Happiness.[24]

Importantly, although explicitly grounded in a theological source, these 'unalienable rights'[25] were connected with the need for protection by consensual

[20] Simpson, *Human Rights and the End of Empire* 20–37; Greer, *The European Convention on Human Rights* 4–5. This common law ideology was reflected especially in the (politically contestable) work of William Blackstone, *Commentaries on the Laws of England* (Oxford, Clarendon Press, 1765) and Albert Venn Dicey, *Lectures Introductory to the Study of the Law of the Constitution* (London, Macmillan & Co, 1885).

[21] On the role of fear in these constitutional settlements note András Sajó, *Constitutional Sentiments* (New Haven, Yale University Press, 2011) 87, 112–15.

[22] Bernard Bailyn, *The Ideological Origins of the American Revolution* (Cambridge, Mass, Harvard University Press, 1967) 112–16; David E Engdahl, 'Soldiers, Riots and Revolution: The Law and History of Military Troops in Civil Disorders' (1971) 57.1 *Iowa Law Review* 1, 22–28.

[23] Griffin, *On Human Rights* 213.

[24] The US Declaration of Independence, 4 July 1776. This was based on the Virginia Declaration of Rights of 12 June 1776, which declared in Section 1: 'That all men are by nature equally free and independent and have certain inherent rights, of which, when they enter into a state of society, they cannot, by any compact, deprive or divest their posterity; namely, the enjoyment of life and liberty, with the means of acquiring and possessing property, and pursuing and obtaining happiness and safety'. Both transcriptions are from the US National Archives and Records Administration, www.archives.gov/founding-docs (consulted 27 August 2018).

[25] Wicks, *The Right to Life and Conflicting Interests* 35 rightly emphasises the narrow scope of these rights of 'all men', which excluded women, black slaves and Native Americans.

government. The rationale for this was that those with a vested interest in the rights were best placed to protect them, and that the powers necessary to do so would be just if grounded in participatory consent. As such, the Declaration echoed both the philosophy of Locke[26] and the common law tradition, despite the revolution against Britain.[27] It is also significant to note that the intended essence of this early right to life was the preservation of life, reflecting the revolutionary context of military action that was seen to take colonists' lives unjustly.[28]

Subsequently, the right to life in the American context received additional legal recognition and protection through the Fifth Amendment to the US Constitution, as ratified in the 1791 Bill of Rights.[29] Focusing on criminal justice and applicable to federal government actions, its penultimate clause linked the protection of life (as well as liberty and property) with due process of law, specifically in the context of capital punishment.[30] This clause expressed the view that the power of the state – in the sense of governmental authority – over the life of one of its subjects, even in an emerging proto-democratic republic, had to be circumscribed by and exercised through law and proper legal procedure. In other words, echoing both the common law heritage and the grievances against British action that had triggered the revolution, state power could not be exercised arbitrarily and without check or control.[31]

Similarly, across the Atlantic, the French Revolution was in large part shaped by the fear of military intervention against the National Assembly,[32] and the formulation of legal control structures to limit state power was catalysed by confidence in the force of law to structure and control the state.[33] This focus on law for the protection of rights culminated in the principal European declaration of this period, the French Declaration of the Rights of Man and the Citizen of 1789. Whereas the

[26] The Lockean view was popularised in North America through the work of Thomas Paine, *Common Sense* (Philadelphia, Robert Bell, 1776). See also Wicks, *The Right to Life and Conflicting Interests* 35.

[27] Simpson, *Human Rights and the End of Empire* 19.

[28] Morton White, *The Philosophy of the American Revolution* (New York, Oxford University Press, 1978) 206–209.

[29] The US Bill of Rights, 15 December 1791, Amendment V: 'No person shall be held to answer for a capital, or otherwise infamous crime, unless on a presentment or indictment of a Grand Jury, except in cases arising in the land or naval forces, or in the Militia, when in actual service in time of War or public danger; nor shall any person be subject for the same offence to be twice put in jeopardy of life or limb; nor shall be compelled in any criminal case to be a witness against himself, nor be deprived of life, liberty, or property, without due process of law; nor shall private property be taken for public use, without just compensation'. Transcription from the US National Archives and Records Administration, www.archives.gov/founding-docs (consulted 27 August 2018).

[30] The Fourteenth Amendment of 1868 subsequently extended this due process protection to actions by the states: see Wicks, *The Right to Life and Conflicting Interests* 37.

[31] Although primarily about France, the importance of the US position on this point is noted in Keith Michael Baker, 'The Idea of a Declaration of Rights' in Dale Van Kley (ed), *The French Idea of Freedom: The Old Regime and the Declaration of Rights of 1789* (Stanford, Stanford University Press, 1994) 154–96, 158.

[32] Lynn Hunt, 'Introduction: The Revolutionary Origins of Human Rights' in Lynn Hunt (ed and trans), *The French Revolution and Human Rights: A Brief Documentary History* (Boston, Bedford/St Martin's, 1996) 1–32, 14.

[33] Dale Van Kley, 'Introduction' in Van Kley, *The French Idea of Freedom* 5, 7.

American Bill of Rights followed the constitution in an effort to curtail governmental power, in the French context that same concern (among others)[34] led to the Declaration being created first, as the source of legitimacy for government and the new constitution, and a nascent connection with democracy.[35] The 1789 Declaration did not explicitly refer to a right to life, which usually means that the Declaration is left out of histories of that right. Even so, protection of life appears to be implicit within the limits on rights that the Declaration envisaged. Significantly, the rights set out were identified first and foremost as having been recognised and declared by the National Assembly, 'in the presence and under the auspices of the Supreme Being'.[36] Thus, although as in the American Declaration of Independence a divine dimension is claimed to endorse the establishment of rights, they were fundamentally the product of political choice and a supposed political expression of Jean-Jacques Rousseau's concept of the general will.[37] Focusing on equality and freedom,[38] the Declaration established a series of rights directed at limiting governmental power through law and processes of accountability,[39] anchoring law in political participation, and recognising the necessity of protection by and from public powers exercised by the state.[40]

In both systems therefore, prefiguring the birth of twentieth-century rights, the creation of a new legal order and within it the adoption of legally expressed rights were due to a historical experience of oppressive practices and the use of force, as well as confidence in the capacity of law to anchor protection by and from the state in an enforceable normative structure. Of significance in both systems is the way in which legal rights were understood in terms of a special relationship with early forms of participatory government and the rule of law. As the beginnings of modern democracy, these factors were a key part of the

[34] Baker, 'The Idea of a Declaration of Rights' 161.

[35] Hunt, 'Introduction' 15.

[36] The translation used here is from 'The Declaration of the Rights of Man and Citizen' in Hunt, *The French Revolution and Human Rights* 77–79.

[37] Article 6 of the Declaration stated that law was the expression of the general will. On this point and the link with Rousseau note Baker, 'The Idea of a Declaration of Rights' 193. Rousseau's influential theory was first published in 1762: see Jean-Jacques Rousseau, (Donald A Cress, ed and trans), *On the Social Contract* (Indianapolis, Hackett, 1987) and Held, 'Central Perspectives on the Modern State' 29, 48–50.

[38] Article 1 famously declared that 'Men are born and remain free and equal in rights', and Article 2 stated that: 'The purpose of all political association is the preservation of the natural and imprescriptible rights of Man. These are Liberty, Property, Safety and Resistance to Oppression'.

[39] Note Article 4 on liberty and Article 5 on the limits on legal prohibition and the requirement of legality; Article 7 and Article 8 establish law as the foundation for and principal limit on state law enforcement and punitive powers; Article 15 covers the accountability of public agents; Article 16 links the guarantee of rights and the separation of powers with the constitutional order. See also Leben, 'Is there a European Approach to Human Rights?' 84.

[40] Article 12 recognised the connection between the state and the protection of rights through 'public powers' (*force publique*), including a prohibition on their misuse for personal gain: note E Picard, 'Commentaire de l'article 12 de la Déclaration des droits de l'homme et du citoyen' (1991) 5 *Les Cahiers de la sécurité intérieure* 201, 202–203, 208–10.

political and ideological processes of self-definition and self-assertion – the creation narratives – that were constructed in each system, justifying and legitimating the new legal developments.[41] The story of the right to life in the ECHR, and its narrative connection with democratic society set up by the ECtHR, even though specifically grounded in the post-war context, arguably reflect deeper historical, contextual and ideological factors that lie at the heart of the Western rights tradition.[42]

That relationship between rights and law continued to be developed theoretically and practically throughout the nineteenth century and into the twentieth,[43] including the slow turn of the tide against slavery.[44] It also saw the introduction of legal protection for human life in the context of international conflict through the Geneva and Hague Conventions on the conduct of warfare, restrictions on weapons, as well as the treatment of sick, wounded and captured soldiers and sailors.[45] Just as the subsequent extension of such war-related legal protection to non-combatants was a product of the Second World War,[46] the development from constitutional rights for citizens to universal human rights for all was a specific product of the mid-twentieth century and the aftermath of that conflict. Thus with regard to the ECHR, the legal formulation of Article 2 and their connections with democracy, attention must focus on the period after 1945.

C. Human Rights, the Right to Life and the ECHR in the Post-War Context

The end of the Second World War saw the first international efforts to express and protect universal human rights, including notably the 1948 UN UDHR. Formed in 1945, the UN had among its foundational purposes respect for human rights, and faith in 'the dignity and worth of the human person' and 'the equal rights of men and women'.[47] The UN's Human Rights Commission proceeded to draft the UDHR, intended as a foundational statement of core values paving the way towards subsequent, enforceable human rights law. Partly influenced by the

[41] On the American Declaration of Independence in this light see Wicks, *The Right to Life and Conflicting Interests* 35.

[42] See also Jeremy McBride, 'Protecting Life: A Positive Obligation to Help' (1999) 24 *European Law Review – Supplement: Human Rights Survey* 43, 54.

[43] Greer, *The European Convention on Human Rights* 5–8.

[44] Note the British Slave Trade Abolition Act 1807 and the first international effort to end slavery in the Treaty of Vienna 1815.

[45] Note the Geneva Convention of 1864 and its revisions in 1906, 1925 and 1929; and the Hague Conventions of 1899 and 1907: www.icrc.org/eng/resources/documents/misc/mouvement-date-011006.htm (consulted 27 August 2018). See also Sandesh Sivakumaran, 'International Humanitarian Law' in Daniel Moeckli, Sangeeta Shah and Sandesh Sivakumaran (eds), *International Human Rights Law* (Oxford, Oxford University Press, 2014) 479, 480.

[46] These extensions to the Geneva and Hague Conventions were signed in 1949.

[47] Charter of the United Nations, San Francisco, 26 June 1945.

philosophical and constitutional heritage outlined above, as well as other political factors, the UDHR was primarily created in response to the horrors of the War and above all the Holocaust.[48] Echoing the UN Charter's recognition of and faith in inherent dignity and equal rights, the UDHR's Preamble explicitly noted how 'disregard and contempt for human rights have resulted in barbarous acts which have outraged the conscience of mankind …'[49] That experience directly influenced the UDHR's Article 3,[50] which stated that 'Everyone has the right to life, liberty and security of person'.[51]

The year after the UDHR, the Council of Europe was formed in 1949 as a regional organisation for achieving greater unity among its members, and for upholding democracy, human rights and the rule of law.[52] The Council of Europe emerged from the complex context of post-war European reconstruction,[53] and its cornerstone and major achievement was the ECHR.[54] The ECHR was signed by its High Contracting Parties, the members of the Council of Europe, in 1950 and entered into force in 1953 with the specific aim of giving effect to elements of the UDHR. As discussed by Steven Greer in his detailed history of the ECHR, 'there are no simple explanations either for what it is or for why it came into being',[55] but he indicates that its main contemporary functions were:

> … to contribute to the prevention of another war between western European states, to provide a statement of common values contrasting sharply with Soviet-style communism (and Nazism/fascism) capable of serving as a Cold War totem, to

[48] Morsink, *The Universal Declaration of Human Rights* 1–40; Mary Ann Glendon, *The Forum and the Tower: How Scholars and Politicians have Imagined the World, from Plato to Eleanor Roosevelt* (New York, Oxford University Press, 2011) 199–220; Henkin, *The Age of Rights* 1; Wicks, *The Right to Life and Conflicting Interests* 38–40; Dupré, *The Age of Dignity* 58–59.

[49] UDHR 1948 Preamble, second paragraph.

[50] On the evolution and meanings of the right to life in the post-war era see BG Ramcharan, 'The Concept and Dimensions of the Right to Life' in Ramcharan (ed), *The Right to Life in International Law* 1; Morsink, *The Universal Declaration of Human Rights* 38–40; Tomuschat, 'The Right to Life – Legal and Political Foundations' 4; Wicks, *The Right to Life and Conflicting Interests* 38–39; and note Paolo De Stefani, 'Il Diritto alla vita e la sua tutela internazionale' in Paolo De Stefani and Francisco Leita (eds), *La Tutela Giuridica Internazionale dei Diritti Umani* (Padova, CEDAM, 1997) 9. See also Jon Yorke, 'Introduction' in Jon Yorke (ed), *The Right to Life and the Value of Life: Orientations in Law, Politics and Ethics* (Farnham, Ashgate, 2010) 1. On the degradation of human life in the Nazi concentration camps see David Fraser, *Law after Auschwitz: Towards a Jurisprudence of the Holocaust* (Durham, NC, Carolina Academic Press, 2005) 31, 59.

[51] This declaration of respect for the value of life and the stated reasons for it were, however, questionable given historical evidence about Soviet gulags, British (and other states') colonial conduct and US treatment of African-Americans, for example. See Morsink, *The Universal Declaration of Human Rights* 40–41 and Wicks, *The Right to Life and Conflicting Interests* 39.

[52] Statute of the Council of Europe, 5 May 1949, European Treaty Series 1: Preamble and Article 1; Article 3 made acceptance of the rule of law and fundamental freedoms, as well as sincere collaboration in achieving the Council's aims, a condition of membership. These aims were reiterated more recently in the 2005 Warsaw Declaration: Warsaw Declaration, 17 May 2005: www.coe.int/t/dcr/summit/20050517_decl_varsovie_EN.asp (consulted 17 July 2018). See Bernadette Rainey, Elizabeth Wicks and Clare Ovey (eds), *Jacobs, White & Ovey: The European Convention on Human Rights* (Oxford, Oxford University Press, 2017) 4–5.

[53] Greer, *The European Convention on Human Rights* 12–17.

[54] Convention for the Protection of Human Rights and Fundamental Freedoms, 4 November 1950, European Treaty Series 5.

[55] Greer, *The European Convention on Human Rights* 17.

> re-enforce a sense of common identity and purpose should the Cold War turn 'hot', and to establish an early warning device by which a drift towards authoritarianism in any member state could be addressed by an independent trans-national tribunal through complaints brought by states against each other.[56]

The ECHR, like the UDHR before it, thus largely reflected the 'never again' ethos[57] of the post-war world and a response to totalitarianism, both with regard to the regimes defeated in the war and fear of their return, and to the perceived threat of Communism beyond the Iron Curtain that divided Europe.[58] Notably, this anti-totalitarian focus was evident in early ECtHR judgments,[59] and in some politicians' understanding of the appropriate scope of ECHR law.[60] Above all, the ECHR was rooted in a foundational connection between post-war democracy and the protection of rights as the key mechanisms for upholding fundamental freedoms, peace and justice.[61] These purposes and values were declared in its Preamble:[62]

> The Governments signatory hereto, being members of the Council of Europe,
>
> Considering the Universal Declaration of Human Rights proclaimed by the General Assembly of the United Nations on 10th December 1948;

[56] Greer, *The European Convention on Human Rights* 20. Note also Emmanuel Decaux, 'Les États parties et leurs engagements' in Louis-Edmond Pettiti, Emmanuel Decaux and Pierre-Henri Imbert (eds), *La Convention Européenne des Droits de l'Homme* (Paris, Economica, 1999) 3–25. It is important to recall the influence of some states' concerns about managing issues arising in their colonies and independence movements: see generally Simpson, *Human Rights and the End of Empire*.

[57] Dupré, *The Age of Dignity* 57–62.

[58] Susan Marks, 'The European Convention on Human Rights and its "Democratic Society"', (1996) 66 *British Yearbook of International Law* 209, 210–11; Klaus Günther, 'The Legacies of Injustice and Fear: A European Approach to Human Rights and their Effects on Political Culture' in Alston (ed), *The EU and Human Rights* 117, 124–27; Elizabeth Wicks, 'The United Kingdom Government's Perceptions of the European Convention on Human Rights at the Time of Entry' (2000) *Public Law* 438, 441–42 and 448; Andrew Moravcsik, 'The Origins of Human Rights Regimes: Democratic Delegation in Post-war Europe' (2000) 54.2 *International Organization* 217, 237; Danny Nicol, 'Original Intent and the European Convention on Human Rights' (2005) *Public Law* 152, 152–53.

[59] This focus became less apparent though as the ECHR developed into a more prospective human rights system: see Marks, 'The European Convention on Human Rights and its "Democratic Society"' 210–11; Ed Bates, *The Evolution of the European Convention on Human Rights* (Oxford, Oxford University Press, 2010) 4–8. On similar processes elsewhere see also Richard Primus, 'A Brooding Omnipresence: Totalitarianism in Postwar Constitutional Thought' (1996–97) 106 *Yale Law Journal* 423 and Margaret Raymond, 'Rejecting Totalitarianism: Translating the Guarantees of Constitutional Criminal Procedure' (1998) 76 *North Carolina Law Review* 1193.

[60] The UK government at the time of signing thought that the ECHR's purpose of protecting democracy meant that it should only be interpreted as an instrument for stopping incipient totalitarian (primarily Communist) activity, rather than potentially undermining a democratic state through human rights challenges. On that basis the UK government initially opposed individual petition and a compulsory ECtHR, mainly due to concerns about misuse of the system by political militants (again primarily Communists), colonial interests and parliamentary sovereignty: see Wicks, 'The United Kingdom Government's Perceptions of the European Convention' 441–42, 444, 448–55.

[61] Compare Marco Duranti, *The Conservative Human Rights Revolution: European Identity, Transnational Politics, and the Origins of the European Convention* (Oxford, Oxford University Press, 2017), who argues that the ECHR was also intended to block left-wing policies by elected governments and conserve Christian values in a conservative form of democracy.

[62] Moravcsik, 'The Origins of Human Rights Regimes' 238; Théo Van Boven, 'Convention des droits de l'homme et des libertés fondamentales' in Pettiti et al, *La Convention Européenne des Droits de l'Homme* 125–34.

> Considering that this Declaration aims at securing the universal and effective recognition and observance of the Rights therein declared;
>
> Considering that the aim of the Council of Europe is the achievement of greater unity between its members and that one of the methods by which that aim is to be pursued is the maintenance and further realisation of Human Rights and Fundamental Freedoms;
>
> Reaffirming their profound belief in those fundamental freedoms which are the foundation of justice and peace in the world and are best maintained on the one hand by an effective political democracy and on the other by a common understanding and observance of the Human Rights upon which they depend;
>
> Being resolved, as the governments of European countries which are likeminded and have a common heritage of political traditions, ideals, freedom and the rule of law, to take the first steps for the collective enforcement of certain of the rights stated in the Universal Declaration,
>
> Have agreed as follows …

The Preamble thus portrayed the ECHR as being based on an agreement rooted in the basic values of the 'likeminded' countries in the Council of Europe, which were said to share a 'common heritage'.[63] This partly referred to a longer-term historical sense of the development of 'political traditions, ideals, freedom and the rule of law', especially democracy and forms of rights, as well as a specifically post-war sense of self-definition through opposition to totalitarianism. As the opening statement of foundational values and purposes, the Preamble is considered to be a key part of the ECHR's interpretive framework.[64] However, the idea of a 'common heritage' was questionable in that it encompassed founding Member States in 1950 that had only recently emerged from dark periods in their history (primarily the Federal Republic of Germany (at the time West Germany) from Nazism, Italy from Fascism, France from the Vichy regime and Norway from the Quisling government).[65] Moreover, the Preamble needs to be understood as a selective politico-legal statement of perceived historical conditions and commonalities that was intended to anchor the ECHR in a legitimating framework of values and circumstances.[66] Both of these points are discussed below in Part II with regard to

[63] See Greer, *The European Convention on Human Rights* 15–16; Van Boven, 'Convention des droits de l'homme et des libertés fondamentales' 131–34.

[64] The ECtHR confirmed this in *Golder v United Kingdom* (1975), relying on Article 31(1) and 31(2) of the Vienna Convention on the Law of Treaties 1969. See also Jens Meyer-Ladewig, 'The Rule of Law in the Case Law of the Strasbourg Court' in Hermann-Josef Blanke and Stelio Mangiameli, *The European Union After Lisbon: Constitutional Basis, Economic Order and External Action* (Berlin, Springer, 2012) 233, 235.

[65] On this issue see generally Christian Joerges and Navraj Singh Ghaleigh (eds), *Darker Legacies of Law in Europe: the Shadow of National Socialism and Fascism over Europe and its Legal Traditions* (Oxford, Hart, 2003).

[66] As Susan Marks has observed, the Preamble's formulation 'no doubt belied a complex mixture of history, ideology, aspiration and cant': Marks, 'The European Convention on Human Rights and its "Democratic Society"' 209–10. Compare on the Preamble's and ECHR's ideological contingency Conor Gearty, 'Democracy and Human Rights in the European Court of Human Rights: A Critical Appraisal' (2000) 51.3 *Northern Ireland Legal Quarterly* 381, 382 and Mario Dogliani, 'I Diritti dell'uomo: Principii

the combination of the real and the imaginary in the concept of democratic society in ECHR law.

In terms of the specific provisions of the ECHR in that context, the first substantive right that it protected was the right to life:

> 1. Everyone's right to life shall be protected by law. No one shall be deprived of his life intentionally save in the execution of a sentence of a court following his conviction of a crime for which this penalty is provided by law.
>
> 2. Deprivation of life shall not be regarded as inflicted in contravention of this Article when it results from the use of force which is no more than absolutely necessary:
>
> (a) in defence of any person from unlawful violence;
> (b) in order to effect a lawful arrest or to prevent the escape of a person lawfully detained;
> (c) in action lawfully taken for the purpose of quelling a riot or insurrection.

Article 2 has a broad range of applications[67] and, as noted in Chapter 1, although it originally reflected retention of capital punishment in post-war Europe, the element of Article 2(1)'s second clause allowing for the death penalty is now considered to be redundant. The way that the right to life is covered in Article 2(1)'s first clause though is of particular importance with regard to its connection with democratic society. Rather than declaring the existence of the right and its fundamental nature, Article 2(1) is based on an assumption that there is such a right and focuses on an imperative statement about its protection by law.[68] Article 2 thus reflects the fundamental ethos of the Council of Europe and the ECHR in terms of the rule of law.

Article 2(2) covers three strictly circumscribed grounds on which an 'absolutely necessary' use of force in domestic policing and law enforcement activities that causes a deprivation of life will not breach the right.[69] This inclusion of narrowly defined ways in which lethal force may be permissible in Article 2(2) goes further than the basic declaration of a right to life in Article 3 UDHR. It can also be seen to be a distinctive feature of Article 2 ECHR in comparison with the

universali o ideologia?' in Mario Dogliani and Stefano Sicardi (eds), *Diritti Umani e Uso della Forza: Profili di diritto costituzionale interno e internazionale* (Turin, Giappichelli, 1999) 45.

[67] The right to life in Article 2 can encompass issues including the beginning and end of life (abortion and euthanasia), deaths in the care of the state (ranging from health care to prison) and armed conflict, but the focus here is on its applicability to policing and law enforcement: see generally Rainey, Wicks and Ovey, *Jacobs, White & Ovey: The European Convention on Human Rights* 150–82 and Pieter van Dijk, Fried van Hoof, Arjen van Rijn and Leo Zwaak, *Theory and Practice of the European Convention on Human Rights* 5th edn (Antwerp, Intersentia, 2018) 353–80.

[68] Ramcharan, 'The Concept and Dimensions of the Right to Life' 3–4; Wicks, *The Right to Life and Conflicting Interests* 44.

[69] On the drafting of these exceptions see Council of Europe, *Collected Edition of the Travaux Préparatoires of the European Convention on Human Rights*, Vol III 158, 186, and the UK's concern with ensuring that the right specified its ambit and limits at 248–80; BG Ramcharan, 'The Drafting History of Article 2 of the European Convention on Human Rights' in Ramcharan (ed), *The Right to Life in International Law* 57–61; Wicks, *The Right to Life and Conflicting Interests* 43; JES Fawcett, *The Application of the European Convention on Human Rights* (Oxford, Clarendon Press, 1987) 33–40.

protection of the right to life in Article 6 of the subsequent International Covenant on Civil and Political Rights (ICCPR, 1966), which only prohibited in more general terms the arbitrary deprivation of life.[70] Although that aspect of Article 6 ICCPR was intended to limit its permissible exceptions,[71] it apparently reflected the US representatives' desire not to list (and so restrict) possible circumstances in which lethal force could be used.[72] Nevertheless, the concept of arbitrariness in the use of force, via Article 6 ICCPR, has supplemented the ECtHR's interpretation of Article 2(2) ECHR (discussed in Chapter 4).[73]

Although the exceptions in Article 2(2) indicate narrowly defined limitations on permissible deprivations of life, the fact that such exceptions are included in the right to life can appear to be problematic. As the first substantive right protected in the ECHR, the right to life in Article 2 can be understood to be the foundational right and the precondition for the other rights: without it all others become meaningless.[74] Indeed, commenting on the main expressions of the right to life in international human rights law, including the UDHR, ECHR and ICCPR, the ECtHR has stated:

> The convergence of the above-mentioned instruments is significant: it indicates that the right to life is an inalienable attribute of human beings and forms the supreme value in the hierarchy of human rights.[75]

[70] The ICCPR was introduced to make rights first set out in the UDHR enforceable. The first paragraph of Article 6 ICCPR states: 'Every human being has the inherent right to life. This right shall be protected by law. No one shall be arbitrarily deprived of his life'. See CK Boyle, 'The Concept of Arbitrary Deprivation of Life' in Ramcharan, *The Right to Life in International Law* 221, 228 and 236; and Wicks, *The Right to Life and Conflicting Interests* 40–42, 44. The prohibition on arbitrary killing is based on the view that a permissible deprivation of life must have a basis in a lawfully recognised exceptional reason, and not be inappropriate, unjust, unpredictable, in breach of due process of law, unreasonable, unnecessary or disproportionate: United Nations Office of the High Commissioner for Human Rights, Human Rights Committee, 'General Comment No 36 on Article 6 of the International Covenant on Civil and Political Rights, on the Right to Life' (draft adopted on first reading during the 120th session, July 2017) paras 16–21 at para 18. See also Christof Heyns, Report of the Special Rapporteur on Extrajudicial, Summary or Arbitrary Executions (1 April 2014), United Nations Human Rights Council A/HRC/26/36, 7–17.

[71] Ramcharan, 'The Concept and Dimensions of the Right to Life' 19. See further BG Ramcharan, 'The Drafting History of Article 6 of the International Covenant on Civil and Political Rights' in Ramcharan, *The Right to Life in International Law* 42–56.

[72] Boyle, 'The Concept of Arbitrary Deprivation of Life' 221–44; see also Daniel D Nsereko, 'Arbitrary Deprivation of Life: Controls on Permissible Deprivations' in Ramcharan (ed), *The Right to Life in International Law* 245, 248.

[73] The Human Rights Committee's development of the concept of arbitrariness under Article 6 ICCPR also reflects the influence of ECHR law through the concepts of necessity and proportionality.

[74] Franciszek Przetacznik, 'The Right to Life as a Basic Human Right' (1976) 9 *Revue des Droits de l'Homme: Revue de Droit International et Comparé* 585, 589–90.

[75] *Streletz, Kessler and Krenz v Germany* (2001) para 94 – this case is discussed in Chapter 6. Compare Yoram Dinstein, 'The Right to Life, Physical Integrity, and Liberty' in Louis Henkin, *The International Bill of Rights: The Covenant on Civil and Political Rights* (New York, Columbia University Press, 1981) 114: the 'inviolability or sanctity of life is, perhaps, the most basic value of modern civilisation'. On the right to life in other European provisions see Bertrand Mathieu, *Le droit à la vie dans les jurisprudences constitutionnelles et conventionnelles européennes* (Strasbourg, Editions du Conseil de l'Europe, 2005) and Nicolae Pavel, 'The Right to Life as a Supreme Value and Guaranteeing the Right to Life' (2012) 4.2 *Contemporary Readings in Law and Social Justice* 970.

Furthermore, given that Article 2 and Article 3 ECHR (the prohibition on torture and inhuman and degrading treatment) are connected by the ECtHR as basic values of democratic societies in the Council of Europe, it can seem strange that Article 3 is absolute while the more fundamental Article 2 is not. As CK Boyle observed:

> It is a paradox that torture of a human being which leaves that person alive is never justifiable, whatever the circumstances, while to kill that person in different circumstances may be. Torture is not permissible even to save life but killing one human being to save another can be.[76]

However, the exceptions in Article 2(2) are based on recognition that the state might need in some situations to protect collective interests above individual interests and use force to do so, which might result in death.[77] In other words, it reflects the understanding that the High Contracting Parties as democratic societies cannot guarantee the protection of all lives in all circumstances. As such Article 2 protects the right to life but situates it pragmatically in a social context in which individual rights, social interests and the need for state action come into conflict and need to be mediated through law. According to Franciszek Przetacznik, 'man is by his nature a social being' and 'designated by nature to live in community, in which he always normally lives', which leads Przetacznik to argue that 'man's right to life must be and can only properly be treated in the aspect of his relationship towards this community' and 'his reciprocal rights and duties with respect to other men and towards the State'.[78] Even though the right to life needs to be considered in this social aspect, it remains a right, entailing the need to respect and protect the individual's life as well as the social interest.[79] This also involves recognition of the fact that the exercise of power by state authorities, even democratic ones, may not always be correct or faultless, and that such imperfection leads to the need for safeguards and limits on permissible state action.[80]

How the ECtHR approaches these competing demands in its interpretation and application of Article 2 is discussed in detail in Chapters 4–6. At this stage though it suffices to note that in applying Article 2 to state uses of force,

[76] Boyle, 'The Concept of Arbitrary Deprivation of Life' 221, 223.

[77] Note Michael O'Boyle, 'The Use of Lethal Force under Article 2 of the European Convention on Human Rights', DH-ED-COLL (90) 9, Council of Europe, 26–28 November 1990; Stefan Trechsel, 'Spotlights on Article 2 ECHR, The Right to Life' in Wolfgang Benedek, Hubert Isak and Renate Kicker (eds), *Development and Developing International and European Law* (Frankfurt am Main, Peter Lang, 1999) 671; Fawcett, *The Application of the European Convention on Human Rights* 40. See also George Fletcher, 'The Right to Life' (1979) 13 *Georgia Law Review* 1371, 1375.

[78] Przetacznik, 'The Right to Life as a Basic Human Right' 585, 590. Przetacznik's use of a gender-specific noun and pronoun is reproduced here, but the intended sense of this discussion is non-gendered and universal.

[79] McBride, 'Protecting Life' 54; this issue is central to Wicks, *The Right to Life and Conflicting Interests*. Emphasis on society over the individual, ignoring the particular aspect of a right that requires respect, would risk veering towards the anti-democratic denial of the importance of individual rights: recall Rocco, 'The Political Doctrine of Fascism' 401–403.

[80] Note David Held, *Models of Democracy* (Stanford, Stanford University Press, 2006) 78.

the fundamental importance of the right to life 'dictates the possible scope of exceptions to the right',[81] which as recognised by the ECtHR should therefore be construed strictly and proportionately with regard to the value being protected;[82] but at the same time the ECtHR has had to accept the thrust of Article 2(2) and limited the right's protection in some circumstances in favour of state action in the name of society. The right to life in Article 2 as a fundamental provision of the ECHR and a basic value of democratic societies in the Council of Europe thus arguably has a thick significance that reflects twentieth-century (and older) concerns about state power and the danger of oppression, involves an inherent tension, and is structured around provisions allowing for the use of lethal force.

II. Democratic Society as Narrative Theme: Interpretations

The ECtHR's references to the connection between the right to life and the 'basic values of the democratic societies making up the Council of Europe', first stated in *McCann* and repeated in subsequent Article 2 case law, open, orient and support its interpretation and application of that right. As such, that connection constitutes the main narrative theme in case law on the use of lethal or potentially lethal force. While the above discussion of the post-war origins of the ECHR and the formulation of Article 2 has included references to the concept of democratic society, this section looks more closely at that concept's possible meanings, not in terms of how it can be understood through an interpretation of Article 2 law's implications, which are addressed in Chapters 6 and 7, but in terms of what the concept appears to mean when used by the ECtHR. It is suggested here that in Article 2 case law 'democratic societies' has (at least) three overlapping senses. First, the reference to the values of the democratic societies making up the Council of Europe can be seen to have a descriptive sense, to the extent that it is intended to refer to Member States' identities and values as a supposed matter of fact, as well as an idealised and legitimating representation of fact. Second, the reference to 'democratic societies' arguably alludes to the ECHR concept of 'democratic society', which relates to the ECtHR's process of proportionately balancing individual rights with collective interests and can be understood in the context of *McCann* and subsequent judgments as a way of qualifying the ECtHR's approach to the 'absolutely necessary' test in Article 2(2). Third, both of these meanings can be understood as feeding into a normative sense of 'democratic societies', expressing the ECtHR's purposive and aspirational development of standards under Article 2.

[81] Boyle, 'The Concept of Arbitrary Deprivation of Life' 223.

[82] As it stated in *McCann* para 150 and subsequent cases, 'in keeping with the importance of this provision in a democratic society, the Court must, in making its assessment, subject deprivations of life to the most careful scrutiny, particularly where deliberate lethal force is used'.

A. 'Democratic Societies' as a Descriptive and Legitimating Concept

The references in Article 2 case law to the values of the democratic societies making up the Council of Europe echo the ECHR Preamble, as well as the Council of Europe's founding statute, and their declarations about 'countries which are likeminded' with 'a common heritage of political traditions, ideals, freedom and the rule of law'.[83] The concept of 'democratic societies' can thus be seen as grounding Article 2 judgments in the foundations of the ECHR order and positioning decisions about lethal or potentially lethal force and the right to life in relation to a larger schema of fundamental values. This concept needs to be unravelled though to address its core elements, its apparent scope and, by critically locating it in European history, its legitimating function.

At the heart of the values of democratic societies and their common traditions in the Council of Europe are adherence to democracy and the rule of law. As famously observed by WB Gallie, democracy as a system of representative social organisation and government is an essentially contested concept,[84] the theoretical and system-specific meanings of which, including its nexus with human rights,[85] are interpreted in various ways.[86] Although the ECHR Preamble declares a certain vision of the High Contracting Parties' values, which can largely be situated historically in their post-war anti-totalitarian stance, an a priori conceptual model of what democracy actually entails is not specified in the ECHR or by the ECtHR.[87] ECtHR judgments have though sought to maintain and promote democratic

[83] ECHR Preamble; Statute of the Council of Europe Preamble and Article 1.

[84] WB Gallie, 'Essentially Contested Concepts' (1956) 56 *Proceedings of the Aristotelian Society* 167, 169, 171–72, 183–87; also note Anna Pintore, *I diritti della democrazia* (Bari, Laterza, 2003) 3 and Alain Zysset, *The ECHR and Human Rights Theory: Reconciling the Moral and the Political Conceptions* (London, Routledge, 2017) 140. An argument that the meaning of democracy is contestable rather than contested is made by David Beetham, *Democracy and Human Rights* (Cambridge, Polity Press, 1999) 2–6.

[85] Notable perspectives on the rights-democracy nexus are outlined in Michael Goodhart, 'Democracy as Human Rights' in Thomas Cushman (ed), *Handbook of Human Rights* (Abingdon, Routledge, 2014) 68; Todd Landman, *Human Rights and Democracy: The Precarious Triumph of Ideals* (London, Bloomsbury, 2013) 25–41; Beetham, *Democracy and Human Rights* 89–114; Martin Loughlin, 'Rights, Democracy, and Law' in Tom Campbell, KD Ewing and Adam Tomkins (eds), *Sceptical Essays on Human Rights* (Oxford, Oxford University Press, 2001) 41; Rosas, 'Democracy and Human Rights' 17–52.

[86] See for example the historical outline in Charles Tilly, *Democracy* (Cambridge, Cambridge University Press, 2007) 25–50; a definitional discussion in terms of two core principles of popular control and political equality in Beetham, *Democracy and Human Rights* 1–29; a reflection on the meaning of democracy in international law in James Crawford, 'Democracy and International Law' (1993) 64 *British Yearbook of International Law* 113; and political analyses of types of democracy in Held, *Models of Democracy*; G Duncan, *Democratic Theory and Practice* (Cambridge, Cambridge University Press, 1983); and CB Macpherson, *The Life and Times of Liberal Democracy* (Oxford, Oxford University Press, 1977).

[87] Zysset, *The ECHR and Human Rights Theory* 151–52; Greer, *The European Convention on Human Rights*, 199–200.

society through a focus on what the ECtHR considers to be democracy's main general characteristics, sometimes based on what it determines to be common standards in the Council of Europe.[88] This has received most attention in relation to matters concerning elections and political parties, where the ECtHR's strategy for fostering democratic political culture has involved primarily promoting the importance of deliberative processes and pluralism.[89]

Fundamental to the meaning of democratic society in the ECHR is the rule of law, which is the central component in the interaction between human rights and democracy in the ECHR system, as declared in the Preamble.[90] By its very nature as a legal instrument, the ECHR embodies and confirms its proclaimed reliance on law. Within it, Article 2(1) expresses and depends on the primacy of the rule of law in its focus on the protection of the right to life by law. The ECtHR's operation as a court seeking to achieve state accountability in terms of ECHR law likewise reflects and fosters the rule of law, and its rulings on Article 2 (as will be discussed in Chapter 4) encompass not only the specific terms of that provision but also a state's broad compliance with principles of legality and legal certainty. Yet, reliance on law, the existence of a legal system and the application of legal principles, whilst important, are not the sole components of the rule of law.

What the rule of law means as a fundamental value and in fact is, like democracy, a matter of debate. Theories and definitions of the rule of law vary around Europe, including its common law meanings, as well as *Rechtsstaat*, *état de droit*, *prééminence du droit* and *Stato di diritto* for example, and its signification at the international level is unclear.[91] These variations and related discussions have been addressed elsewhere,[92] but it is informative to note that the European

[88] Marks, 'The European Convention on Human Rights and its "Democratic Society"' 213; François Ost, 'The Original Canons of Interpretation of the European Court of Human Rights' in Mireille Delmas-Marty (Christine Chodkiewicz, trans), *The European Convention for the Protection of Human Rights: International Protection versus National Restrictions* (Dordrecht, Martinus Nijhoff Publishers, 1992) 283; Mireille Delmas-Marty, 'The Richness of Underlying Legal Reasoning' in Delmas-Marty, *The European Convention for the Protection of Human Rights* 319, 327–30.

[89] Marks, 'The European Convention on Human Rights and its "Democratic Society"' 231–34; Alistair Mowbray, 'The Role of the European Court of Human Rights in the Promotion of Democracy' (1999) *Public Law* 703 and 'Contemporary Aspects of the Promotion of Democracy by the European Court of Human Rights' (2014) 20.3 *European Public Law* 469; note the critical view in Gearty, 'Democracy and Human Rights in the European Court of Human Rights'; see also Rabinder Singh, 'The Place of the Human Rights Act in a Democratic Society' in Jeffrey Jowell and Jonathan Cooper (eds), *Understanding Human Rights Principles* (Oxford, Hart, 2001) 179, 186–95.

[90] Jens Meyer-Ladewig, 'The Rule of Law in the Case Law of the Strasbourg Court' in Blanke and Mangiameli, *The European Union After Lisbon* 233; Tomuschat, 'Democracy and the Rule of Law' 471, 475–82; see generally Geranne Lautenbach, *The Concept of the Rule of Law and the European Court of Human Rights* (Oxford, Oxford University Press, 2013); also note Xavier Souvignet, *La prééminence du droit dans le droit de la Convention européenne des droits de l'homme* (Brussels, Bruylant, 2012).

[91] Robert McCorquodale, 'Defining the International Rule of Law: Defying Gravity?' (2016) 65.2 *International and Comparative Law Quarterly* 277–80, 288–96.

[92] For in-depth treatment see Lautenbach, *The Concept of the Rule of Law and the European Court of Human Rights.*

Commission for Democracy through Law (the Council of Europe's 'Venice Commission') has identified 'the essential elements of the rule of law'[93] in six key points:

(1) Legality, including a transparent, accountable and democratic process for enacting law
(2) Legal certainty
(3) Prohibition of arbitrariness
(4) Access to justice before independent and impartial courts, including judicial review of administrative acts
(5) Respect for human rights
(6) Non-discrimination and equality before the law.[94]

The essence of the rule of law can thus be seen to focus on the nature of law, its centrality to the exercise of power, and its interdependency with justice, human rights and equality. The importance of the rule of law is based on the view that in the context of democracy law prescriptively and protectively grounds and limits state power, governs society and (at least in theory) provides the principal mechanism for vertical and horizontal relations within and among states.[95] As Geranne Lautenbach notes, it is aimed at providing stable rules by which society can live, protecting individuals from arbitrary power and supporting liberal ideology, and promoting a just legal system for the adequate protection of individual rights, even though the rule of law can itself involve an inherent tension between the demands of certainty and stability ('law and order') and the needs of individual rights protection.[96] The rule of law in democratic systems is therefore, at least in principle, the keystone that ties their institutional and procedural aspects together with their fundamental values, reflecting and supporting confidence in rules as a source of certainty, fairness and due process in the exercise of power and management of the tensions that governing society generates. In that sense, the rule of law is meant to be the rule of an overarching control system – the impersonal law and its assumed concomitant of (at least formal) justice – instead of the rule of a

[93] European Commission for Democracy through Law, *Report on the Rule of Law*, adopted by the Venice Commission at its 86th plenary session (Venice, 25–26 March 2011) Study no 512/2009, CDL-AD(2011)003rev (Strasbourg, Council of Europe, 2011) 9, para 36. The Venice Commission quotes Tom Bingham, *The Rule of Law* (London, Allen Lane, 2010) 8: 'The core of the existing principle is, I suggest, that all persons and authorities within the state, whether public or private, should be bound by and entitled to the benefit of laws publicly made, taking effect (generally) in the future and publicly administered in the courts'. The eight components of Bingham's definition of the rule of law are set out in Chs 3–10 of his book and include: accessibility of the law; the normal supremacy of law over discretion; equality before the law; power must be exercised lawfully, fairly and reasonably; protection of human rights; dispute resolution without undue cost or delay; fair trials; and compliance by the state with national and international legal obligations.

[94] Venice Commission, *Report on the Rule of Law* 10, para 41.

[95] Note especially Duncan Fairgrieve, 'État de droit and Rule of Law: Comparing Concepts: A Tribute to Roger Errera' (2015) *Public Law* 40; see generally Pietro Costa and Danilo Zolo, *The Rule of Law: History, Theory and Criticism* (Berlin, Springer, 2007) and Brian Tamanaha, *On the Rule of Law: History, Politics, Theory* (Cambridge, Cambridge University Press, 2004).

[96] Lautenbach, *The Concept of the Rule of Law and the European Court of Human Rights* 5, 21–23.

person, office-holder or tyrant.[97] While the rule of law can merely involve what is sometimes called a 'thin' or formal adherence to procedural requirements (important as these are), it should ideally entail a 'thick' or substantive interlocking of democratic legal values and systemic practices.[98] As such, the rule of law needs to be understood as 'intricately bound up with the historical, ideological, and institutional context in which it has developed'.[99]

Accountability under the rule of law, as noted in Chapter 2, is fundamental to the control of power in democracy and is one of the principal ends of human rights law under the ECHR as well as its means, in an endeavour to tie together systemic values and rights protection processes.[100] Whereas a form of democracy can exist with a form of rule of law but without human rights, a true democracy arguably only exists where it incorporates and supports human rights, which can only be meaningful in a system under the rule of law.[101] Rather than adhering solely to a purely parliamentary model of democracy focused on popular sovereignty, the concept of democratic society in the ECHR order is essentially grounded in the conceptual ideal of a combination of political pluralism, representative government, the rule of law, legally protected human rights, and properly functioning courts.[102] Although the predominant legalistic discourse of human rights protection is open to criticism as a mask for power and injustice,[103] and can be seen as a manifestation of the closed-circuitry of legal systems that espouse the foundations and means of their own operation as inherent goods, the ECHR system is based on the understanding that the rule of law can both structure and guarantee human rights in the democratic context.

The ECtHR's connection in *McCann* and subsequent cases between the right to life and the basic values of the democratic societies making up the Council of Europe can be understood as an expression of this fundamentally interdependent and defining conjunction of democracy, the rule of law and human rights. In that regard it is not without significance that the ECtHR refers to 'democratic societies' instead of democracy or democratic states. By including 'societies' the

[97] Tomuschat, 'Democracy and the Rule of Law' 475.

[98] McCorquodale, 'Defining the International Rule of Law' 282–83; Landman, *Human Rights and Democracy* 26–31; Paul P Craig, 'Formal and Substantive Conceptions of the Rule of Law: An Analytical Framework' (1997) *Public Law* 467. 'Thick' in the context of theoretical discussions of the rule of law does not appear to have an intentionally Geertzian connotation.

[99] Lautenbach, *The Concept of the Rule of Law and the European Court of Human Rights* 24.

[100] Tomuschat, 'Democracy and the Rule of Law' 469; Greer, *The European Convention on Human Rights* 201–203.

[101] For example, Landman, *Human Rights and Democracy* 38–42.

[102] Michael Hamilton and Antoine Buyse, 'Human Rights Courts as Norm Brokers' (2018) 18 *Human Rights Law Review* 205, 230.

[103] For example, Michael Freeman, *Human Rights: An Interdisciplinary Approach* (Cambridge, Polity Press, 2011) 8; Amartya Sen, 'Human Rights and the Limits of Law' (2006) 27.6 *Cardozo Law Review* 2913; Neil Stammers, 'A Critique of Social Approaches to Human Rights' (1995) 17 *Human Rights Quarterly* 488; Roland Axtmann, *Democracy: Problems and Perspectives* (Edinburgh, Edinburgh University Press, 2007) 58–60; and see Marie-Bénédicte Dembour, *Who Believes in Human Rights? Reflections on the European Convention* (Cambridge, Cambridge University Press, 2006) 114–54 on the Marxist critique of rights.

ECtHR arguably seeks to express a broad concept, combining social and political dimensions, rather than just referring to a form of state or legal system, thereby indicating the role of heritage and culture that tie democracy, rights and the rule of law into a meaningful whole. Moreover, the reference to 'democratic societies' in the plural indicates a recognition that they might be varied in their specificities, but the essential idea is that they share common values in the Council of Europe.[104] The reference to democratic societies can thus be understood to some extent as being intended to have a descriptive sense, as an appeal to shared values and practices, or a claimed consensus and commonality, to support the ECtHR's interpretation and application of Article 2.[105] Like the Preamble, that reference can be seen as a purportedly factual statement, supposedly reflecting reality, including the self-identification of democratic societies in post-war Europe through rejection of totalitarianism, and as systems upholding the values declared in the ECHR. Referring to the idea of democratic societies and their values in right to life cases is a way of linking judgments to a benchmark of existing standards.

At the same time, due to questionable aspects of the concept's selective temporal and systemic bases in fact, the reference to democratic societies in *McCann* and subsequent cases, as noted in Part I above with regard to the Preamble, also needs to be understood as reflecting a contingent and selective politico-legal representation of historical and systemic factors with a legitimating objective. This is not only because some of the original High Contracting Parties at the time of the formation of the ECHR had only recently ceased to be totalitarian or authoritarian, but also because subsequent members of the Council of Europe included former military dictatorships in southern Europe[106] and former Communist states in Central and Eastern Europe. In other words, although a declared (prospective) adherence to basic values of democracy and human rights, including respecting the right to life, was part of being a signatory of the ECHR, the apparent universality of the ECtHR's references to democratic societies in a descriptive (contemporary and retrospective) sense is limited and glosses over a number of fault-lines in that concept as a homogenous point of reference.[107]

[104] In *Hirst v United Kingdom (No 2)* (2005), para 61, the ECtHR observed that there is 'a wealth of differences, inter alia, in historical development, cultural diversity and political thought within Europe which it is for each Contracting State to mould into their own democratic vision'. Tomuschat, 'Democracy and the Rule of Law' 471. See also Leben, 'Is there a European Approach to Human Rights?', 69–97 but compare (with an EU focus) Päivi Leino, 'A European Approach to Human Rights? Universality Explored' (2002) 71 *Nordic Journal of International Law* 455.

[105] See further Kanstantsin Dzehtsiarou, 'Does Consensus Matter? Legitimacy of European Consensus in the Case Law of the European Court of Human Rights' (2011) *Public Law* 534 and note his discussion of the ECtHR's appeal to supposedly shared values in Kanstantsin Dzehtsiarou, *European Consensus and the Legitimacy of the European Court of Human Rights* (Cambridge, Cambridge University Press, 2015) 11–12.

[106] Moravcsik, 'The Origins of Human Rights Regimes' 231–32.

[107] Note also Stephen Skinner, 'Crimes Against the State and the Intersection of Fascism and Democracy in the 1920s–30s: Vilification, Seditious Libel and the Limits of Legality' (2016) 36.3

The statements in Article 2 law linking that right with the basic values of democratic societies in the Council of Europe can thus be understood in narrative terms as a combination of the real (historical fact and legal source) and the imaginary (an idealised systemic self-image). In Cover's interpretation, this is a way of supplying a legal prescription with history, of giving it a point, of producing a narrative 'plotted upon material reality by our imaginations'.[108] In Ricoeur's terms, this shows the combination of facts and symbolic factors, in this case the symbolic declaratory force of the ECHR and Council of Europe's mission statement, and their inclusion in a narrative that uses them to configure meaning about the right to life based on an imagined ideal of democratic society.[109] The narrative theme of democratic societies is therefore in part factual and in part fictional, as a way of grounding the ECtHR's argument and legitimating Article 2's normative force.[110] This observation is not intended to challenge the veracity of post-war efforts in Europe to maintain democracy through human rights and the rule of law, or the importance of the connections among them, but to point to the layers of fact and politically charged symbolism and self-representation that feed into the ECtHR's case narratives.[111] Given that the *McCann* judgment involved the actions of the UK, a founding member of the Council of Europe, and that in 1995 the judgment came just after the beginning of the Council's post-Communist expansion in the aftermath of 1989, this reference to the values of democratic societies served to anchor the ruling in the ECHR's foundational purposes and provide a strategic reminder of them in a period of change. Ongoing repetitions of that connection in subsequent judgments on the right to life have served to link them, not only cohesively with each other, but also with this representation of the right's significance and the ECHR's roots and aims. The concept of democratic societies is therefore a fundamental part of Article 2 narratives, but at the same time, when considered in a 'thicker' sense, is also contextually questionable. Yet these are not the only possible interpretations of the ECtHR's stated connection between the right to life and democratic society.

B. 'Democratic Societies', 'Democratic Society': A Concept within a Concept?

The reference to 'democratic societies' serves a related purpose in setting up how the ECtHR anchors and orients its interpretation and application of Article 2,

Oxford Journal of Legal Studies 482–504, 501–503; and Vivian Curran, 'Law's Past and Europe's Future' (2005) 6.2 *German Law Journal* 483–512.

[108] Cover, 'Foreword: Nomos and Narrative' 4–5.

[109] Ricoeur *Time and Narrative, Volume 1* 54–71.

[110] Günter Frankenberg, *Comparative Law as Critique* (Cheltenham, Edward Elgar, 2016) 195–99.

[111] See also Bernard Jackson, *Law, Fact and Narrative Coherence* (Liverpool, Deborah Charles Publications, 1988) 157–61 on the combination of fact and a layer of interpretation in legal analysis.

by arguably alluding to the concept – or term of art – of 'democratic society' in its more technical sense as an interpretive device that is integral to the ECHR and has been developed by the ECtHR through its case law.[112] This sense of 'democratic society' is primarily concerned with the interpretation and application of qualified rights in the ECHR, specifically Articles 8–11. The ECtHR has interpreted the 'necessary in a democratic society' clause in these rights and the extent to which the right in question may be permissibly curtailed by seeking to balance the right in relation to other key values and objectives in the democratic context.[113] The ECtHR has addressed this through the concept of proportionality,[114] which it outlined in the *Soering* judgment: 'inherent in the whole of the Convention is a search for a fair balance between the demands of the general interest of the community and the requirements of the protection of the individual's fundamental rights'.[115] Even though in *McCann* and subsequent rulings the ECtHR has declared that the 'absolutely necessary' test in Article 2(2) requires 'a stricter and more compelling test of necessity' than that 'normally applicable when determining whether state action is "necessary in a democratic society"' under the qualified rights in the ECHR, thus using a test of strict proportionality between the force used and the aim pursued,[116] the ECtHR's connection between Article 2 and 'democratic societies' nevertheless links it with the same conceptual framework.

As noted in Chapter 2, the process of interpreting and applying a right, including any element of proportionality in its permissible limitation, can affect both the meaning and scope of the right in question,[117] and indicates the adjudicator's understanding of priorities among the competing values and interests at stake. This can include questions of socio-political concern, as well as degrees

[112] Phédon T Vegleris, 'Valeur et Signification de la Clause "Dans une Société Démocratique" dans la Convention Européenne des Droits de l'Homme' (1968) 1.2 *Les Droits de l'Homme: Revue de Droit International et Comparé* 219; O Jacot-Guillarmod, 'The Relationship Between Democracy and Human Rights' in *Democracy and Human Rights*, Proceedings of the Colloquy organised by the Government of Greece and the Council of Europe, 24–26 September 1987 (Kehl, NP Engel, 1990) 43; Ost, 'The Original Canons of Interpretation of the European Court of Human Rights' 283, 294–303.

[113] See generally Rainey, Wicks and Ovey, *Jacobs, White & Ovey: The European Convention on Human Rights* 359–368 and note for example *Dudgeon v UK* (1981) paras 52–53.

[114] Vegleris, 'Valeur et Signification de la Clause "Dans une Société Démocratique"' 219–42; Alastair Mowbray, 'A Study of the Principle of Fair Balance in the Jurisprudence of the European Court of Human Rights' (2010) 10.2 *Human Rights Law Review* 289–317; Alain Zysset, 'Searching for the Legitimacy of the European Court of Human Rights: The Neglected Role of "Democratic Society"' (2016) 5.1 *Global Constitutionalism* 16, 22–27; see also Aileen McHarg, 'Reconciling Human Rights and the Public Interest: Conceptual Problems and Doctrinal Uncertainty in the Jurisprudence of the European Court of Human Rights' (1999) 62.5 *Modern Law Review* 671–96.

[115] *Soering v UK* (1989) para 89. See also Greer's analysis of interpretive principles in the ECHR: Greer, *The European Convention on Human Rights* 196–97, 203.

[116] *McCann* para 149. Note also Pietro Pustorino, *L'Interpretazione della Convenzione Europea dei Diritti dell'Uomo nella Prassi della Commissione e della Corte di Strasburgo* (Naples, Editoriale Scientifica, 1998) 71–72.

[117] Janneke Gerards and Hanneke Senden, 'The Structure of Fundamental Rights and the European Court of Human Rights' (2009) 7.4 *International Journal of Constitutional Law* 619, 619–20.

of subordination in the relationship between national and trans-national decision making.[118] As such, it is a contested aspect of ECHR law,[119] especially when its conjunction with subsidiarity stretches into the margin of appreciation.[120] It is thus important to observe how the ECtHR configures its interpretation in terms of an underlying narrative theme, which indicates its guiding justificatory rationale. By referring to the right to life as a basic value of democratic societies when introducing its analysis of Article 2 in the *McCann* and subsequent rulings, the ECtHR both underlined the right's fundamental importance, and arguably alluded to the concept of 'democratic society' as a way of contextualising and supporting its approach to the proportionate application of the right to life. In Cover's narrative terms, this suggests the 'interpretive commitments' that shape the ECtHR's normative world,[121] and these commitments in this context have two main aspects.

First, the idea that ECHR rights could be limited in the democratic context was derived from the UDHR, which made allowances for legally prescribed restrictions on certain rights in the name of upholding others' rights or collective interests, such as public order.[122] The idea of democratic society in ECHR law was thus intended to encapsulate an understanding of democracy as the framework in which human rights may best be demanded, fostered and protected. Yet at the same time, through its inclusion and, ideally, appropriate balancing of competing individual and collective interests, democratic society signified a system requiring the justifiable and proportionate limitation of some rights in certain situations, involving both a process for achieving such limitation and awareness of the network of beliefs, perceptions and contextual pressures in which it occurs.[123]

At the heart of this interpretive (politico-legal) concept of democratic society, therefore, is recognition of the possible tensions among individual rights and between them and collective interests. Indeed, in theoretical terms some commentators note that that tension is inherent in the relationship between rights and democracy, which are mutually essential and yet incompletely compatible, due to the potential conflict between individual worth and the inevitable relativity

[118] Marks, 'The European Convention on Human Rights and its "Democratic Society"' 209–18; Alastair Mowbray, 'Subsidiarity and the European Convention on Human Rights' (2015) 15 *Human Rights Law Review* 313.

[119] For example, Başak Çali, 'Balancing Human Rights? Methodological Problems with Weights, Scales and Proportions' (2007) 29 *Human Rights Quarterly* 251; Julian Rivers, 'Proportionality and Variable Intensity of Review' (2006) 65.1 *Cambridge Law Journal* 174; Stavros Tsakyrakis, 'Proportionality: An Assault on Human Rights?' (2009) 7.3 *International Journal of Constitutional Law* 468.

[120] See Steven Greer, 'The Interpretation of the European Convention on Human Rights: Universal Principle or Margin of Appreciation?' (2010) 3 *UCL Human Rights Review* 1 and Dean Spielmann, 'Allowing the Right Margin: The European Court of Human Rights and the National Margin of Appreciation Doctrine: Waiver or Subsidiarity of European Review?' (2012) 14 *Cambridge Year Book of European Legal Studies* 381.

[121] Cover, 'Foreword: Nomos and Narrative' 7, 10.

[122] Vegleris, 'Valeur et Signification de la Clause "Dans une Société Démocratique" dans la Convention Européenne des Droits de l'Homme' 219, 229.

[123] Jacot-Guillarmod, 'The Relationship Between Democracy and Human Rights' 43, 46–47.

involved in assessing communitarian interests.[124] Democracy in democratic society thus supports human rights but, with the limited exceptions of absolute rights, at times requires, mediates and moderates their restriction through proportionate limits and judicial processes of interpretation.[125]

Second, the importance of 'democratic society', as the context in which proportionate balancing between individual and collective interests takes place, also needs to be understood with reference to a key socio-political concern in the post-war European context with the ability of democratic society to protect itself. This is based on recognition of the fact that a democratic society may have enemies, within and without, and that by adhering to values of liberalism and the protection of rights, it potentially opens the way for freedoms and rights to be used against it and weakens its own ability to respond to threats.[126] In other words, fundamental characteristics of democratic societies may constitute their points of weakness. Beginning in the interwar period, due to the failings of some democratic orders to face the threat of anti-democratic movements internally, or anti-democratic regimes elsewhere, the concept of 'militant democracy' was formulated by Karl Loewenstein to express the idea of firm but carefully circumscribed action by democratic states to preserve themselves and their liberal values against such threats.[127] The concept continued into the post-war era (especially in the German constitutional system) as a way of expressing the need for continued vigilance and strong action by democracies in dealing with matters that might threaten them, such as the resurgence of fascist movements, the perceived dangers of Communism during the Cold War and other subsequent political risks.[128] As Patrick Macklem notes, it involves 'a form of constitutional democracy authorized

[124] Mariano Croce, 'La Democrazia come Reciproco Processo di Apprendimento: Procedure Giuridiche e Diritti Umani' (2005) 24 *Ragion Pratica* 281.

[125] Delmas-Marty, 'The Richness of Underlying Legal Reasoning' 319, 322–30. Note Paul Ricoeur's observation that the act of judging per se is about determining a party's 'fair share in that model of cooperation that is society': Paul Ricoeur, 'The Act of Judging' in Paul Ricoeur (David Pellauer, trans), *The Just* (Chicago, University of Chicago Press, 2000) 127, 132. See generally Grant Huscroft, Bradley W Miller and Grégoire Webber (eds), *Proportionality and the Rule of Law: Rights, Justification, Reasoning* (Cambridge, Cambridge University Press, 2014).

[126] Torkel Opsahl, 'The Right to Life' in R St J Macdonald, F Matscher and H Petzold (eds), *The European System for the Protection of Human Rights* (Dordrecht, Martinus Nijhoff Publishers, 1993) 207, 215; Samy Cohen, 'Introduction: Dilemmas in the War against Terrorism' in Samy Cohen (ed), *Democracies at War against Terrorism: A Comparative Perspective* (Basingstoke, Palgrave Macmillan, 2008) 1, 3, 6.

[127] Karl Loewenstein, 'Militant Democracy and Fundamental Rights, I' (1937) 31.3 *The American Political Science Review* 417 and 'Militant Democracy and Fundamental Rights, II' (1937) 31.4 *The American Political Science Review* 638.

[128] Ost, 'The Original Canons of Interpretation of the European Court of Human Rights' 283, 298; Paul Harvey, 'Militant Democracy and the European Convention on Human Rights' (2004) 29.3 *European Law Review* 407–20; András Sajó (ed), *Militant Democracy* (Utrecht, Eleven International Publishing, 2004); Markus Thiel, 'Introduction' in Markus Thiel (ed), *The 'Militant Democracy' Principle in Modern Democracies* (Farnham, Ashgate, 2009) 1–5 and Markus Thiel, 'Comparative Aspects' in Thiel (ed), *The 'Militant Democracy' Principle*, 379–421; Svetlana Tyulkina, *Militant Democracy: Undemocratic Political Parties and Beyond* (Abingdon, Routledge, 2015).

to protect civil and political freedom by pre-emptively restricting the exercise of such freedoms'.[129]

On the one hand, this is perhaps merely an acute expression of the need for proportionate balance between individual and collective interests and a way of conceptualising a robust approach to it. However, on the other hand, it is a specific reflection of European historical experience and a fundamental aspect of the construction of democracy, rights and the rule of law in the post-war era. As a 'militant' concept, it expresses the idea that democratic states may be proactively, even 'aggressively', defensive in the face of dangers, especially in today's world the threat of terrorism.[130] This then brings with it an enhanced need for ways of ensuring that the resultant balance in rights protection is appropriate, and is as fair as possible, all things considered; that it is carefully scrutinised and evaluated; and that it does not bring about a change in systemic attitude and approach, so that the values in the name of which action is militantly taken are not eroded to the extent that they resemble the threat against which the action is deemed justified.[131]

In that light, the ECtHR's reference to 'democratic societies' can be seen to orient the *McCann* and subsequent judgments in terms of those two sets of 'interpretive commitments'. As discussed in Part I above, state concerns with law enforcement and maintaining order had shaped the formulation of Article 2(2), and through its interpretation of the 'absolutely necessary' provision[132] – untested in the ECtHR before *McCann* – the ECtHR had to balance the importance of the right to life with those state concerns. By linking that interpretation with its longer-standing approach to proportionate determination of the scope of rights in the context of 'democratic society', the ECtHR arguably brought Article 2 into the established fold of qualified rights and positioned it in the essential context of 'democracy' and 'society', in relation to which life, force and state action had to be evaluated. Notably in *McCann* this involved the context of terrorism, and in subsequent cases a range of policing and law enforcement situations bringing these matters into conflict. However, as discussed in the following chapters, in so

[129] Patrick Macklem, 'Militant Democracy, Legal Pluralism, and the Paradox of Self-Determination' (2006) 4.3 *International Journal of Constitutional Law* 488.

[130] See Emanuel Gross, 'Legal Aspects of Tackling Terrorism: The Balance between the Right of a Democracy to Defend Itself and the Protection of Human Rights' (2001) 6 *UCLA Journal of International Law and Foreign Affairs* 89–168; and generally Benjamin J Goold and Liora Lazarus (eds), *Security and Human Rights* (Oxford, Hart, 2007); Andrea Bianchi and Alexis Keller with Steven J Barela (eds), *Counterterrorism: Democracy's Challenge* (Oxford, Hart, 2008); and Daniel Moeckli, 'Human Rights Strategies in an Age of Counter-Terrorism' in Reza Banakar (ed), *Rights in Context: Law and Justice in Late Modern Society* (Farnham, Ashgate, 2012) 215.

[131] See for example *Klass and Others v Germany* (1978) paras 42–60; Bingham, *The Rule of Law* 158–59.

[132] Mathieu, *Le droit à la vie dans les jurisprudences constitutionnelles et conventionnelles européennes* 58. See also Nsereko, 'Arbitrary Deprivation of Life' 245, 246.

doing the ECtHR blurred the distinction between identifying the meaning and the scope of the right to life.

C. 'Democratic Societies' as a Normative Concept

As noted in relation to its descriptive and legitimating senses, the concept of democratic societies is partly a statement of what is, and partly a statement of what is imagined to be. Similarly, in its more technical, proportionate balancing sense, it is a way of indicating the contextual framework for determining what might be needed in adjudication on competing interests. Both of these involve a third, normative dimension of the ECtHR's references to 'democratic societies', as a way of setting up an interpretive narrative theme to support a prospective and purposive protection of the right to life in the context of democratic society, and what its values could or should be.[133] As considered in Chapter 2, Cover referred to the ways in which law is rooted in narratives that are the 'trajectories plotted upon material reality by our imaginations', involving 'visions of what the world might be'.[134] For Ricoeur, the configuration of narrative is a way of making meaning through a narrative theme in a purposive way, to move from the ordering of fact and experience, to project a meaning from it.[135] The role of the link with democratic societies in Article 2 case law can thus also be seen to have a purposive aspect.

This more open-textured sense of democratic society as the narrative theme in Article 2 judgments is arguably relied on by the ECtHR not only to legitimate the way in which it holds a state to account according to purportedly existing standards, applied proportionately, but also to develop those standards (albeit as a minimum[136]) with a view to achieving the telos of the right in question, to make it practical and effective, and to require particular conduct and practice in democratic societies.[137] As the ECtHR stated in *Soering*, 'any interpretation of the rights and freedoms guaranteed has to be consistent with "the general spirit of the Convention, an instrument designed to maintain and promote the ideals and values of a democratic society"'.[138] Focusing on the ECHR's purpose when

[133] On the ECtHR's teleological methodology see also Zysset, *The ECHR and Human Rights Theory* 123, 207.

[134] Cover, 'Foreword: Nomos and Narrative' 4–5, 10.

[135] Ricoeur, *Time and Narrative Volume 1* 66–67.

[136] Note for example, *Brecknell v United Kingdom* (2007) para 70: 'It is also salutary to remember that the Convention provides for minimum standards, not for the best possible practice, it being open to the Contracting Parties to provide further protection or guarantees'.

[137] Recall *Artico v Italy* (1980) para 33 on the practical aims of ECHR law, as noted in Chapter 2.

[138] *Soering* para 87, citing a previous judgment in *Kjeldsen, Busk Madsen and Pedersen v Denmark* (1976) para 53. Such purposive interpretation is based on Articles 31–33 of the Vienna Convention on the Law of Treaties 1969, see Greer, *The European Convention on Human Rights* 195.

interpreting it necessarily involves the ECtHR in projecting what that purpose should be and how it should be developed. Indeed, it has been argued in general terms that the fundamental role of judges in a democracy has been to identify and express essential aspects of that system and how they should be protected.[139] These interpretive and systemic roles regarding democratic aims and the democratic context can be understood to outweigh concerns about the ECtHR's own democratic status in so doing.[140] The narratives configured around the right to life in the context of lethal and life-threatening force can thus be seen to reflect and develop a model of democratic society that the ECtHR seeks to promote.[141] As the following chapters show, through its judgments about Article 2 and state uses of force, the ECtHR's case law points to core substantive, procedural and qualitative dimensions that provide a purposive, and aspirational, vision of the nature of democratic society in the context of the exercise of state power in policing and law enforcement.

In conclusion, by narratively positioning the right to life in connection with the basic values of democratic societies in the Council of Europe the ECtHR encapsulates, explicitly and implicitly, a range of factors. As discussed in Part I, these include the narrative influences that can be understood to show why the right to life can be said to be a fundamental provision of the ECHR and to enshrine a basic value of democratic societies, comprising the longer history of rights protection, confidence in legal control mechanisms, as well as the (re)consolidation of democracy against totalitarianism in the post-war era. As discussed in Part II, the connection also indicates how the ECtHR's narratives are configured around the

[139] Aharon Barak, *The Judge in a Democracy* (Princeton, Princeton University Press, 2006) 20–21 and Aharon Barak, 'On Judging' in Martin Scheinin, Helle Krunke and Marina Aksenova (eds), *Judges as Guardians of Constitutionalism and Human Rights* (Cheltenham, Edward Elgar, 2016) 32–33. On the importance of judicial reasoning in identifying and consolidating democratic principles and human rights see Dupré, *The Age of Dignity* 82–112, including the ECtHR, 92–93; see also Andreas Follesdal, 'Why the European Court of Human Rights might be Democratically Legitimate – A Modest Defence' (2009) 27.2 *Nordisk Tidsskrift for Menneskerettigheter* 289, 293–294.

[140] For example, see Zysset, 'Searching for the Legitimacy of the European Court of Human Rights' 16, 17, 46–47; Kanstantsin Dzehtsiarou and Alan Greene, 'Legitimacy and the Future of the European Court of Human Rights: Critical Perspectives from Academia and Practitioners' (2011) 12 *German Law Journal* 1707; Jean-Paul Costa, 'On the Legitimacy of the European Court of Human Rights' Judgments' (2011) 7.2 *European Constitutional Law Review* 173; David Thór Björgvinsson, 'The Role of Judges of the European Court of Human Rights as Guardians of Fundamental Rights of the Individual' in Scheinin, Krunke and Aksenova (eds), *Judges as Guardians of Constitutionalism and Human Rights* 329, 329–38; and Luzius Wildhaber, 'Criticism and Case-Overload: Comments on the Future of the European Court of Human Rights' in Spyridon Flogaitis, Tom Zwart and Julie Fraser (eds), *The European Court of Human Rights and its Discontents: Turning Criticism into Strength* (Cheltenham, Edward Elgar, 2013) 9–11. See also Thorbjorn Jagland, 'Don't Reject Europe Court as Caricature' (13 December 2016) *New York Times* 1 and 17; and more generally compare Robert A Dahl, 'Can International Organizations be Democratic? A Skeptic's View' in Ian Shapiro and Casiano Hacker-Cordón (eds), *Democracy's Edges* (Cambridge, Cambridge University Press, 1999) 19–36.

[141] Tomuschat, 'Democracy and the Rule of Law' 482–83, 494–95. On the apparent tension between democracy and the work of the ECtHR in light of this teleological approach see Zysset, 'Searching for the Legitimacy of the European Court of Human Rights' 16.

concept of democratic society – singular and plural – as a core narrative theme or rationale. This is a way of reflecting what the actual attributes and values of the High Contracting Parties are deemed to be, in fact and through an imaginary, legitimating representation of them; how the right to life needs to be balanced proportionately with the wider social interest, specifically framed in terms of the democratic social context; and how the ECtHR normatively develops the standards to be attained under Article 2. The connection made by the ECtHR between Article 2 and the concept of democratic societies is thus a fundamental aspect of its narratives about the right to life in the context of state uses of lethal and potentially lethal force.

4

Substantive Dimensions of the Right to Life and Democratic Society

Since its first decision on lethal force under Article 2 in the 1995 *McCann* judgment the ECtHR has developed an extensive body of case law on the right to life in the context of lethal and potentially lethal force in domestic policing and law enforcement operations. Through these judgments the ECtHR has interpreted the right to life in the ECHR to involve two principal dimensions, one substantive, addressed in this chapter, and the other procedural, examined in the following chapter. These two dimensions indicate how the scope of Article 2 has been enlarged by the ECtHR beyond its basic wording and establish the minimum standards that that right entails. The substantive dimension involves three aspects: the resort to force by state agents in the specific incident (to which the ECtHR sometimes refers as operational conduct) and whether or not it is covered by the provisions of Article 2(2); the domestic legal, regulatory and administrative framework for state agents' action, including whether or not it complies with the general injunction in Article 2(1) and the provisions of Article 2(2); and the wider issues preceding and surrounding the operation in question, involving its planning and control. As the framework through which the ECtHR has applied the right to life in substantive terms, these aspects provide the grounds on which applicants may base a claim.

This chapter draws on the narrative theories introduced in Chapter 2, in order to examine how the ECtHR's case law on Article 2 and lethal or potentially lethal force demonstrates its understanding of the relationship between the right to life and the concept of democratic society, as addressed in Chapter 3. Based generally on Robert Cover's call to attend to the narratives that locate legal prescriptions and give them meaning, this chapter turns from the broad contextual narratives considered in the previous chapter, to focus on ECtHR judgments on Article 2. The chapter explores these judgments as narratives by considering how they engage with what Paul Ricoeur referred to as the 'world of action' from which meaning is configured through narrative processes. For Ricoeur, the world of action provides the subject matter, or raw material of narrative, including structural, symbolic and temporal elements. Of these, structural (facts, circumstances and human conduct and perceptions) and to some extent temporal elements are considered in this chapter and in the following, Chapter 5, while symbolic and cultural factors, as well as the underlying values apparent in the judgments discussed in Chapters 4 and 5, are considered in Chapter 6. It is essential to recall though that in his reflection, Ricoeur was not concerned with legal narratives, which as noted in Chapter 2 are bounded by the parameters of the applicable law. Consequently, the structural element that underpins all of this discussion, although not envisaged by Ricoeur, is the law itself, namely Article 2 and other relevant provisions of the ECHR. However, the focus here is on the second, dynamic aspect of Ricoeur's model of narrative, which concerns the production of meaning from the subject matter through a process of configuration. In the legal realm, this has two interlinked layers. One is the configuration of meaning from the facts and conduct in question. In addressing the world of action, case narratives include the applicants' and state's competing versions of events, involve a process of selection of relevant evidence and make connections among facts and conduct in consequentialist terms of causation and responsibility.[1] In so doing, ECtHR judgments are configured, or plotted, around the central question of whether or not state conduct can be said to have been compatible with, or to have breached, the right in question. That depends on the other layer of meaning, that is, how the right to life and its connections with democratic society are interpreted. These two layers are interlinked in that the ECtHR's narratives for making sense of concrete experience in terms of Article 2 depend on its choices about how the facts fit into the schema of the law, and how the schema of the law should be interpreted in the context of the facts. While not losing sight of the legal specificities of the case law, the focus here is on these two layers of narrative configuration by the ECtHR.

This chapter argues first, that by situating the right to life in relation to democratic society as a way of emphasising the right's importance the ECtHR has produced a strict and extended interpretation of Article 2's substantive aspects. However, the chapter argues, second, that by applying the right to life with reference to democratic society as a way of qualifying and limiting Article 2's application through proportionate evaluation of conduct in context, and within the ECtHR's understanding of the boundaries of subsidiarity, the ECtHR has introduced limits on the right's protective capacity. Overall, therefore, the chapter serves to demonstrate the tension at the heart of Article 2 and how that provision's application in terms of the narrative theme of democratic society leads to flexibility in the case law and a potentially problematic uncertainty in the generation of protective standards.

I. The Importance of the Right to Life in Democratic Society

Starting with its initial analysis in *McCann*, the ECtHR has always reiterated that Article 2 enshrines a basic value of democratic societies in order to emphasise

[1] On the 'forensic paradigm' note Sanneke Kuipers and Paul 't Hart, 'Accounting for Crises' in Mark Bovens, Robert E Goodin and Thomas Schillemans (eds), *The Oxford Handbook of Public Accountability* (Oxford, Oxford University Press, 2014) 589, 592.

the right's importance, and for that reason has 'strictly construed' its provisions so as to restrict the permissible exceptions in Article 2(2).[2] It has also expanded Article 2's scope by treating it as a living instrument to achieve the primary objective of ECHR law that was recalled in *McCann*, namely making rights protection practical and effective.[3] The ECtHR has thus extended its analysis to the evaluation of domestic legal and regulatory provisions in relation to those strict standards on the use of force and their relevance beyond the incident in question, in terms of training. At the same time, the emphasis on the importance of the right to life in democratic society has enabled the ECtHR to enlarge its conception of what is relevant to its narrative in forensic and temporal terms, by extending its analysis to the prior and parallel elements of state planning and control.

A. Extended Scope and Strict Interpretation

To begin with, the ECtHR has interpreted the scope of Article 2 more widely than its text appears prima facie to envisage.[4] As confirmed in *McCann*, following the earlier Commission decision in *Stewart*,[5] the ECtHR has strictly construed Article 2 read as a whole to cover both intentional deprivation of life by a state agent and situations in which force is used that unintentionally results in death.[6] This has since been interpreted as going beyond 'the use of weapons or physical violence' to include all conduct, with any means, that may involve the use of force against another that causes death or endangers life.[7] Moreover, as held in *Ilhan v Turkey* and *Makaratzis v Greece*, the use of force under Article 2 can extend beyond lethal force to include serious threats to life, with or without physical harm, provided the use of force is of sufficient gravity.[8] The ECtHR has thus used

[2] The ECtHR's emphasis on 'strictly' appears to echo its reference to the UN Basic Principles on the Use of Force and Firearms, Article 9, which says: 'intentional lethal use of firearms may only be made when strictly unavoidable in order to protect life': *McCann v United Kingdom* (1995) paras 138–39.

[3] *McCann* para 146.

[4] For a comparative perspective see Paul Tavernier, 'Le recours à la force par la police' in Christian Tomuschat, Evelyne Lagrange and Stefan Oeter (eds), *The Right to Life* (Leiden, Martinus Nijhoff Publishers, 2010) 41.

[5] *Stewart v United Kingdom* (1984) para 15.

[6] *McCann* para 148.

[7] *McShane v United Kingdom* (2002) para 101. In this case 'use of force' was held to include the use of an armoured vehicle to clear a barricade, killing a man hiding behind it, although the ECtHR then declined to address this issue in Article 2 terms due to ongoing domestic litigation: paras 102–103.

[8] This was accepted in principle in *Ilhan v Turkey* (2000) paras 73–78, in which the applicant's brother had been badly beaten by gendarmes, although the ECtHR did not ultimately find that the beating constituted life-threatening harm. It was found in *Makaratzis v Greece* (2004) paras 49–55 where police fired their weapons wildly in an uncontrolled chase during which the applicant suffered some physical harm. A life-threatening use of force was also identified for example in *Soare et autres c Roumanie* (2011) paras 107–110, in which the victim was shot in the head by police and paralysed but not killed; and *Haász and Szabó v Hungary* (2015) paras 43–48 in which a police officer fired his gun towards the applicants at night, without intending to hit them or actually hitting them. See also *Trévalec c Belgique* (2011) paras 10, 60–61. In contrast note *Tzekov c Bulgarie* (2006) paras 40–44, in which an

the argument of the fundamental importance of the right to life in democratic society to enlarge the ambit of its protection.

As for the scope of the right to life in terms of what interferences with it may be justifiable, in and since *McCann* the ECtHR has similarly used the importance in a democratic society argument to construe Article 2(2) strictly, that is, to narrow the range of permissible exceptions. As the ECtHR stated in this regard in *McCann*, Article 2 'not only safeguards the right to life but sets out the circumstances when the deprivation of life may be justified'.[9] In other words, the right to life also establishes the parameters for permissible killing, which must be absolutely necessary in the circumstances and within the finite range of possible objectives set out in Article 2(2)(a), (b) and (c). Where a use of force causes death or life-threatening harm and can be attributed to a state agent beyond reasonable doubt, it is for the state to establish that the force used was covered by those provisions.[10] The ECtHR has interpreted Article 2(2) strictly in terms of both the permissible reasons and the applicable test. In *McCann* it declared the 'absolutely necessary' test to be 'a stricter and more compelling test of necessity' than that 'normally applicable when determining whether state action is "necessary in a democratic society"', including a requirement that 'the force used must be strictly proportionate to the achievement of the aims' in that provision.[11] However, where a use of force is clearly unnecessary and disproportionate, a breach of Article 2 can be found without engaging in analysis of the provisions of Article 2(2).[12]

The ECtHR has interpreted the 'defence of any person from unlawful violence' in Article 2(2)(a) to require a defensive response to a threat to life.[13] In that sense, the ECtHR has determined that only violence threatening life may justify a use of lethal (or potentially lethal) force by a state agent that takes or endangers the life of another, provided that the degree of force is strictly proportionate to the threat in the circumstances. In *McCann* this was expressed in terms of lethal force 'to prevent [the victims] from detonating a bomb and causing serious loss of life'

insufficiently serious non-lethal use of force was excluded from the ambit of Article 2 and so considered under Article 3. See also *Zelilof v Greece* (2007) paras 35–37.

[9] *McCann* para 147.

[10] As stated by the ECtHR in, for example, *Giuliani and Gaggio v Italy* (2011) para 181.

[11] *McCann* paras 147–49. The ECtHR followed on this point the Commission decision in *McCann* (1994) para 182, and the earlier Commission decision in *Kelly v United Kingdom* (1993) 7.

[12] For example, in *Ciorcan and Others v Romania* (2015) paras 116–17, in which special police forces had fired on a crowd causing danger to life during a heavily-armed operation to serve court summonses, the ECtHR held that even if the crowd attacked the police officers as they claimed, 'it was not sufficiently established that the attack was so extremely violent as to justify shooting at random with live ammunition', and so found a breach of Article 2 without considering Article 2(2). See also *Nagmetov v Russia* (2015) paras 40–41 and (2017) [GC] paras 9–37 and 47 in which the firing of a tear-gas cannister at a demonstrator, against regulations, causing fatal injuries was an undisputed breach of Article 2.

[13] Note pre-*McCann* Michael O'Boyle, 'The Use of Lethal Force under Article 2 of the European Convention on Human Rights', DH-ED-COLL (90) 9, Council of Europe, 23 October 1990. See generally Jan Arno Hessbruegge, *Human Rights and Personal Self-Defense in International Law* (Oxford, Oxford University Press, 2017) 1–3, 93–96, 172.

and thus 'to safeguard innocent lives'.[14] Similarly, in *Ramsahai and Others v The Netherlands*, the ECtHR Grand Chamber found that the fatal shooting by a police officer of an armed robber who ignored warnings and raised his weapon was absolutely necessary force.[15] The ECtHR thus interprets the right to life on the basis of the fundamental value it protects, infringement of which can only be justified if that value is itself under threat.

In that light, the ECtHR has interpreted the permissible exceptions in Article 2(2)(b) and (c) to make them consistent with that strict approach, thus effectively reducing their prima facie coverage. This focus is particularly clear in the ECtHR's limitation of the apparently nonsensical scope of Article 2(2)(b), in that it would not be possible to arrest or meaningfully recapture someone who has been killed.[16] Moreover, in the broader ECHR schema, lawful arrest in terms of Article 5 requires an aim of bringing the arrestee before a court for trial.[17] The apparent rationale of Article 2(2)(b) with regard to justifying lethal force in the context of the right to life therefore seems to be flawed. In its case law, the ECtHR has rectified this oddity by interpreting Article 2(2)(b) in line with its reading of Article 2(2)(a) and Article 2's overall importance and purpose. For example, in *Nachova v Bulgaria*, which involved the fatal shooting of two young men during an operation conducted by military police officers to arrest them for being absent without leave from an army construction unit, with reference to the objectives of Article 2 and the UN Basic Principles on the Use of Force and Firearms,[18] the ECtHR Grand Chamber held that:

> the legitimate aim of effecting a lawful arrest can only justify putting human life at risk in circumstances of absolute necessity. The Court considers that in principle there can be no such necessity where it is known that the person to be arrested poses no threat to life or limb and is not suspected of having committed a violent offence, even if failure to use lethal force may result in the opportunity to arrest the fugitive being lost.[19]

Due to the established facts in the case that neither of the victims was armed or dangerous, and had clearly been observed to be unarmed and unthreatening,

[14] *McCann* para 200.

[15] *Ramsahai and Others v The Netherlands* (2007) [GC] paras 281, 282, 288.

[16] John Smith, 'The Right to Life and the Right to Kill in Law Enforcement' (1994) *New Law Journal* 354, 356.

[17] David Harris, 'The Right to Life under the European Convention on Human Rights' (1994) 1 *Maastricht Journal of European and Comparative Law* 122, 136.

[18] United Nations Basic Principles on the Use of Force and Firearms by Law Enforcement Officials, adopted on 7 September 1990 by the Eighth United Nations Congress on the Prevention of Crime and the Treatment of Offenders, following on from the United Nations Code of Conduct for Law Enforcement Officials, adopted by UN General Assembly resolution 34/169 of 17 December 1979. See Stuart Casey-Maslen, 'The Use of Firearms in Law Enforcement' in Stuart Casey-Maslen (ed), *Weapons Under International Human Rights Law* (Cambridge, Cambridge University Press, 2014) 3; and on the ECtHR's non-systematic references to such sources note Magdalena Forowicz, *The Reception of International Law in the European Court of Human Rights* (Oxford, Oxford University Press, 2010) 382–83.

[19] *Nachova and Others v Bulgaria* (2005) para 95. On similar facts and the same finding see *Putintseva v Russia* (2012) paras 68–72.

the resort to a type and degree of force that resulted in death was held not to be proportionate to the claimed legitimate objective.[20] Lethal or potentially lethal force may therefore only be deemed justifiable under Article 2(2)(b) if, during an endeavour lawfully to effect an arrest or prevent an escape, it is used against an intended arrestee or prisoner who behaves in a way that represents a threat to life.[21] In that sense Article 2(2)(b) in effect indicates only the initial context, with the situation needing to evolve into one covered by Article 2(2)(a) for a permitted use of force to be found.[22]

Article 2(2)(c), which focuses on quelling a riot or insurrection, foregrounds the maintenance of public order as a paradigmatically collective interest, and a key concern of the modern state in its policing functions. Although riot and insurrection may involve protest against the state order, the assumption seems to be that protest in European democracies should be peaceful, so that activities fitting the autonomous definition of riot and insurrection[23] are merely group violence that can justify a forceful state response. In that sense, the assumption in Article 2(2)(c) is that a democratic society within the Council of Europe is entitled to protect itself and preserve its internal order by suppressing such violence, even through the use of lethal force, provided it is lawful and absolutely necessary.[24] As with the other two justifications under Article 2(2), the ECtHR has indicated that force

[20] Similarly, in *Alikaj et autres c Italie* (2011) paras 66–77, a breach of Article 2 (implicitly 2(2)(b)) was found after a police officer shot and killed an escaping suspect after drawing his weapon while giving chase on slippery ground and in the absence of any apparent threat to life. Moreover, in *Guerdner et autres c. France* (2014) paras 71–73, a gendarme's shots in the dark at a suspect escaping from custody were held to be excessive due to the absence of any reason to believe he represented a threat at that time.

[21] On the linkage between Article 2(2)(a) and (b) see for example *Saoud c France* (2007) para 91, in which the use of force by police seeking to apprehend a mentally disturbed man, who was behaving violently towards his family and the intervening officers, was found to be justified, as was the force used in *Altin et Kiliç c Turquie* (2016) paras 47–48, involving a police assault on terrorists inside a flat. Contrast *Kalkan c Turquie* (2016) involving excessive force used during a purported arrest operation. See also Hessbruegge, *Human Rights and Personal Self-Defense in International Law* 115–17, 172–73.

[22] In *Wasilewska and Kałucka v Poland* (2010) paras 52–53, police officers apparently trying to arrest some suspects fired repeatedly at their vehicles as they sought to escape, but the force was held to be unnecessary and excessive because there was no apparent danger to the officers as the vehicles had already passed them when they opened fire. In *Kitanovski v The Former Yugoslav Republic of Macedonia* (2015) para 71, the use of potentially lethal force supposedly to try to stop a suspect after he had driven his vehicle past a police roadblock was found not to be absolutely necessary, due to the absence of any evidence that he was at that point putting the lives of police officers or others at risk. On similar facts see also *Juozaitienė and Bikulčius v Lithuania* (2008) paras 73–84. In the case of *Kakoulli v Turkey* (2006) paras 120–21, in which a man was shot dead by soldiers of the Turkish Republic of Northern Cyprus in unclear circumstances during an apparent arrest operation near a sensitive border crossing, the lethal force was not justified under Article 2(2)(a) or (b) because it was used when the victim had already been wounded and neutralised, so did not represent a threat and could have been arrested. Compare *Anik and Others v Turkey* (2007) paras 65–67. See also Hessbruegge, *Human Rights and Personal Self-Defense in International Law* 107–108.

[23] *Stewart* paras 24–25; Hannah Russell, 'Understanding "Quelling a Riot or Insurrection" under Article 2 of the ECHR' (2015) 5 *European Human Rights Law Review* 495.

[24] The wording of Article 2(2)(c) requires that such action be lawfully taken: note *X v Belgium* (1969).

used in response to a riot must be strictly proportionate to the severity of the threat involved, assessed with regard to the core value of life.[25]

Thus for example in *Güleç v Turkey*, the victim died after being shot (in uncertain circumstances) during a confrontation between state forces and demonstrators, in which the evidence indicated that the Turkish gendarmes had used the only weapons at their disposal, namely heavy machine guns mounted on the roofs of their armoured vehicles.[26] Shots were not fired as a warning over the crowd, but downwards towards the ground, raising the risk of potentially and actually fatal ricochets, and there was no evidence that the gendarmes had themselves come under armed attack. The ECtHR held that although some force could have been justified under Article 2(2)(c),[27] the degree of force used was not absolutely necessary because less lethal means than firearms should have been deployed.[28] Here too, the ECtHR required strict proportionality between the purported justificatory objective and the means used in the circumstances.[29] Relying on the importance of the right to life in democratic society, the ECtHR has therefore interpreted the terms of Article 2(2) in ways intended to give that right a strict level of protection.

B. Protection of the Right to Life by Law and the State's Legal and Regulatory Framework

The ECtHR's emphasis on the importance of the right to life in democratic society and the need for its practical and effective protection in light of the aims of the ECHR have led it to interpret Article 2 to include assessment of the state's legal, regulatory and administrative framework for state agents' resort to lethal or potentially lethal force. Given that the focus of the ECHR system is on the protection of human rights by the High Contracting Parties, and Article 2(1) requires protection of the right to life by law, this aspect of Article 2 firmly puts the spotlight on state compliance beyond individual agents' conduct, whilst recognising that the latter will primarily be guided by domestic law. The legal framework dimension of the right to life was addressed in *McCann* for the first time and as the first issue arising, with regard to the compatibility between domestic law and Article 2. However, as discussed in Part II below, the ECtHR's approach focused

[25] Russell, 'Understanding "Quelling a Riot or Insurrection" under Article 2 of the ECHR'; also, Hannah Russell, *The Use of Force and Article 2 of the ECHR in Light of European Conflicts* (Oxford, Hart, 2017) 37–49. Note *McShane* in this context on the scope of interpretation of the 'use of force'. See also Hessbruegge, *Human Rights and Personal Self-Defense in International Law* 106–10.

[26] *Güleç v Turkey* (1998).

[27] In *Stewart* para 27 the Commission indicated that ECHR law does not require state agents to back down in order to avoid using force altogether.

[28] *Güleç* paras 71–73. See also Hessbruegge, *Human Rights and Personal Self-Defense in International Law* 168–70.

[29] Note also *Şimşek and Others v Turkey* (2005) paras 104–13.

on the need for flexibility in determining compatibility.[30] In subsequent cases the ECtHR confirmed that the Article 2(1) protection by law clause establishes a positive obligation for states to protect and safeguard life, including through domestic legal provisions, such as criminal laws prohibiting the taking of life.[31] In this aspect of Article 2 law the ECtHR has focused on compliance with the right to life and other international provisions, as well as with the broader rule of law criteria of legality and certainty.[32]

The major example of these issues was *Makaratzis*, in which the ECtHR Grand Chamber considered the legal framework dimension of Article 2 law in relation to the planning and control (discussed in the next section) of the police operation in question.[33] In evaluating the Greek regulations in place at the time, the ECtHR considered them in light of Article 2 and other provisions of international law.[34] In this instance the ECtHR referred to the prohibition on arbitrary killing in Article 6(1) of the 1966 ICCPR,[35] which as noted in Chapter 3 is less specific than Article 2 ECHR, as well as the UN Basic Principles on the Use of Force and Firearms, which similarly seek to prevent arbitrary uses of force.[36] The ECtHR combined these references when indicating the importance of an adequate domestic legal framework:

> As the text of Article 2 itself shows, the use of lethal force by police officers may be justified in certain circumstances. Nonetheless, Article 2 does not grant a *carte blanche*. Unregulated and arbitrary action by State agents is incompatible with effective respect for human rights. This means that, as well as being authorised under national law, policing operations must be sufficiently regulated by it, within the framework of a system of adequate and effective safeguards against arbitrariness and abuse of force.
>
> … police officers should not be left in a vacuum when performing their duties, whether in the context of a prepared operation or a spontaneous chase of a person perceived to be dangerous: a legal and administrative framework should define the limited circumstances in which law-enforcement officials may use force and firearms, in the light of the international standards which have been developed in this respect (see, for example, the "United Nations Force and Firearms Principles" …).[37]

From the analysis in *Makaratzis* it is apparent that in the ECtHR's interpretation, a democratic society under the rule of law must have a legal framework for the use of force by state agents that complies with the ECHR and other international

[30] *McCann* para 151.

[31] Anja Seibert-Fohr, *Prosecuting Serious Human Rights Violations* (Oxford, Oxford University Press, 2009) 112–20.

[32] See also Hessbruegge, *Human Rights and Personal Self-Defense in International Law* 117–24.

[33] *Makaratzis* para 57.

[34] See fn 18 above.

[35] Confirmed in *Makaratzis* paras 28–29, 58.

[36] Confirmed in *Makaratzis* paras 30–32, 59. The prevention of arbitrariness is also the focus of Articles 1–2 of the UN Principles on the Effective Prevention and Investigation of Extra-legal, Arbitrary and Summary Executions, Recommended by Economic and Social Council resolution 1989/65 of 24 May 1989, but these were not referred to by the ECtHR in this case.

[37] *Makaratzis* paras 58 and 59.

standards, and that is sufficiently clear and robust in its authorisation and control of state action. At the time of the events in question, the applicable law in Greece consisted of broad and imprecise provisions enacted in 1943 (when, as the ECtHR mentions twice,[38] the country was under German occupation) supplemented by a later presidential decree adding an absolute necessity clause.[39] Describing it as 'somewhat slender' the ECtHR determined that that legal framework 'would not appear sufficient to provide the level of protection "by law" of the right to life that is required in present-day democratic societies in Europe'.[40] The ECtHR linked this inadequate legal framework to the way in which the 'chaotic' police response to the situation unfolded,[41] noting that 'when the event took place, a law commonly acknowledged as obsolete and incomplete in a modern democratic society was still regulating the use of weapons by State agents'.[42] Referring to 'democratic societies' and 'democratic society', the ECtHR concluded that Greece had failed in its positive obligation under Article 2(1) to provide adequate safeguards for the right to life, thus violating it.[43] The ECtHR reference to 'democratic societies' here, as considered in Chapter 3, can be seen to encapsulate a sense of an appropriate standard in the democratic context, based on a perceived common approach to essential values, in order to support and legitimate its criticism of the High Contracting Party.

Similarly, in *Nachova*, the applicants' principal argument under Article 2 was that the victims had died as a result of an inadequate domestic regulatory framework.[44] As in *Makaratzis*, the ECtHR's analysis of this claim encompassed the compatibility of the domestic regulations with Article 2 and other international provisions,[45] as well as with the principles of legality and certainty under the rule of law. The ECtHR found them to be inadequate on both fronts, due to the domestic regulations' overly broad terms and because they were unpublished.[46] The ECtHR thus held, echoing but going further than its finding in *Makaratzis*, that the legal framework in *Nachova* was 'fundamentally deficient and falls well short of the level of protection "by law" of the right to life that is required by the

[38] *Makaratzis* para 25 and para 62.

[39] This deficient legal framework was replaced with a new law in 2003: *Makaratzis* paras 25–27.

[40] *Makaratzis* para 62. In *Sunday Times v United Kingdom (No 1)* (1979) para 49, in relation to the concept of 'prescribed by law' under Article 10 ECHR, the ECtHR had determined that 'law' requires adequate accessibility to a citizen and sufficient precision to enable him or her to regulate his or her conduct.

[41] *Makaratzis* paras 67 and 70.

[42] *Makaratzis* para 70.

[43] *Makaratzis* paras 60–63, 70–72. Similar criticisms were made of the inadequacy of the Greek legal framework in controlling police conduct in *Karagiannopoulos c Grèce* (2007) para 63, involving the non-fatal but devastating shooting of the applicant after he tried to escape arrest and police officers sought to recapture him; *Celniku c Grèce* (2007) para 57, involving a fatal shooting while the victim was apparently seeking to resist arrest; and *Leonidis v Greece* (2009) para 65, in which the victim was fatally shot while being arrested by the police.

[44] *Nachova* para 87.

[45] UN Basic Principles on the Use of Force and Firearms, *Nachova* paras 71–74, 96.

[46] *Nachova* paras 50–54, 60–61, 93–102.

Convention in present-day democratic societies in Europe'.[47] Again, the ECtHR anchored its analysis of the legal framework dimension in the concept of democratic society and addressed issues of substance and legality.[48]

The legal and regulatory framework dimension also involves extending the factual and temporal scope of the ECtHR's evaluation of a High Contracting Party's compliance with Article 2 in this respect, to include conduct prior to the incident in question, as well as subsequent to it. This is because the ECtHR considers the domestic legal framework not only as the parameters for state agents' use of force in an incident, but also and essentially as the principal basis for their training at the national level.[49] The ECtHR assesses this point with regard to how state agents should have been trained, and how training should be improved in the future. Consequently, the ECtHR's development of a strict interpretation of Article 2 provides grounds for evaluating a High Contracting Party's compliance with the obligation under Article 2(1), including both the domestic legal framework as an object of analysis per se, and its broader implications for the state's preparation of its agents. The ECtHR's case narratives thus go beyond the use of force, with the focus on protection by law being opened up to its terms and applications at different temporal stages. Essentially, the narrative of the right to life and democratic

[47] *Nachova* paras 100–101. Compare *Guerdner* paras 66–69, in which the basic provisions of the Defence Code, which were not prima facie compatible with Article 2, had been modified by a series of administrative circulars and Court of Cassation judgments, leading to a legal framework that was not as clear as it could be, but was nevertheless held to be sufficient in Article 2 terms. In contrast, in *Alikaj* para 73, the absence of regulations on the operational use of weapons by police officers contributed to a breach of Article 2. In *Putintseva* para 65 the ECtHR held that the legal framework was 'fundamentally deficient and falls well short of the level of protection "by law" of the right to life that is required by the Convention', with no reference to 'democratic societies'.

[48] Similar problems with the legal and administrative framework in Bulgaria were subsequently considered in relation to the civil police: see *Vasil Sashov Petrov v Bulgaria* (2010) paras 43–50, and *Karandja v Bulgaria* (2010) paras 55–63, referring to similar issues in the earlier judgment in *Tzekov* (in relation to Article 3). An inadequate domestic legal framework for the use of force by Turkish gendarmes in anti-smuggling operations resulted in a breach of Article 2 in *Halis Akin c Turquie* (2009) para 32, *Beyazgül c Turquie* (2009) paras 55–57, and *Atiman v Turkey* (2014) paras 34–38. The domestic legal framework for the operational use of firearms by the police was also found to be inadequate in *Soare* para 132: on the context and legislative shortcomings relating to this case see Lorena Zidaru, 'Încălcarea art. 2 din Convenția Europeană a Drepturilor Omului prin utilizarea în mod nejustificat a armelor de foc' (2012) 2 *Revista Forumul Judecătorilor* 163. On similar issues relating to the point-blank fatal shooting by a police officer of the applicant's son see *Gheorghe Cobzaru c Roumanie* (2013) paras 58–64. In *Sašo Gorgiev v The Former Yugoslav Republic of Macedonia* (2012) paras 50–54, the legal framework for controlling the carrying of arms by police officers and their training was held to be insufficient, contributing to a finding that Article 2 had been breached. On similar issues see also *Gorovenky and Bugara v Ukraine* (2012) paras 38–40.

[49] Note *Nachova* para 97 and for example *Celniku* para 57. See further Ralph Crawshaw, Barry Devlin and Tom Williamson, *Human Rights and Policing* (The Hague, Kluwer Law International, 1998); Ralph Crawshaw, 'International Standards on the Right to Life and the Use of Force by Police' (1999) 3.4 *International Journal of Human Rights* 67; Francesco de Sanctis, 'What Duties do States Have with Regard to the Rules of Engagement and the Training of Security Forces under Article 2 of the European Convention on Human Rights?' (2006) 10.1 *International Journal of Human Rights* 31; Jim Murdoch and Ralph Roche, *The European Convention on Human Rights and Policing: A Handbook for Police Officers and Other Law Enforcement Officials* (Strasbourg, Council of Europe Publishing, 2013).

society in this respect focuses on compliance with the rule of law, substantively and systemically.

C. Expanding the Factual and Temporal Frame of Relevance: State Responsibility for Planning and Control

An extension of the factual and temporal frame of reference, as indicated above in relation to the domestic legal framework and the training of state agents, is even more apparent in the third substantive aspect of the ECtHR's interpretation of Article 2. Based on the need for practical and effective protection of the right to life, reinforced by that right's importance in democratic society, the ECtHR has configured its way of making sense of the structural, factual origins of cases so as to expand the range of causal factors it deems relevant to the incident in question. This enlarges the time frame under consideration, and thereby the scope of pertinent facts and phases of state agents' involvement.

This was first undertaken in *McCann*, in which the ECtHR extended its purview from the fatal incident itself, based on the argument that as the UK had had advance warning of the terrorist plot and so had had time to prepare, its planning and control of the operation shaped how the incident unfolded and how the state agents understood and perceived the situation. The ECtHR thus gave itself grounds on which to stretch its analysis of causality and responsibility under Article 2, and therefore the range of factors for which the state could be held accountable.[50] This extension of Article 2 was anchored in the ECtHR's recognition of the provision's special status:

> In keeping with the importance of this provision (art 2) in a democratic society, the Court must, in making its assessment, subject deprivations of life to the most careful scrutiny, particularly where deliberate lethal force is used, taking into consideration not only the actions of the agents of the State who actually administer the force but also all the surrounding circumstances including such matters as the planning and control of the actions under examination.[51]

After finding that the resort to force by the soldiers did not breach Article 2, the ECtHR considered 'whether the anti-terrorist operation as a whole was controlled and organised in a manner which respected the requirements of Article 2' and 'whether the information and instructions given to the soldiers which, in effect, rendered inevitable the use of lethal force, took adequately into consideration the

[50] See generally AR Mowbray, *The Development of Positive Obligations under the European Convention on Human Rights by the European Court of Human Rights* (Oxford, Hart, 2004) 7–22; Hessbruegge, *Human Rights and Personal Self-Defense in International Law* 164–70 and note Keir Starmer, *European Human Rights Law* (London, Legal Action Group, 1999) 194–200 and 'Positive Obligations Under the Convention' in Jeffrey Jowell and Jonathan Cooper (eds), *Understanding Human Rights Principles* (Oxford, Hart, 2001) 139.

[51] *McCann* para 150.

right to life of the three suspects'.[52] This formulation was shaped by the ECtHR's preliminary recognition of the dilemma raised for the UK by the operation (that is, the need to protect citizens and security personnel, and yet also respect the suspects' right to life[53]), the involvement of known terrorists, and the fact that the operation had been prepared but inevitably involved some incomplete information.[54] The ECtHR was especially concerned with the UK's positive obligation under Article 2, to 'minimise, to the greatest extent possible, recourse to lethal force'.[55] In that light, the ECtHR held by a marginal majority (of ten votes to nine) that the UK's planning and control of the operation involved three main failings: not authorising an earlier intervention against the suspects to stop them crossing into Gibraltar from Spain; not making adequate allowances for possible inaccuracies in the information given to the soldiers; and the use of special forces soldiers (members of the SAS), whose training and apparently 'automatic' use of firearms to kill rather than wound was called into question.[56] These findings were though challenged by the dissentients, who preferred the Commission's view that there had been no breach of Article 2,[57] arguing that the ECtHR should 'studiously resist the temptations offered by the benefit of hindsight'[58] and pointing to the seriousness of the information received by the UK authorities about the bomb threat.[59] Even though views on the evaluation of the facts differed, the key point here was the ECtHR's extension of its narrative sense-making frame of reference due to the stated importance of Article 2 in democratic society.

After *McCann* the ECtHR confirmed that it would extend its analysis to planning and control matters in *Andronicou and Constantinou v Cyprus*, involving an intervention by armed police in a hostage situation, although in this case no breach was found on this ground.[60] The ECtHR clarified its interpretation of a positive obligation under Article 2 in *LCB v United Kingdom*,[61] a case about how the UK had exposed servicemen to the risk of radiation during nuclear tests. In this decision, the ECtHR declared that 'the first sentence of Article 2(1) enjoins the State not only to refrain from the intentional and unlawful taking of

[52] *McCann* para 201.

[53] Note Fionnuala Ní Aoláin, 'Truth Telling, Accountability and the Right to Life in Northern Ireland' (2002) 5 *European Human Rights Law Review* 572, 576 on the 'equality approach' adopted in this case. See also Sarah Joseph, 'Denouement of the Deaths on the Rock: The Right to Life of Terrorists' (1996) 14.1 *Netherlands Quarterly of Human Rights* 5, 22.

[54] *McCann* paras 192–194.

[55] *McCann* para 194.

[56] *McCann* paras 205–14.

[57] *McCann*, Joint Dissenting Opinion of Judges Ryssdal, Bernhardt, Thór Vilhjálmsson, Gölcüklü, Palm, Pekkanen, Freeland, Baka and Jambrek, paras 7 and 11–25.

[58] *McCann*, Joint Dissenting Opinion para 8.

[59] *McCann*, Joint Dissenting Opinion para 10.

[60] *Andronicou and Constantinou v Cyprus* (1997) paras 171, 181–86. The ECtHR's five to four conclusion in this regard was challenged by the dissentients. See also the critical view of Axelle Reiter-Korkmaz, 'Usage de la force meutrière lors d'une opération de sauvetage d'une jeune fille kidnappée' (1999) 39 *Revue trimestrielle des droits de l'homme* 555, 569–73.

[61] *LCB v United Kingdom* (1998).

life, but also to take appropriate steps to safeguard the lives of those within its jurisdiction'.[62] As this was not a case in which the state had 'intentionally sought to deprive the applicant of her life' the issue was rather whether 'the State did all that could have been required of it to prevent the applicant's life being avoidably put at risk'.[63]

The following month and without referring to the *LCB* judgment, in *Ergi v Turkey* the ECtHR interpreted the state's responsibility to avoid or minimise risk to life under Article 2 as extending beyond the conduct of its own personnel, and as providing the basis for presumptive liability in unclear situations.[64] In this case the applicant's sister was killed in crossfire during an operation by the Turkish gendarmerie. Even though it was not established beyond reasonable doubt that the security forces had fired the fatal shot, the ECtHR held that:

> … under Article 2 of the Convention, read in conjunction with Article 1, the State may be required to take certain measures in order to 'secure' an effective enjoyment of the right to life.
>
> … the responsibility of the State is not confined to circumstances where there is significant evidence that misdirected fire from agents of the State has killed a civilian. It may also be engaged where they fail to take all feasible precautions in the choice of means and methods of a security operation mounted against an opposing group with a view to avoiding and, in any event, minimising, incidental loss of civilian life.[65]

The ECtHR thus drew on a combined reading of Article 1, which enjoins the High Contracting Parties to 'secure to everyone within their jurisdiction the rights and freedoms' in the ECHR, and Article 2 to find a positive requirement under the latter for the state to plan adequately in order to avoid risks to life from its own agents and others involved in, and affected by, their operations. On that basis, despite the uncertainty about the cause of death and in the absence of direct evidence from the state about how the operation had been planned and conducted, the ECtHR held 'that it can reasonably be inferred that insufficient precautions had been taken to protect the lives of innocent civilians'.[66]

Consequently, in this series of judgments, the ECtHR confirmed the factual and temporal expansion of the scope of its analysis under Article 2, allowing it to extend its narrative of causality and responsibility into various aspects of state

[62] *LCB* para 36.
[63] *LCB* para 36.
[64] *Ergi v Turkey* (1998).
[65] *Ergi* para 79.
[66] *Ergi* para 81. See also *Dimov and Others v Bulgaria* (2012) para 78, involving use of rocket-propelled grenades against a house in which an armed fugitive was besieged by police seeking to arrest him. In *Vlaevi c Bulgarie* (2010), in which a taxi driver was shot by police after failing to stop when ordered to do so, in paras 70–76 the ECtHR was ready to give the benefit of the doubt to the state agents for a subjective perception of the need to open fire in the circumstances, but found a breach of Article 2 as the planning and control of the operation was inadequate for failing to minimise the risk of resort to lethal force. See also for example *Makbule Kaymaz et Autres c Turquie* (2014) paras 106–13, involving insufficient care by the authorities in a planned operation to arrest suspected terrorists in a residential building due to failings in surveillance and preparation.

planning and control, including in some cases the interconnection between this substantive aspect and the domestic legal and regulatory framework.[67] This approach has continued in numerous subsequent decisions, which have gradually indicated the range of factors that the ECtHR is prepared to scrutinise and that will be required for state planning and control to satisfy Article 2.[68] While these cases have been interpreted as indicating possible inconsistencies in the ECtHR's approach,[69] the rulings perhaps mainly demonstrate how fact-dependent and thus potentially divergent (even divisive) such decisions are.[70] Overall, as this section has shown, the reference to democratic society has served to emphasise the importance of Article 2 and allow the ECtHR to enlarge its narrative engagement with it, tightening the protective scope of Article 2 and allowing a wider range of facts to be taken into account. However, this connection with democratic society interpreted in another sense has also grounded the development of significant limitations on the standards established under the right to life, emphasising the inherent tension in its terms.

II. Article 2, Democratic Society and Flexibility

Although the right to life in relation to uses of lethal and potentially lethal force is said to enshrine a basic value of European democratic societies, the protection of which is a fundamental provision of the ECHR, Article 2 nevertheless

[67] For example, in *Makaratzis* para 71, the inadequate legal and administrative framework supported the ECtHR's decision that the 'hot-pursuit' operation in question was inadequately structured and controlled. Likewise, in *Nachova* paras 104–105, the unsatisfactory national legal and regulatory framework was central to the ECtHR's ruling that the operation breached Article 2 in its planning and control. See also *Hamiyet Kaplan c Turquie* (2005) paras 51–55, involving inadequate regulations and training in relation to a police operation to capture suspects from a house where other family members and children were resident. In contrast, two cases involving police operations to deal with apparently armed men who had taken refuge inside residential buildings were found not to have involved planning and control failings due to the adequacy of the domestic legal framework: *Bubbins v United Kingdom* (2005) para 150 and *Huohvanainen v Finland* (2007) paras 106–107.

[68] Brice Dickson, 'The Planning and Control of Operations Involving the Use of Lethal Force' in Lawrence Early, Anna Austin, Clare Ovey and Olga Chernishova (eds), *The Right to Life under Article 2 of the European Convention on Human Rights: Twenty Years of Legal Developments since McCann v the United Kingdom* (Oisterwijk, Wolf Legal Publishers, 2015) 47; also, Alec Samuels, 'The Police Officer Shoots and Kills: the Strasbourg Jurisprudence' (2006) 1 *Archbold News* 7, 8.

[69] Juliet Chevalier-Watts, 'A Rock and a Hard Place: Has the European Court of Human Rights Permitted Discrepancies to Evolve in their Scrutiny of Right to Life Cases?' (2010) 14.2 *The International Journal of Human Rights* 300. For example, in the admissibility decision in the case of *Brady v United Kingdom* (2001), the ECtHR found that the planning and control dimension of the operation to arrest a group of suspected armed robbers did not breach Article 2, discounting the possibility that the suspects could have been arrested earlier and distinguishing the case from *McCann* on the grounds that the planning and control did not affect the police officer's mistake about the need to shoot the suspect. See also Claire de Than, 'Mistaken Belief in Self-Defence May Justify the Use of Lethal Force' (2001) 65 *Journal of Criminal Law* 417.

[70] Dickson, 'The Planning and Control of Operations Involving the Use of Lethal Force' 47, 49.

explicitly provides for proportionate balance with regard to collective interests and concerns. As discussed in Chapter 3, the ECtHR's approach to applying this provision can be seen to have been set up by its reference to democratic societies, as arguably implying the ECHR interpretive concept of 'democratic society' and stressing the need for contextually sensitive proportionate balancing. As the ECtHR underlined in *Soering v United Kingdom*, proportionality between individual and community interests lies at the heart of the human rights adjudication framework in the ECHR.[71] Even though it emphasises strict limitations on the taking of life at the heart of Article 2, and a 'stricter and more compelling' test of necessity and proportionality than under other provisions of the ECHR, the ECtHR has configured its case narratives to justify making allowances for uses of force, due to concerns about effectiveness, social need and its own subsidiarity in the democratic context. As a result, the ECtHR's interpretation and application of Article 2(2) has resulted in a difficult combination of apparently robust norms with a generally sympathetic approach to contextual contingencies. This is examined here in three steps: the scope of the absolute necessity test in Article 2(2); the domestic legal framework and the ECtHR's approach to its compatibility with Article 2; and the ECtHR's recognition of limits on state responsibility in the area of planning and control.

A. Democratic Society, 'Absolute Necessity' (?) and Human Fallibility

In the ECtHR's judgments, the interpretation and application of Article 2(2), and of the absolute necessity test in the circumstances of the incident in question, give rise to a difficult and controversial problem where the state agent's perception is based on error. This involves the need to temper strict assessment of absolute necessity with a circumstantially-informed understanding of its subjective element, that is, the state agent's perspective when using force. At the same time, this raises the difficulty of reconciling mistaken or putative defensive action with the ostensibly high level of protection for the right to life declared in Article 2's 'absolutely necessary' test and advocated by the ECtHR.

The absolute necessity test, as it was interpreted in *McCann*, apparently involved a subjective and an objective element. While the absolute necessity standard was said by the ECtHR in *McCann* to be a stricter and more compelling test than mere necessity, it was nevertheless one of proportionality. The ECtHR thus approached the test on the basis of an understanding of the need to be aware of the contextual realities of the operation, specifically the predicament at the heart of the operation in *McCann* due to the known terrorist plot, which raised the UK's duties to protect civilians and its own personnel in Gibraltar, while still being under an obligation to

[71] *Soering v United Kingdom* (1989) para 89.

have minimum resort to lethal force.[72] The ECtHR also noted the related circumstances shaping the state response to that plot, that is, the involvement of known, active members of the IRA and the prior warning of their activity, albeit involving imperfect knowledge of the details.[73] By opening its analysis with a statement about the connection between the right to life and the values of democratic societies in the Council of Europe, the ECtHR was arguably paving the way to weighing up that right against other democratic values in dealing with terrorism.[74]

This narrative construction of the issues served to establish the ECtHR's concern with the setting of the operation and the competing interests at stake, and thus the need to make allowances for human error and for the stresses and strains that state agents might experience during challenging operations. The ECtHR thus sought to apply what it considered to be a just and feasible standard of human rights protection, which would not impose excessive limits on what agents could do and so give rise to unintended negative consequences by impairing their ability to protect themselves and the public. It therefore took account of the state agents' understanding of the situation at the time, including the influence of the information given to them about the car-bomb plot and the likely response of the suspects, and making allowances for mistakes. On that basis it declared:

> The Court accepts that the soldiers honestly believed, in the light of the information that they had been given, as set out above, that it was necessary to shoot the suspects in order to prevent them from detonating a bomb and causing serious loss of life … The actions which they took, in obedience to superior orders, were thus perceived by them as absolutely necessary in order to safeguard innocent lives.
>
> The Court … considers that the use of force by agents of the State in pursuit of one of the aims delineated in paragraph 2 of Article 2 of the Convention may be justified under this provision where it is based on an honest belief which is perceived, for good reasons, to be valid at the time but which subsequently turns out to be mistaken. To hold otherwise would be to impose an unrealistic burden on the State and its law-enforcement personnel in the execution of their duty, perhaps to the detriment of their lives and those of others.[75]

In reaching this decision, the majority in the ECtHR followed the Commission's view that in light of the information available to them, the soldiers' decision to shoot the suspects 'cannot be said to have been perverse or unreasonable'[76] and also seemed to comply with the third party intervenors' suggestion that the ECtHR

[72] *McCann* para 192.

[73] *McCann* para 193.

[74] Compare Julen Etxabe, 'The Legal Universe after Robert Cover' (2010) 4.1 *Law and Humanities* 115, 143, who discusses how the ECtHR approached the 'necessary in a democratic society' clause of Article 11 (freedom of association) in a case concerning the banning of a Basque political party. He draws attention to 'the narrative construction with which the Court chooses to frame the issue', formulating its argument about democracy in terms of international terrorist threats, in order to find the Spanish government's banning of the party to be justified.

[75] *McCann* para 200.

[76] Report of the Commission (1994) para 231.

undertake 'a close examination of the genuineness and reasonableness of each killer's belief that the decision to kill the person was absolutely unavoidable'.[77] The ECtHR thus established a test that appeared to require evidence of the state agent's honest belief in the circumstances, based on good reasons, rather than requiring an entirely subjective or entirely objective test of absolute necessity. Although the ECtHR subsequently criticised the soldiers' training and especially what it considered to be their 'reflex action' in shooting the suspects[78] it held that the use of force in the circumstances did not breach Article 2.

In the subsequent case of *Andronicou and Constantinou* the ECtHR considered similar issues. In this case a special unit of police officers armed with machine guns stormed a flat to try to rescue a hostage held by her boyfriend, who was armed with a shotgun. In the course of the rescue the police opened fire and killed both the hostage and the gunman. The ECtHR affirmed its approach to the question of the use of force set out in *McCann* and the need to make allowances for honest and reasonable mistakes, apparently extending that allowance to include the stresses and strains of a dangerous situation more generally. As in *McCann*, finding that there was no breach of Article 2 regarding the State agents' use to force, the ECtHR concluded:

> … the [officers] honestly believed in the circumstances that it was necessary to kill him [Andronicou, the hostage taker] in order to save the life of Elsie Constantinou [the hostage] and their own lives and to fire at him repeatedly in order to remove any risk that he might reach for a weapon … It is clearly regrettable that so much fire power was used in the circumstances to neutralise any risk presented by Lefteris Andronicou. However, the Court cannot with detached reflection substitute its own assessment of the situation for that of the officers who were required to react in the heat of the moment in what was for them a unique and unprecedented operation to save life.[79]

The majority in *Andronicou and Constantinou* thus sought to give weight to the officers' perception of the rapidly unfolding events. Although they found that the use of machine guns in the victims' flat was 'regrettable', it did not result in a breach of Article 2. As the above extract indicates, the ECtHR decided that it was the officers' perception at the time that should carry most weight, making allowances for the 'heat of the moment', and thus avoiding retrospective second-guessing of their conduct. In contrast, the minority (four out of nine judges) found that such a degree of force could not be said to be absolutely necessary.[80] The test as elaborated

[77] *McCann*, Third Party Intervention made jointly by British Irish Rights Watch, the Committee on the Administration of Justice, Inquest and Liberty (the National Council for Civil Liberties) (November 1994) para 3.4.

[78] *McCann* para 212.

[79] *Andronicou* para 192.

[80] Partly Concurring, Partly Dissenting Opinions of Judge Palm, Judge Pekkanen paras 5–6, Judge Jungwiert ('Using machine guns in a small confined space without proper lighting and knowing that the very person to be rescued was next to or in front of the person being aimed at … seems to me more than irresponsible'), and Judge Pikis part (c).

in *McCann* and *Andronicou and Constantinou* has grounded rulings that a use of lethal force has not breached Article 2 in a number of cases, involving mistaken perceptions that a victim was armed, and other reactions to stressful and confusing circumstances.[81]

However, the ECtHR Grand Chamber seemed to change its interpretation of this test in *Armani da Silva v United Kingdom* so as to emphasise the subjective dimension.[82] This case stemmed from the fatal shooting on the London Underground of the applicant's cousin, Jean Charles de Menezes, by armed police who mistook him for a suspected suicide bomber during an operation beset by a number of communication and organisational problems.[83] In its ruling, the Grand Chamber declared that the test of 'an honest belief perceived for good reasons' is not in fact one with a subjective core and an objective caveat, but rather an entirely subjective test.[84] The ECtHR stated that the 'good reasons' are also to be determined from the state agent's perspective, and relate to the honesty and genuineness of the belief formed about the circumstances, rather than constituting a partially objective limitation on the allowances made.[85] Although this appears to go against general understanding since *McCann* that the test is not totally subjective, the ECtHR has now stated that the key point in its approach to the absolute necessity test is not to determine it from the viewpoint of a 'detached observer', but from the state agent's perspective, unless the belief is deemed not to have been honestly held.[86] Although the ECtHR's application of this test in

[81] For example, the response of the police officers to the suspect vehicle in *Makaratzis* para 66 was understood by the ECtHR on this basis, as was the response of the police officer when the suspect pointed a replica gun at him in *Bubbins* para 138. In *Huohvanainen* paras 35 and 96–97, the ECtHR did not find a breach of Article 2 where armed officers in an armoured vehicle fired at the applicant's brother as he was crawling out of a burning house. The officers' assessment of the need to shoot the man in order to protect other police officers in the vicinity, who were not in protective vehicles, was deemed reasonable given the deceased's earlier violent conduct, even though at the moment of the shooting he was on the ground and not pointing a weapon. See also *Leonidis* paras 63–66; *Giuliani and Gaggio* (2011) paras 189–94; and note the admissibility decisions in *Brady* 8 and *Oláh v Hungary* (2004) 14, in both of which the victim was perceived to be holding something resembling a weapon. See also Hessbruegge, *Human Rights and Personal Self-Defense in International Law* 143–46.

[82] *Armani da Silva v United Kingdom* (2016). See Natasa Mavronicola, 'Taking Life and Liberty Seriously: Reconsidering Criminal Liability Under Article 2 of the ECHR' (2017) 80.6 *Modern Law Review* 1026, 1042–43 and Hessbruegge, *Human Rights and Personal Self-Defense in International Law* 133–39 on the ECtHR's apparent dilution of the test.

[83] See also Deborah Coles, Inquest, 'European Court of Human Rights – family to challenge UK government failure to prosecute police officers: background briefing on the broader context of the shooting of Jean Charles de Menezes' (4 June 2015), www.inquest.org.uk/jean-charles-de-menezes-family-challenge-uk-government (consulted 28 August 2018).

[84] *Armani da Silva* paras 244–48.

[85] Echoing the conclusion in *Nachova*, para 114, three of the dissentients in *Armani da Silva* disagreed with the majority on this point, arguing that the officers' subjective perception of the need to use force in the circumstances giving rise to the *Da Silva* case was shaped by failings in the police operation overall, which were excluded from the investigation because the objective bases for the officers' perception were not addressed: *Armani da Silva*, Joint Dissenting Opinion of Judges Karakaş, Wojtyczek and Dedov paras 4–7, 12.

[86] *Armani da Silva* paras 245, 247. A suggestion that the state agent acted in the heat of the moment will also be discounted if the situation leading to his perceived need to use force is of his own making: note *Haász and Szabó* para 57.

a number of judgments appears to have been the same in its effect, the shift in emphasis in the explanation of the test is problematic given that Article 2 requires a standard of 'absolutely necessary' in determining whether a deprivation of life is permissible.

The ECtHR has though found a breach of Article 2 where state agents have resorted to force in circumstances where the possibility of making allowances for mistake, human error or stress is questionable *and* where the degree of force used is clearly disproportionate to an aim falling within Article 2(2). In *Gül v Turkey* the ECtHR found that the use of lethal force had not been absolutely necessary.[87] In this case, during a search operation following a tip-off about suspected terrorists, police officers fired numerous shots with their automatic weapons through the door of a flat in a residential building, killing the occupant inside. There was a suggestion that the police officers thought that the sound of a door bolt being pulled back was the sound of a bolt-action weapon being prepared to fire, but the ECtHR noted that this was unconvincing and acknowledged it only as a hypothetical factor influencing the police use of force. The essential issue was the grossly disproportionate degree of force used against an unseen target in a residential setting, in contrast with the majority view on the situation in *Andronicou and Constantinou*.[88]

Where the ECtHR does take mistakes and stress into account, it opens the possibility of bringing killings that were not objectively absolutely necessary within the ambit of Article 2(2) exceptions.[89] This arguably reduces the high level of protection that the right to life in Article 2 in principle requires and introduces the difficult dimension of making allowances for putative defensive action. Although it is important to recall that ECHR law is not criminal law,[90] there is nevertheless an apparent difficulty, even lacuna, in the theoretical rationale for exceptions to the right to life under Article 2 in some cases, which can usefully be indicated by comparison with a criminal law approach.

As some theoretical engagement with the moral and legal status of killing in self-defence in criminal law has shown, the abstract concept of a right to life in

[87] *Gül v Turkey* (2000).

[88] *Gül* para 82. See also on similar facts *Bektaş and Özalp v Turkey* (2010) para 69, in which no evidence that the officers acted in the heat of the moment and multiple operational and procedural failings led to a breach of Article 2. In *Dimov* para 78, a breach of Article 2 was found due to the use of excessive force during a police operation to capture a fugitive even though the cause of death was not clear. On similar facts see also *Vachkovi v Bulgaria* (2010) para 76. In contrast, as in *Andronicou and Constantinou* a proportionate use of force during police interventions was found in *Usta and Others v Turkey* (2008), *Kasa v Turkey* (2008) and *Gülen v Turkey* (2008).

[89] Elizabeth Wicks, *The Right to Life and Conflicting Interests* (Oxford, Oxford University Press, 2010) 140; Mavronicola, 'Taking Life and Liberty Seriously' 1042, 1045; and Hessbruegge, *Human Rights and Personal Self-Defense in International Law* 135–36.

[90] Note *Giuliani and Gaggio* (2011) para 182: 'Responsibility under the Convention is based on its own provisions which are to be interpreted in the light of the object and purpose of the Convention, taking into account any relevant rules or principles of international law. The responsibility of a State under the Convention, arising for the acts of its organs, agents and servants, is not to be confused with the domestic legal issues of individual criminal responsibility under examination in the national criminal courts'.

moral terms can be understood as being a qualified (or specified) right that is dependent on conduct.[91] If a person becomes an unjust aggressor threatening the life of another, that other may use necessary and proportionate lethal force against the aggressor in a way that is morally permissible and, in criminal law terms, legally justifiable in the sense of a result-focused emphasis on the right reason for acting.[92] These theories also show that a classification in terms of justification cannot extend to a defensive use of force that causes the death of an unconnected bystander or someone who does not in fact represent a genuine threat.[93] That sort of killing can instead be considered excusable due to mistaken perceptions, that is, causally attributable to the actor but without blameworthy responsibility.[94]

In the human rights logic of the ECHR system, even though the ECtHR refers to the justification of a use of force, the theoretical distinction between a justified killing as opposed to one that may be excused is not addressed, because the focus of analysis is not on determining the existence and degree of a state agent's culpability, or the worth or desert of the person harmed or killed.[95] Instead, Article 2 and the ECtHR's application of it focus on the explicability and permissibility of a use of force as established by the terms of Article 2(2) and related case law. The analysis thus concentrates on the nexus between the state agent and the perceived threat in response to which he or she acted, assessment of which need not necessarily require the response to be to a specific aggressor or to be directly linked with the victim (the deceased or person whose life is otherwise endangered). Where the victim did represent a threat covered by Article 2(2)(a) then in addition to there being a permissible deprivation of life under the ECHR, the victim's right to life may also be qualified in moral terms, but this is not always the case. This is particularly evident in cases involving a use of lethal or potentially lethal force against a threat, resulting in harm or death being caused to one or more individuals who were not themselves perceived at the time to be connected with that

[91] Suzanne Uniacke, *Permissible Killing: The Self-Defence Justification of Homicide* (Cambridge, Cambridge University Press, 1994) 194; Fiona Leverick, *Killing in Self-Defence* (Oxford, Oxford University Press, 2006) 43; Wicks, *The Right to Life and Conflicting Interests* 130. See also George P Fletcher, 'The Right to Life' (1979) 13 *Georgia Law Review* 1371; David Wasserman, 'Justifying Self-Defense' (1987) 16.4 *Philosophy and Public Affairs* 356 and Judith Jarvis Thomson, 'Self-Defense' (1991) 20.4 *Philosophy and Public Affairs* 283.

[92] Leverick, *Killing in Self-Defence* 66–67. Although as George Fletcher noted in the context of criminal law, a court's finding that a state agent's use of force was not only not unlawful, but justified, can be highly contentious and give rise to a public perception of 'whitewashing': see George P Fletcher, *Basic Concepts of Criminal Law* (Oxford, Oxford University Press, 1998) 88–91.

[93] Leverick, *Killing in Self-Defence* 44.

[94] On these distinctions and their relevance in the criminal law of England and Wales see Alan Norrie, 'The Problem of Mistaken Self-Defense: Citizenship, Chiasmus and Legal Form' (2010) 13.2 *New Criminal Law Review* 357. While the distinctions tend to be implicit or invisible in the common law outside theoretical discussion, they are more explicit in legal analysis of culpability in civil law systems: see for example on Italian criminal law Stephen Skinner, 'Death in Genoa: the G8 Summit Shooting and the Right to Life' (2003) 11.3 *European Journal of Crime, Criminal Law and Criminal Justice* 233–52.

[95] See Fletcher, 'The Right to Life' 1391; Wicks, *The Right to Life and Conflicting Interests* 16; and Mavronicola, 'Taking Life and Liberty Seriously' 1037.

threat, specifically or at all. In such situations, the assessment of absolute necessity under Article 2 requires the probability of harm from the perceived threat, assessed prospectively, to outweigh the possibility of harm to those present, including bystanders.[96] However, whereas the death or endangerment of a victim is what triggers the analysis, and the case is brought to hold the state to account and to try to achieve a form of justice in the name of the victim (as the ECtHR said in *McCann*, the ECHR is an 'instrument for the protection of individual human beings'[97]), the prospective, threat-focused analysis under Article 2 means that in some cases the resulting narrative about the permissibility of the use of force based on the state agent's perspective can appear to ignore the individual who has been harmed or killed.[98]

It can therefore be seen that the ECtHR has constructed a way of valuing the right to life highly, but in the context of proportionate balance as required by Article 2(2) and in the context of democratic society. While unexplained and disproportionate uses of force are not tolerated,[99] this socially contextualised approach involves making allowances for state agents' action, apparently with a view to the wider benefit to society of not being overly demanding about what is required from them.[100] The balancing act that is central to the ECtHR's protection of the right to life in a democratic society appears as a result to lean considerably towards a concern with flexibility and feasibility, even though

[96] See further Hessbruegge, *Human Rights and Personal Self-Defense in International Law* 180–83. For example, *Andronicou and Constantinou v Cyprus* (1998), in which the hostage was shot during a police intervention against the hostage taker; and *Giuliani and Gaggio v Italy* (2009) and (2011), in which a member of a group attacking a police vehicle was shot dead, but the ECtHR did not appear to require a link between the deceased and the perceived threat for the purposes of the absolutely necessary use of force, a point criticised by the dissentients: note Stephen Skinner, '*Giuliani and Gaggio v Italy*: the Context of Violence, the Right to Life and Democratic Values' (2010) *European Human Rights Law Review* 85, 91–92. In the early Commission decision in *Stewart* paras 29–30, no breach of Article 2 was found where a baton round fired at a rioting crowd killed the applicant's son, in circumstances where the soldier in question was held to have been hit by a missile as he depressed the trigger, thus disrupting his aim; focusing on the use of force in the circumstances, the Commission did not require there to be a connection between the deceased's conduct specifically and the state agent's actions. In contrast in *Aydan c Turquie* (2013) paras 97–103, soldiers fired on a demonstration, killing a member of the crowd who was no threat to them. As there was no reason to shoot at all, and the gun had not been fired upwards as a warning, a breach of Article 2 was found. This is avoided in some cases where causation is not accepted or the focus is placed on another aspect of Article 2: compare *Bakan c Turquie* (2007) paras 55–56, in which a bystander unconnected with the operation in question was killed by a ricochet following warning shots fired by the police, but the use of force did not breach Article 2 as the death was deemed to be accidental. In *Evrim Öktem c Turquie* (2008) paras 45–51, the victim was seriously injured by a stray bullet during a police chase that did not involve him, but a breach of Article 2 was found due to inadequate control over the state agents concerned.

[97] *McCann* para 146.

[98] In contrast note for example relatives' victim-centric reactions to a use of lethal force by the police: azellerodneycampaignforjustice.wordpress.com/2015/06/29/victim-of-police-shooting-did-not-deserve-to-die-court-told/ (accessed 7 February 2019).

[99] For example, see also *Timus and Tarus v The Republic of Moldova* (2013) para 53 and *Gül* para 82.

[100] On the importance of a contextualised approach compare Norrie, 'The Problem of Mistaken Self-Defense' 373, 377.

vertical protection of human rights could be deemed to require a more demanding approach.[101]

B. Flexibility, Subsidiarity and the Compatibility of the Domestic Legal and Regulatory Framework

Despite the extended scope of Article 2, the stated need for strictness in its interpretation, and the ECtHR's recognition of a positive obligation in Article 2(1) requiring compatibility of the domestic legal and regulatory framework with the ECHR, this substantive aspect of the right to life is similarly circumscribed by a concern with flexibility and the subsidiary nature of ECHR law. The ECtHR mainly focuses in this regard on effective rather than terminologically specific compatibility, based on respect for High Contracting Parties' diverse approaches to compliance with human rights norms.

In *McCann*, in which this substantive aspect was first addressed, the ECtHR's approach to the legal framework issue was primarily concerned with these areas of leeway for the state. The key legal question raised in the case was whether the applicable 'reasonably justifiable' test for the resort to force, as set out in the Gibraltar Constitution, was compatible with the 'absolutely necessary' test in Article 2. Noting that there was no obligation under the ECHR for the latter's terms to be implemented exactly in national law or for their compatibility to be assessed in abstract conceptual terms,[102] the ECtHR found that the provisions in question were similar but that 'the Convention standard appears on its face to be stricter than the relevant national standard'.[103] Although non-committal about the UK Government's submission that the strict interpretation and application of domestic law meant that it was in effect compatible with Article 2, the ECtHR concluded that 'the difference between the two standards is not sufficiently great' that a violation of Article 2(1) could be established.[104] In *McCann* this dimension of Article 2 meant therefore that compatibility appeared to depend on the

[101] On this argument in the context of England and Wales see Wicks, *The Right to Life and Conflicting Interests* 138, 140 and Stephen Skinner, 'Citizens in Uniform: Public Defence, Reasonableness and Human Rights' (2000) *Public Law* 266. On the need for informed debate about determining the scope of allowances for mistaken uses of force note Norrie, 'The Problem of Mistaken Self-Defense' 377, considered further in Chapter 8. Note also Hessbruegge, *Human Rights and Personal Self-Defense in International Law* 145.

[102] *McCann* para 153. This rejection of *in abstracto* analysis drew on the ECtHR's earlier decision that issues of compatibility had to be approached *in concreto*: *Ireland v United Kingdom* (1978) para 240; discussed further in Russell, *The Use of Force and Article 2 of the ECHR in Light of European Conflicts* 70.

[103] *McCann* para 154.

[104] *McCann* para 155.

approximate similarity of wording and the general thrust of interpretation and application.[105]

The questions of effective compatibility with Article 2 and the avoidance of abstract evaluation, as in *McCann*, were also questions in the *Giuliani and Gaggio v Italy* case.[106] Resulting from the shooting of a demonstrator during the G8 Summit protests in Genoa in 2001, the case included a challenge by the applicants to the compatibility of the domestic legal framework with the ECHR. The domestic law in question involved provisions dating from the Italian Fascist era, namely the 1925 Public Safety Law and two articles in the 1930 Penal Code, Article 52 on legitimate defence and Article 53 on the legitimate use of arms.[107] The applicants argued that because of the historical and political origins, as well as the terms of the 1925 law and Article 53 (the latter does not explicitly include a proportionality requirement), those provisions could not be deemed compatible with the spirit of the ECHR and the requirements of Article 2.[108] The ECtHR focused instead on the interpretation and application of Article 53 in practice, which does involve an implied proportionality provision, with the Chamber avoiding the other issues on this point by deeming them abstract, and the Grand Chamber ignoring them entirely.[109] Again, the broad compatibility and effectiveness in practice of the domestic provisions in achieving the Article 2 objectives were the ECtHR's primary concern, ignoring the deeper 'abstract' question of the origins, apparent character and symbolic force of domestic law in relation to ECHR objectives and the nature of democratic society.[110]

The ECtHR's approach to the domestic legal framework aspect shows how its analysis is tempered by allowances for the plurality and sovereignty of High Contracting Parties. Unwilling to be seen to overstep its subsidiary status and be over-demanding about domestic legal provisions enacted or retained by democratically-elected governments, the ECtHR has instead shaped its engagement with this substantive aspect in more general terms and categorised problematic conceptual and political challenges as abstract questions lying beyond its concern with practical and effective human rights. The emphasis on democratic society can thus be seen to limit this aspect of the ECtHR's substantive analysis of Article 2 as well.

[105] This decision echoed the finding of the Commission Report (4 March 1994, para 190) but differed from the contrary view expressed in the Third Party Intervention (1994) para 3.11. The ECtHR reached the same conclusion about the domestic legal test, worded similarly to the Gibraltarian provision in *McCann*, in the admissibility decisions in *Caraher v United Kingdom* (2000) paras 17–18 and *Bennett v United Kingdom* (2010) paras 71–74.

[106] *Giuliani and Gaggio v Italy* (2009) and (2011).

[107] See generally Skinner, 'Death in Genoa' 233–52.

[108] *Giuliani and Gaggio* (2009) para 149 and (2011) paras 202–204.

[109] *Giuliani and Gaggio* (2009) para 226 and (2011) paras 211–15. See further Stephen Skinner, '*Giuliani and Gaggio v Italy*: The Context of Violence, the Right to Life and Democratic Values' 85 and 'The Right to Life, Democracy and State Responsibility in "Urban Guerilla" Conflict: The Grand Chamber Judgment in *Giuliani and Gaggio v Italy*' (2011) 11.3 *Human Rights Law Review* 567.

[110] See further Stephen Skinner, 'Tainted Law? The Italian Penal Code, Fascism and Democracy' (2011) 7.4 *International Journal of Law in Context* 423.

C. Contingency and Flexibility in Planning and Control: Narrating Degrees of Risk

The ECtHR's expansion of its factual and temporal frame of relevance to include planning and control issues in its decisions under Article 2 has, as with the two previous examples, similarly been circumscribed by allowances for difficult circumstances and a concern with the feasibility and subsidiarity of human rights standards in democratic society. This has involved the establishment of parameters for planning and control obligations and recognition by the ECtHR that fair and feasible standards in this regard must involve allowing leeway for operational contingencies, represented in terms of degrees of risk. These factors have been particularly important in the area of policing and law enforcement operations, with regard to which the ECtHR has stressed the importance of the democratic context.

The leading decision on this aspect of Article 2 law is *Osman v United Kingdom*,[111] a case based on an argument that the Metropolitan Police Service had inadequately responded to the apparent danger to a schoolboy and his family posed by a man who had become obsessed with him, and whose threatening behaviour culminated in his fatal shooting of the boy's father. Although not about the use of lethal or potentially lethal force, the judgment highlights the ECtHR's understanding of policing in democratic society and how in that light it moderates its consideration of state responsibility in this expanded dimension of factual and temporal analysis under Article 2. Evidencing its concern with proportionality and the feasibility of rights protection, the ECtHR Grand Chamber in *Osman* confirmed its interpretation in *LCB* that Article 2 included a positive obligation on the state to take preventive measures to protect life[112] but at the same time determined its limits. In particular it noted the difficulties and uncertainties of policing 'modern societies' and the need to comply with legal limits on the exercise of police powers.[113] In that light, the positive obligation would only encompass situations in which

> the authorities knew or ought to have known at the time of the existence of a real and immediate risk to the life of an identified individual or individuals from the criminal acts of a third party and that they failed to take measures within the scope of their powers which, judged reasonably, might have been expected to avoid that risk.[114]

[111] *Osman v United Kingdom* (1998).

[112] *Osman* para 115. On the wider application of *Osman* see Franz Christian Ebert and Romina I Sijniensky, 'Preventing Violations of the Right to Life in the European and the Inter-American Human Rights Systems: From the *Osman* Test to a Coherent Doctrine on Risk Prevention?' (2015) 15 *Human Rights Law Review* 343, 349. Note also Dimitris Xenos, *The Positive Obligations of the State under the European Convention of Human Rights* (Abingdon, Routledge, 2012) 111–12.

[113] *Osman* para 116.

[114] *Osman* para 116.

The ECtHR ultimately found (by a seventeen to three majority) no breach of this obligation.[115]

The *Osman* principles have been particularly important in shaping the ECtHR's assessment of domestic policing in Article 2 cases and of the competing pressures faced by police forces. In particular, the ECtHR has sought not to make the right to life a disproportionate fetter on necessary police activities.[116] In so doing, the ECtHR has refined its determination of state responsibilities in relation to degrees of risk to life, excluding from the positive obligation situations involving general risks and chance events.[117] On that basis, in *Giuliani and Gaggio* the Grand Chamber held (by a ten to seven majority) that the state cannot be expected to guarantee everyone's safety during large scale and widespread disorders involving numerous unexpected risks and unpredictable developments.[118] The ECtHR thus constructed its case narrative so as to focus its assessment of the state's responsibility for minimising risk to life on the specific circumstances in which the applicant's relative had been killed. By disaggregating those circumstances from the wider context of public disorder on the day in question, the ECtHR excluded the wider situation from the category of events that arguably led up to the fatal incident in question.[119] Consequently no breach of Italy's planning and control obligations under Article 2 was found in this case,[120] a result that was disputed by the dissentients.[121] Furthermore, where 'extreme' unpredictable events are involved, the ECtHR has also introduced a limitation in its analysis of the planning and control dimension on the ground of subsidiarity, by recognising that states will be better placed to determine which means and strategies should be deployed, and even going so far as to allow a margin of appreciation.[122] In other circumstances though, where extreme

[115] *Osman* paras 121-122–22.

[116] For example, *Makaratzis* para 69. See also Ebert and Sijniensky, 'Preventing Violations of the Right to Life' 358–68. Emphasising the feasibility aspect see Linos-Alexandre Sicilianos, 'Preventing Violations of the Right to Life: Positive Obligations under Article 2 of the ECHR' (2014) 3.2 *Cyprus Human Rights Law Review* 117, 118, 122.

[117] *Mastromatteo v Italy* (2002) paras 69 and 76.

[118] *Giuliani and Gaggio* (2011) para 255.

[119] *Giuliani and Gaggio* (2011) paras 253–62. Compare on this issue how domestic judges have been shown to construct narrative interpretations of case facts in order to expand or contract the applicability of justifications for the use of force: Fionnuala Ní Aoláin, *The Politics of Force: Conflict Management and State Violence in Northern Ireland* (Belfast, The Blackstaff Press, 2000) 112.

[120] See further Skinner, 'The Right to Life, Democracy and State Responsibility in "Urban Guerilla" Conflict' 575–77.

[121] *Giuliani and Gaggio* (2011) Joint Partly Dissenting Opinion of Judges Rozakis, Tulkens, Zupančič, Gyulumyan, Kalaydjieva and Karakaş, paras 2, 12.

[122] *Finogenov v Russia* (2011) para 213. See Stephen Skinner, 'Deference, Proportionality and the Margin of Appreciation in Lethal Force Case Law under Article 2 ECHR' (2014) 1 *European Human Rights Law Review* 32; Sarabeth M Zielonka, 'The Universality of the Right to Life: Article 2 and the Margin of Appreciation in the Jurisprudence of the European Court of Human Rights' (2014) 47 *NYU Journal of International Law and Politics* 245. Note the Third Party Intervention in *McCann*, Section III para 1.5 on the special status of Article 2 and the argument that the state should not have a margin of appreciation under it. Compare Linos-Alexander Sicilianos, 'Out of Harm's Way: Positive Obligations under Article 2 of the European Convention on Human Rights' in Early et al, *The Right to Life under*

security crises are deemed to have been predictable, the ECtHR has been critical of disproportionate responses and inadequate planning.[123]

Although this positive obligation and evaluation of planning and control matters constitute a vital extension of the ECtHR's analytical narratives under Article 2, in their application much depends on the way the ECtHR determines – narratively configures – the nature of the risks involved in a situation and the extent to which it is prepared to find that they were within the control of the state. This is a sensitive aspect of the relationship between lethal force under Article 2 and democratic society, in terms of both the substance of the tests (the extent of and relationship between standards and allowances for state action), the very role of the ECtHR in the democratic context (its status and relationship with the governments of High Contracting Parties), and the purpose of human rights judges in ensuring robust accountability of state authorities or democratically-disguised deference to them.

Overall, this chapter has shown how, in its interpretation and application of Article 2, the ECtHR has constructed its analytical narratives around the fundamental importance of the right to life in democratic society, so as to ground a strict and extended interpretation of that provision and to read into it three substantive aspects in order to make its protection practical and effective. However, at the same time the emphasis on democratic society has shaped the ECtHR's focus on proportionate compromise, limiting the demands of Article 2 in relation to the operational exigencies facing individual state agents, the compatibility of domestic law with the ECHR and the pressures of modern policing in the democratic context more generally. This duality is indicative of, and due to, the tension at the heart of Article 2, which is meant to protect the most fundamental human right whilst making provision for state action in the name of society; and at the heart of the concept of democratic society itself, the value system that simultaneously values the individual's right to life and allows it to be relativised with regard to others' rights and social interests more generally. This reveals a contestable flexibility, even uncertainty, at the heart of the right to life, which the ECtHR seeks to manage through case-by-case justificatory narratives, interlinked by a shared appeal to a concept of democratic society that both reinforces and restricts the standards applied.

the European Convention on Human Rights 29, 34–35. For a critical view on the margin of appreciation see also David Thór Björgvinsson, 'The Role of Judges of the European Court of Human Rights as Guardians of Fundamental Rights of the Individual' in Martin Scheinin, Helle Krunke and Marina Aksenova (eds), *Judges as Guardians of Constitutionalism and Human Rights* (Cheltenham, Edward Elgar, 2016) 329, 347–50.

[123] Note *Tagayeva and Others v Russia* (2017) paras 492 and 595, in which Russia's handling of the infamous Beslan school siege was found to have breached Article 2. In paras 523–27, 584–90 and especially 608–61, the ECtHR expressed particular concern about the indiscriminate use of lethal force. Notably the ECtHR was less lenient than in *Finogenov*: see anon, 'Case Comment: Terrorist Hostage Taking and Rescue Missions' (2017) 4 *European Human Rights Law Review* 400, 403.

5

Procedural Dimensions of the Right to Life and Democratic Society

Like the substantive dimension of Article 2, the procedural dimension has been developed by the ECtHR on the basis of the same declaration about the importance of the right to life in the ECHR and the democratic societies making up the Council of Europe. In order to make protection of that right practical and effective, and in light of its special importance, the ECtHR has similarly interpreted the scope of Article 2 as going beyond its original terms by reading into it a duty on the state to investigate suspicious deaths, especially from incidents in which lethal or life-threatening force has been used. As with the substantive dimension and outlined at the start of Chapter 4, the ways in which the ECtHR has configured the meaning of Article 2, its temporal application and the scope of the duty to investigate reflect the ECtHR's narrative engagement with the concept of democratic society, as a factor both underpinning and delimiting the importance and reach of the right to life.

The procedural dimension differs from the substantive dimension though in two important ways. Whereas the ECtHR's narrative approach to the substantive dimensions of Article 2 involves, in Ricoeur's terms, analysis of the 'world of action' or structural elements of the incident in question, including facts, conduct and circumstances, the procedural dimension concerns the ECtHR's development of a narrative about the state authorities' process for constructing a narrative about what happened in an incident. This is still about how the ECtHR makes sense of what a state has done, giving an incident and state conduct in relation to it meaning, and justifying how they are to be evaluated in terms of the right to life, but the procedural dimension involves a step back from the use of force itself.

Furthermore, the procedural dimension of Article 2 can be seen to have a dual significance, as an end in itself and a means to an end. The duty to investigate has been developed into a key part of the ECtHR's narrative about what a High Contracting Party has done in response to an incident of lethal or potentially lethal force, establishing important standards for state investigations and forming a distinct ground for liability under Article 2. Yet, at the same time, the procedural dimension is also concerned with the extent to which the state's investigation is sufficiently reliable for the ECtHR to use its findings as the source of information and forensic interpretation underpinning its own assessment of the substantive aspects of Article 2. In other words, it involves evaluating the reliability of the state narrative about the use of force as a foundation for the ECtHR's narrative. This indicates an evidential reliance on the High Contracting Party, which in the context of a resource-fettered transnational judicial process and the implications of the institutional changes to the ECHR system in 1998, reflects a pragmatic need for reliable information provided by the party best able to ascertain what happened, namely the state. Even so, it also appears to suggest the apparent dependency of the accountability process on the party being held to account.

As a last introductory point, it is important to note that the duty to investigate under Article 2 has been developed in relation to all aspects of that provision's application, including state uses of force, disappearances, deaths in custody and in psychiatric care, as well as other cases of death in circumstances including murders, hospital treatment, road accidents and environmental disasters.[1] Although the procedural dimension of Article 2 has some connections with the broader considerations of Article 13 (on the right to an effective remedy), it has primarily been developed by the ECtHR as an autonomous aspect of the right to life, with a distinct lineage and set of objectives.[2] A similar duty has also been developed by the ECtHR in relation to Article 3 (freedom from torture and inhuman or degrading treatment or punishment) and Article 5 (liberty and security).[3] The focus here though is specifically on how the procedural dimension, or duty to investigate, has been developed under Article 2 in cases of lethal and life-threatening force in domestic policing and law enforcement operations.

As in Chapter 4, the aim in this chapter is to consider the ECtHR's decisions about the procedural dimension as narratives and how they are configured both factually and legally in terms of the relationship between the right to life and democratic society in this context. The broader symbolic and cultural aspects of these issues, as well as the values underpinning them, are then addressed in Chapter 6. First, by way of background, this chapter begins by tracing the emergence of the implied duty to investigate under Article 2, with regard to the ECtHR's emphasis on the importance of the right to life, and to the ECtHR's

[1] Bernadette Rainey, Elizabeth Wicks and Clare Ovey (eds), *Jacobs, White & Ovey: The European Convention on Human Rights* (Oxford, Oxford University Press, 2017) 168–77; Eva Brems, 'Procedural Protection: An Examination of Procedural Safeguards Read into Substantive Convention Rights' in Eva Brems and Janneke Gerards, *Shaping Rights in the ECHR* (Cambridge, Cambridge University Press, 2013) 137; Alastair Mowbray, 'Duties of Investigation under the European Convention on Human Rights' (2002) 51 *International and Comparative Law Quarterly* 437, 438.

[2] Rainey, Wicks and Ovey, *Jacobs, White & Ovey: The European Convention on Human Rights* 169; Egbert Myjer, 'Investigation into the Use of Lethal Force: Standards of Independence and Impartiality' in Lawrence Early, Anna Austin, Clare Ovey and Olga Chernishova (eds), *The Right to Life under Article 2 of the European Convention on Human Rights: Twenty Years of Legal Developments since McCann v the United Kingdom* (Oisterwijk, Wolf Legal Publishers, 2015) 115; Hannah Russell, *The Use of Force and Article 2 of the ECHR in Light of European Conflicts* (Oxford, Hart, 2017) 155–82.

[3] Rainey, Wicks and Ovey, *Jacobs, White & Ovey: The European Convention on Human Rights* 214–15, 243–44 relating to disappearances. For example, in *Kitanovski v Former Yugoslav Republic of Macedonia* (2015), in which life-threatening force was used during a police operation to stop a suspect vehicle, the ECtHR found a breach of the procedural dimension of Article 2 and Article 3 together.

structural reform. Second, the chapter explores how the procedural dimension has been developed by the ECtHR to encompass the key criteria of adequacy, independence, transparency, promptness and duration of investigations. The chapter shows how, in developing these procedural criteria, the ECtHR uses the theme of the right to life's relationship with the concept of democratic society both as the rationale for robust accountability processes and the contextual justification for pragmatic limits on them.

I. Effective Protection under Article 2 and Systemic Necessity

The procedural dimension of the right to life, establishing the duty to investigate, is not to be found in the wording of Article 2 itself. Read into that provision by the ECtHR in *McCann*, it demonstrates the application of the living instrument principle and overlapping concerns with systemic need and functional objectives. Under this duty, a High Contracting Party must investigate in a satisfactory way any suspicious death (or endangerment of life) occurring in its jurisdiction that may engage its responsibility,[4] a requirement that is especially important where such an outcome has resulted from force used by the state. On that basis the duty has become an essential aspect of Article 2, both as a key dimension on its own terms, establishing the requisite investigatory steps where this fundamental right is in question, and as a crucial element of the ECtHR's ability to evaluate the substantive dimensions of the right to life. Before addressing its application though, the development of the procedural dimension needs to be understood in its systemic setting, which involves its emergence and development before and after the reform of the ECtHR in 1998. This systemic angle underlines the potentially problematic nature of the procedural dimension and contextualises the ECtHR's development of the procedural principles addressed in the following section.

A. Reading the Duty to Investigate into Article 2 pre-1998: Effective Protection and Pragmatism

While Article 2's procedural dimension has been developed by the ECtHR since *McCann* to encompass a range of criteria, the first set of judgments invoking it were more limited in scope. These rulings occurred between 1995 and 1998, the last few years of operation of the Human Rights Commission and the original

[4] See generally Rainey, Wicks and Ovey, *Jacobs, White & Ovey: The European Convention on Human Rights* 168.

part-time pre-Protocol 11 ECtHR,[5] and were primarily concerned with three factors. These were the interpretive goal of making Article 2 practical and effective;[6] the ECtHR's pragmatic need to try to ensure that High Contracting Parties provided it with reliable information about the circumstances giving rise to cases, due to the limits on what the Commission could achieve; and the aim of establishing the duty to investigate as a fundamental element of accountability under the ECHR to complement the right to life in its substantive aspects.

In *McCann*, the applicants submitted in their arguments before the Commission that Article 2 'should be interpreted as including a procedural element, namely, the provision of an effective procedure after the event for establishing the facts'.[7] Considering this to be part of Article 2's requirement that the right to life be protected by law, the Commission reasoned – as subsequently echoed by the ECtHR – that a 'general legal prohibition of arbitrary killing by state authorities would be rendered nugatory if, in practice, there was no mechanism for reviewing the action of the State agents', which it interpreted to mean a need 'for an ex post facto review of the circumstances of a killing'.[8] This was because the Commission recognised in practical terms that the state, rather than victims or relatives, is best placed to establish exactly what happened, and because it is 'essential both for the relatives and for public confidence in the administration of justice and in the State's adherence to the principles of the rule of law that a killing by the State is subject to some form of open and objective oversight'.[9] In the Commission's view, this procedural requirement had to involve a minimum standard of 'public and independent scrutiny', the nature and degree of which would vary according to the circumstances of the case.[10] On that basis it ultimately determined that the inquest held in Gibraltar satisfied the requisite Article 2 standard.[11]

The Third Party Intervention brought by various NGOs in *McCann* also gave considerable attention to the evidential burden on the state and the claimed procedural dimension of Article 2.[12] With regard to the burden of proof, the Third Party Intervention, like the Commission, emphasised that key information about the events in question would lie within the control of the state, which places it under a duty to investigate in good faith all alleged human rights violations made

[5] Alastair Mowbray, 'A New European Court of Human Rights' (1994) *Public Law* 540, 545–46 and 'The Composition and Operation of the New European Court of Human Rights' (1999) *Public Law* 219, 228.

[6] Alastair Mowbray, 'The Creativity of the European Court of Human Rights' (2005) 5 *Human Rights Law Review* 57, 77–78.

[7] *McCann, Farrell and Savage v UK*, Report of the Commission (4 March 1994), para 185.

[8] *McCann*, Report of the Commission, para 191.

[9] *McCann*, Report of the Commission, para 192.

[10] *McCann*, Report of the Commission, para 193.

[11] *McCann*, Report of the Commission, paras 194–201.

[12] *McCann*, Third Party Intervention made jointly by British Irish Rights Watch, The Committee on the Administration of Justice, Inquest and Liberty (the National Council for Civil Liberties) (November 1994).

against it.[13] Agreeing with the Commission's finding in principle that Article 2 raised a duty to investigate, the Third Party Intervention questioned the sufficiency of the inquest and called on the ECtHR to consider in particular the UN Principles on the Effective Prevention and Investigation of Extra-Legal, Arbitrary and Summary Executions, which reflected pre-existing international law standards, and especially the need for an investigation to be thorough, prompt and impartial.[14]

Both of these opinions on the duty to investigate fed, to some extent, into the ECtHR's reasoning. In its judgment, the Grand Chamber included in its survey of relevant international law the investigation requirements in Articles 22–23 of the UN Basic Principles on the Use of Force and Firearms by Law Enforcement Officials,[15] as well as in Article 9 of the UN Principles on the Effective Prevention and Investigation of Extra-Legal, Arbitrary and Summary Executions,[16] although it did not subsequently draw explicitly on these provisions when elaborating its analysis of the domestic investigation process.[17] The ECtHR did though conclude that a procedural dimension was a necessary element in protecting the right to life under Article 2, read together with Article 1:

> The Court confines itself to noting, like the Commission, that a general legal prohibition of arbitrary killing by the agents of the State would be ineffective, in practice, if there existed no procedure for reviewing the lawfulness of the use of lethal force by State authorities. The obligation to protect the right to life under this provision (Article 2),

[13] *McCann*, Third Party Intervention, Section III, para 3.12, referring to the UN Human Rights Committee's Views on Communication No 30/1978, *Bleier Lewenhoff v Uruguay*, Comm. 30/1978, UN Doc. A/37/40, at 130 (HRC 1982), para 13.3.

[14] UN Principles adopted on 24 May 1989 by Economic and Social Council Resolution 1989/65. *McCann*, Third Party Intervention, Section IV, paras 1.1–5.3. In para 3.1 the Intervention also referred to the earlier Inter-American Court of Human Rights judgment in *Velasquez Rodriguez v Honduras*, 29 July 1988, Series C, No 4, para 177.

[15] Article 22: 'Governments and law enforcement agencies shall ensure that an effective review process is available and that independent administrative or prosecutorial authorities are in a position to exercise jurisdiction in appropriate circumstances. In cases of death and serious injury or other grave consequences, a detailed report shall be sent promptly to the competent authorities responsible for administrative review and judicial control'; Article 23: 'Persons affected by the use of force and firearms or their legal representatives shall have access to an independent process, including a judicial process. In the event of the death of such persons, this provision shall apply to their dependants accordingly'.

[16] Article 9: 'There shall be a thorough, prompt and impartial investigation of all suspected cases of extra-legal, arbitrary and summary executions, including cases where complaints by relatives or other reliable reports suggest unnatural death […]. Governments shall maintain investigative offices and procedures to undertake such inquiries. The purpose of the investigation shall be to determine the cause, manner and time of death, the person responsible, and any pattern or practice which may have brought about that death. It shall include an adequate autopsy, collection and analysis of all physical and documentary evidence and statements from witnesses. The investigation shall distinguish between natural death, accidental death, suicide and homicide'.

[17] Fionnuala Ní Aoláin, 'The Evolving Jurisprudence of the European Convention Concerning the Right to Life' (2001) 19.1 *Netherlands Quarterly of Human Rights* 21, 39. Also Magdalena Forowicz, *The Reception of International Law in the European Court of Human Rights* (Oxford, Oxford University Press, 2010) 382–83.

> read in conjunction with the State's general duty under Article 1 … of the Convention to 'secure to everyone within their jurisdiction the rights and freedoms defined in [the] Convention', requires by implication that there should be some form of effective official investigation when individuals have been killed as a result of the use of force by, *inter alios*, agents of the State.[18]

The application of this principle in *McCann* resulted in a finding that the duty to investigate had in fact been satisfied. Whereas the victims' families had complained that the inquest into the killings had not enabled them to be independently represented and had not been sufficiently effective as an investigative mechanism,[19] the ECtHR concluded that the inquest had been a 'thorough, impartial and careful examination of the circumstances surrounding the killings'.[20] The decisive factors in determining the satisfactoriness of the investigation were thus its apparent thoroughness and objectivity, despite the close links between the inquest jury and the military community from which it had been drawn, and the limits on questioning the soldiers involved. This first decision now appears to be out of line with the ECtHR's subsequently more rigorous approach to the criteria of an investigation.

The crucial points in this aspect of the *McCann* judgment were matters of principle and practicality. The implied duty to investigate was introduced as an additional positive obligation, buttressing the effectiveness of Article 2 by requiring it to be actively supported by the state through an ex post facto learning process.[21] In so doing the ECtHR effected a significant extension of Article 2's protection, apparently based on that provision's fundamental importance as enshrining a basic value of democratic societies, as underlined at the start of the ECtHR's legal analysis, and in line with other international provisions. At the same time, this extension was driven by recognition of the fact that the High Contracting Party was best placed to know what had happened in a given incident, and that the needs of truth and justice meant that an acceptable investigation, from which evidence could inform claims brought on behalf of a victim, was a crucial requirement in the event of a death. Whilst at this stage the ECtHR could still rely on evidence gathered by the Commission, the latter's role was limited, and a state investigation was an important source of information. In that connection, practicality concerns also placed a pragmatic limit on how demanding the ECtHR was initially prepared to be regarding the duty to investigate, so as not to impose too great a burden on states or breach subsidiarity by interfering disproportionately in domestic

[18] *McCann* para 161.

[19] On these concerns see also Hilary Kitchin, *The Gibraltar Report: Inquest into the Deaths of Mairead Farrell, Daniel McCann & Sean Savage, Gibraltar, September 1988* (London, National Council for Civil Liberties, 1989).

[20] *McCann* paras 162–64; also 165–73.

[21] Juliet Chevalier-Watts, 'Effective Investigations under Article 2 of the European Convention on Human Rights: Securing the Right to Life or an Onerous Burden on a State?' (2010) 21.3 *European Journal of International Law* 701, 703, drawing on Mowbray, 'The Creativity of the European Court of Human Rights' 78.

processes.[22] In that sense the ECtHR's relationship with states in the democratic context was a restrictive factor on its interpretation of the procedural dimension.

The Grand Chamber's confirmation of the existence of a duty to investigate under Article 2 in *McCann*, focusing on effective protection and requiring High Contracting Parties to support the evidence-gathering process in Article 2 cases, had also been influenced by other practical issues arising within the Council of Europe. These involved investigatory problems in cases against Turkey, which had been hampered by insufficient evidence.[23] Against that backdrop, it seems that the *McCann* case, involving an established democracy that had been a leading state in the formation of the Council of Europe and ECHR, provided the ECtHR with an opportunity to start embedding responses to these difficulties in ECHR law. Even though a breach of this procedural dimension was not found in *McCann*, the high-profile nature of the Grand Chamber decision and its status as the first judgment on Article 2 gave the extended reading of the provision particular authority. These same issues involving cases against Turkey led to the affirmation of the duty to investigate in a series of decisions after *McCann*, in the final years of the part-time ECtHR.[24]

The first of these judgments was *Kaya v Turkey*,[25] a case resulting from the death of the applicant's brother in unclear circumstances. Given that neither the Commission nor the ECtHR were persuaded that it was proven beyond reasonable doubt that the deceased had been killed by a state use of force,[26] the case focused on the applicant's claims that the Turkish authorities had not carried out a sufficiently thorough investigation into the death.[27] Despite the government's arguments that due to dangerous circumstances the investigation could legitimately be kept to a minimum, the Commission found that that investigation was so inadequate that it breached Article 2.[28] In its judgment on this point, the ECtHR relied on the general principles stated in *McCann* and explained their importance in terms of accountability:

> the procedural protection of the right to life inherent in Article 2 of the Convention secures the accountability of agents of the State for their use of lethal force by

[22] Chevalier-Watts, 'Effective Investigations' 705.

[23] See also Aisling Reidy, Françoise Hampson and Kevin Boyle, 'Gross Violations of Human Rights: Invoking the European Convention on Human Rights in the Case of Turkey' (1997) 15.2 *Netherlands Quarterly of Human Rights* 161, 167–69; Alastair Mowbray, *The Development of Positive Obligations under the European Convention on Human Rights by the European Court of Human Rights* (Oxford, Hart, 2004) 228; and Onder Bakircioglu and Brice Dickson, 'The European Convention in Conflicted Societies: The Experience of Northern Ireland and Turkey' (2017) 66 *International and Comparative Law Quarterly* 263, 281–82.

[24] See further Carla Buckley, 'The European Convention on Human Rights and the Right to Life in Turkey' (2001) 1.1 *Human Rights Law Review* 35, 46–51; also focusing on Article 2 judgments involving Turkey note Stuart E Hendin QC, 'The Evolution of the Right to Life by the European Court of Human Rights' (2004) 4.1 *Baltic Yearbook of International Law* 75.

[25] *Kaya v Turkey* (1998).

[26] *Kaya* paras 39, 74–78.

[27] *Kaya* paras 79–81.

[28] *Kaya* paras 82–85.

> subjecting their actions to some form of independent and public scrutiny capable of leading to a determination of whether the force was or was not justified in a particular set of circumstances.[29]

At this stage in its case law, the ECtHR's outline of the duty to investigate was relatively limited, but it nevertheless identified the importance of independence and publicity, as well as the requirement that the investigation be capable of determining whether or not the force used was justified, a criterion of potential rather than outcome. After a detailed discussion of the investigation's technical shortcomings, especially the public prosecutor's unquestioning acceptance of the soldiers' version of events and the limited autopsy, the ECtHR found a breach of Article 2, noting that:

> loss of life is a tragic and frequent occurrence in view of the security situation in south-east Turkey … However, neither the prevalence of violent armed clashes nor the high incidence of fatalities can displace the obligation under Article 2 to ensure that an effective, independent investigation is conducted into deaths arising out of clashes involving the security forces, more so in cases such as the present where the circumstances are in many respects unclear.[30]

This statement of the importance of the duty to investigate shows the ECtHR emphasising both the principle of accountability and the practical need for evidence-gathering by the state. The fact that it could not be displaced in difficult conditions reflected the right's non-derogable status (under Article 15) other than in the context of lawful acts of war.[31] Building on *McCann*, the *Kaya* judgment therefore represented a notable step in developing the extended interpretation of Article 2.[32]

These key points were confirmed by the ECtHR in two further cases against Turkey later in the same year. In *Güleç v Turkey*,[33] in which a boy was shot dead during a large public demonstration, with evidence suggesting he was killed by gendarmes who responded to it with automatic weapons (see Chapter 4), the ECtHR reiterated the above principles. It found the investigation inadequate due to its lack of thoroughness and independence, and because it did not involve the applicant, thus adding an expectation of family involvement.[34] Similarly, in *Ergi v Turkey*, in which a woman was killed when security forces opened fire on a village, the ECtHR echoed the principles in the previous decisions and found a violation of the duty to investigate due to the public prosecutor's reliance on the gendarmerie report and general lack of rigour.[35] The ECtHR affirmed that the duty to investigate arose as soon as the state became aware of a death, even where it was

[29] *Kaya* para 87.
[30] *Kaya* para 91.
[31] Ní Aoláin, 'The Evolving Jurisprudence' 34, 41.
[32] Ní Aoláin, 'The Evolving Jurisprudence' 32–33.
[33] *Güleç v Turkey* (1998).
[34] *Güleç* paras 77–82.
[35] *Ergi v Turkey* (1998) paras 83–85.

not established that the killing was caused by a state agent, and therefore that the scope of the duty had been expanded beyond the initial outline in *McCann*.[36] The need to be able to rely on a state's investigation into an incident of lethal force was a key part of these decisions, and was to become even more important following the institutional reforms of 1998, which ended the Commission's role.[37]

B. The Duty to Investigate post-1998: Systemic Limits and Reliance on States

Following the removal of the Commission from the ECHR procedure in the 1998 reform, the ECtHR was left with a limited investigatory capability.[38] Due to resource restrictions it needed to be able to rely on information provided by state parties, even though they are not its only source of information.[39] In particular, the ECtHR relies on factual evidence as established and confirmed by domestic courts,[40] which its subsidiary status requires it to respect unless serious doubts are raised.[41] The duty to investigate has thus continued to be important not only as a mechanism for supporting justice and seeking to make Article 2 effective at the state level, but also as the means for trying to ensure that state processes are

[36] *Ergi* para 82; Chevalier-Watts, 'Effective Investigations' 706.

[37] Rainey, Wicks and Ovey, *Jacobs, White and Ovey: The European Convention on Human Rights* 8–9.

[38] ECHR Article 38. See Russell, *The Use of Force and Article 2 of the ECHR in Light of European Conflicts* 205–11. Note also Council of Europe, 'Explanatory Report to Protocol No. 11 to the Convention for the Protection of Human Rights and Fundamental Freedoms, restructuring the control machinery established thereby', European Treaty Series no 155 (11 May 1994) 16.

[39] Rainey, Wicks and Ovey, *Jacobs, White and Ovey: The European Convention on Human Rights* 26–28; Philip Leach, Costas Paraskeva and Gordana Uzelac, *International Human Rights and Fact Finding: An Analysis of the Fact-Finding Missions Conducted by the European Commission and Court of Human Rights*, Report by the Human Rights and Social Justice Research Institute at London Metropolitan University (2009) 4–6; Philip Leach, Costas Paraskeva and Gordana Uzelac, 'Human Rights Fact-Finding. The European Court of Human Rights at a Crossroads' (2010) 28.1 *Netherlands Quarterly of Human Rights* 41, 42; Michael O'Boyle and Natalia Brady, 'Investigatory Powers of the European Court of Human Rights' (2013) 4 *European Human Rights Law Review* 378, 386. As the latter point out at 387–88, the ECtHR also relies on evidence submitted by the parties and 'on the reports of other investigatory bodies such as UN bodies, Organisation for Security and Cooperation in Europe (OSCE), Committee for the Prevention of Torture (CPT) or the Parliamentary Assembly of the Council of Europe (PACE) or the reports of reputable and well-established NGOs'. The ECtHR may draw on other sources of information including the media: for example in *Ciorcan v Romania* (2015) para 82, the ECtHR considered newspaper reports on police conduct towards Roma communities in order to address the context of the use of force.

[40] For example, in *Leonidis v Greece* (2009) paras 69–74, the ECtHR found that the state's investigation had been satisfactory because the domestic courts had been able to rely on it and had not identified any shortcomings; similarly see also *Dölek c Turquie* (2007) para 60.

[41] Note for example the clear statement on this point by the Grand Chamber in *Giuliani and Gaggio v Italy* (2011) para 180 and *Mustafa Tunç and Fecire Tunç v Turkey* (2015) para 182; see also *Erdoğan and Others v Turkey* (2006) paras 71–73, 90–95. See further O'Boyle and Brady, 'Investigatory Powers' 378, 388; Alastair Mowbray, 'Subsidiarity and the European Convention on Human Rights' (2015) 15 *Human Rights Law Review* 313, 323–24, 331–32; and Matthew Smith, 'The Adjudicatory Fact-Finding Tools of the European Court of Human Rights' (2009) 2 *European Human Rights Law Review* 206.

good enough for the ECtHR to rely on. This could appear to involve a potentially problematic circularity, in that the ECtHR has to determine a state's compliance with human rights standards essentially on the basis of evidence predominantly in the control of and provided by that state.[42] The procedural standards set by the ECtHR are, though, intended to provide an inherent guarantee of quality and reliability.[43]

For example, in *Giuliani and Gaggio v Italy*, finding (by ten votes to seven) that the investigation was satisfactory in all respects, the Grand Chamber explicitly underlined the connection between the investigation by the High Contracting Party and its own ability to decide on a case.[44] Emphasising that it had found no substantive breach of Article 2 'on the basis of the information provided by the domestic investigation' which had furnished it with 'sufficient evidence',[45] the Grand Chamber concluded that:

> It follows that the investigation was sufficiently effective to enable it to be determined whether the use of lethal force had been justified in the present case [...] and whether the organisation and planning of the policing operations had been compatible with the obligation to protect life.[46]

Given that key information in a case involving the use of lethal force by state agents will predominantly lie within the control of the state, rather than victims or applicants, and that the ECtHR cannot investigate independently in every case, or investigate productively if the case arises long after the events in question, this is the pragmatic solution under the ECHR.[47] Where a state investigation is not reliable, provided that the apparent procedural shortcoming made a material difference,[48] there can be a procedural breach of Article 2 separately from a decision about the substantive elements,[49] or a finding that an investigation by the

[42] Note Chevalier-Watts, 'Effective Investigations' 718. This was already problematic in Commission decisions: Ní Aoláin, 'The Evolving Jurisprudence' 26–27.

[43] Even if the ECtHR notes that the evidence submitted is incomplete, it may still base its assessment of both substantive and procedural dimensions on the evidence before it: for example, *Wasilewska and Kałucka v Poland* (2010) para 60.

[44] *Giuliani and Gaggio* paras 298–26.

[45] *Giuliani and Gaggio* para 308.

[46] *Giuliani and Gaggio* para 309. This was questioned by some of the dissentients: on criticisms of the linkage between the evidential base and the substantive finding see Joint Partly Dissenting Opinion of Judges Rozakis, Tulkens, Zupančič, Gyulumyan, Ziemele, Kalaydjieva and Karakaş para 14; and Joint Partly Dissenting Opinion of Judges Tulkens, Zupančič, Gyulumyan and Karakaş paras 7, 10 and 14.

[47] See for example the statement on this point in the Admissibility Decision in *Romijn v Netherlands* (2005) 20, a case about a fatal shooting during a police raid on a house.

[48] Note on this point for example the Admissibility Decision in *Grams c l'Allemagne* (1999) 11, in which the applicants' son had been killed in unclear circumstances during a police anti-terrorist operation. The ECtHR decided that even without various failings in the investigation the domestic decision not to prosecute the police officers involved would not have been different.

[49] O'Boyle and Brady, 'Investigatory Powers' 383. For example, in *Abik c Turquie* (2013), in which the applicant's son and another person had been shot dead by the police in unclear circumstances, in paras 37, 42–50 the ECtHR found a procedural breach of Article 2 when it could not determine the substantive dimension due to an inadequate state investigation; see also *Akpinar and Altun v Turkey* (2007) paras 60–61; *Behçet Söğüt c Turquie* (2015) paras 57–66; *Hakim İpek c Turquie* (2015) paras 67–69.

state was inadequate may serve to support the view that a substantive dimension of Article 2 has also been breached.[50] The ECtHR has focused on the duty to investigate in relation to discrimination where it has been unwilling to address racial prejudice in the use of force itself,[51] and has even decided that the duty to investigate can constitute an autonomous ground for state responsibility under Article 2 (and Article 3), applicable to events that occurred before the ECHR came into force for the state in question.[52] In the post-1998 period of the full-time ECtHR, the duty to investigate is thus a crucial part of the accountability process under Article 2, constituting both a means and an end in the legal protection of the right to life. In that sense as an independent ground for state liability it represents a significant extension of the right to life, due to the need for practical and effective protection of that right and its importance in democratic society, as well as a crucial foundation for the ECtHR's ability to address the substantive dimensions of Article 2. In that light, the scope of the duty to investigate can now be addressed in more detail.

II. The Duty to Investigate and its Elements

The procedural dimension of Article 2, as applied to cases of lethal and potentially lethal force in the domestic policing and law enforcement context, has been developed by the ECtHR to involve a number of elements. In terms of outcomes, a deficiency in any one of these elements, assessed by the ECtHR as undermining

In *Scavuzzo-Hager et autres c Suisse* (2006) the applicants' son had died from a pre-existing medical condition while being restrained and arrested by police officers. The ECtHR could not find a causal connection between the state agents' conduct and the death in substantive terms, but in paras 80–86 found a breach of the duty to investigate partly because the state authorities had inadequately addressed that point. Contrast *Boukrourou et autres c France* (2017) on similar facts in which the investigation was not challenged. The 'detachability' of the procedural dimension under Article 2, or its evolution into a separate and autonomous duty, was confirmed in *Šilih v Slovenia* (2009) paras 153–59, a case involving medical negligence.

[50] For example, in the context of anti-terrorist operations note *Gülbahar and Özer and Others v Turkey* (2013) paras 74–76 and *Taydaş v Turkey* (2013) paras 44–45. In *Timus and Tarus v Republic of Moldova* (2013) paras 51–58, in which the applicants' brother had been shot in the head during a police operation to arrest a different person, multiple investigatory and evidential failings resulted in substantive and procedural breaches of Article 2. See also on this point *Karataş and Others v Turkey* (2017) para 90.

[51] The question whether lethal or life-threatening force was used in a discriminatory way in individual cases requires a separate line of argument in ECHR law, using Article 14 in relation to Article 2. Despite the ECtHR's emphasis on the relationship between non-discrimination and democracy (*Nachova* para 145), in *Nachova* para 168 and *Ciorcan* paras 159–67 a breach of Article 14 was found in relation to Article 2's procedural dimension when the ECtHR's focus 'on subjective intent, and its refusal to infer race discrimination from the evidence of excessive force' meant that it could not, or would not, find discrimination in substantive terms: see Sandra Fredman, 'Emerging from the Shadows: Substantive Equality and Article 14 of the European Convention on Human Rights' (2016) 16 *Human Rights Law Review* 273, 285–86; note also Marie-Bénédicte Dembour, *Who Believes in Human Rights? Reflections on the European Convention* (Cambridge, Cambridge University Press, 2006) 133.

[52] See section II.D below.

the duty to investigate, can lead to a finding that it has been breached. In terms of their scope and significance, the elements also point to essential components of the ECtHR's analytical and justificatory case narratives about Article 2 and its nexus with democratic society. In relation to each of these procedural elements, as with the substantive dimensions of Article 2, the ECtHR relies on the importance of the right to life in democratic society as the compelling rationale for seeking to achieve practical and effective protection of that right, but also recognises that the procedural dimension may require some proportionate circumscription in the democratic context. The ECtHR thus draws on the concept of democratic society in a descriptive and idealised sense to bolster the right to life, as well as that concept's indication of the need for limits, in the form of subsidiarity, and the proportionate balancing of individual and social interests. Together these show teleologically how the ECtHR envisages the investigatory needs of Article 2 and the appropriate range of measures to be taken by state authorities in democratic society. This section explores these points by outlining how the ECtHR has developed the procedural dimension and its various elements in order to evaluate state investigations. As noted in the previous section about the significance of the duty to investigate per se and its role in supporting the ECtHR's substantive analysis, the main element of the procedural dimension is its effectiveness, which encompasses questions of adequacy and independence, but the procedural dimension also includes elements relating to the transparency and the timing of an investigation.[53]

A. Adequacy

The effectiveness of an investigation primarily concerns its adequacy, which comprises its thoroughness,[54] the legal standard applied in it, and the investigatory procedure's potential, that is, not whether it produces a particular outcome, but whether it is capable of producing a decision about the use of force in light of Article 2. The adequacy limb of the effectiveness of an investigation reflects the fundamental importance of evidence-gathering in supporting the construction of an account of events that can accurately represent what occurred.

The gathering of evidence about the facts of an incident is perhaps the most basic aspect of any investigation into a use of lethal or potentially lethal force. For example, in four joined cases against the United Kingdom concerning deaths that occurred in Northern Ireland, namely *McKerr*, *Hugh Jordan*, *Kelly* and

[53] Rainey, Wicks and Ovey, *Jacobs, White & Ovey: The European Convention on Human Rights* 168–77; Anja Seibert-Fohr, *Prosecuting Serious Human Rights Violations* (Oxford, Oxford University Press, 2009) 132–41; Chevalier-Watts, 'Effective Investigations' 707; Mowbray, 'Duties of Investigation' 437; Russell, *The Use of Force and Article 2 of the ECHR in Light of European Conflicts* 121–54; see also Stuart Casey-Maslen and Sean Connolly, *Police Use of Force under International Law* (Cambridge, Cambridge University Press, 2017) 377–86.

[54] Mowbray, 'Duties of Investigation' 440–41.

Shanaghan,[55] the applicants raised a number of arguments about the adequacy of the state investigation in this regard. In so doing, they referred to the international 'Minnesota Protocol' in the UN Manual on the Effective Prevention and Investigation of Extra-legal, Arbitrary and Summary Executions.[56] This Protocol was drawn up to supplement and give further effect to the UN Principles of the same name[57] by setting out guidelines on the purpose and elements of investigations, including evidentiary standards. In all of these cases the ECtHR found that there were various shortcomings in the investigations, including upholding the applicants' claims about inadequacies in the state authorities' evidence-gathering processes.[58]

Similarly, in *Makaratzis v Greece*,[59] the Grand Chamber held that an investigation must be capable of ascertaining the principal facts and circumstances, and found a breach of the procedural obligation largely because the Greek authorities failed to identify all of the police officers involved in the operation in which potentially lethal force had been used.[60] The ECtHR's evaluation of the state's approach

[55] *McKerr v United Kingdom* (2001), *Hugh Jordan v United Kingdom* (2001), *Kelly and Others v United Kingdom* (2001) and *Shanaghan v United Kingdom* (2001). In *McKerr*, paras 11–16, the applicant's father and two others had been killed when a special unit of the Royal Ulster Constabulary (RUC) fired at least 109 rounds of ammunition at them during an anti-terrorist operation to prevent a suspected murder plot. In *Hugh Jordan*, paras 11–27, the applicant's son had been shot dead by members of the RUC after they had forcefully stopped his car as part of an operation to prevent the suspected distribution of terrorist equipment. In *Kelly*, paras 11–25, nine of the applicants' relatives had been killed during an operation by the RUC and soldiers against a terrorist attack on a police station. In *Shanaghan*, paras 11–26, the applicant's son had been shot dead by a member of a loyalist terrorist group, allegedly with the collusion of the RUC.

[56] Model Protocol for a legal investigation of extra-legal, arbitrary and summary executions, UN Doc E/ST/CSDHA/.12 (1991). The 'Minnesota' or Model Protocol for a legal investigation of extra-legal, arbitrary and summary executions, in Section B, Purposes of an Inquiry, states: 'As set out in paragraph 9 of the Principles, the broad purpose of an inquiry is to discover the truth about the events leading to the suspicious death of a victim. To fulfil that purpose, those conducting the inquiry shall, at a minimum, seek: (a) to identify the victim; (b) to recover and preserve evidentiary material related to the death to aid in any potential prosecution of those responsible; (c) to identify possible witnesses and obtain statements from them concerning the death; (d) to determine the cause, manner, location and time of death, as well as any pattern or practice that may have brought about the death; (e) to distinguish between natural death, accidental death, suicide and homicide; (f) to identify and apprehend the person(s) involved in the death; (g) to bring the suspected perpetrator(s) before a competent court established by law'. See also Russell, *The Use of Force and Article 2 of the ECHR in Light of European Conflicts* 122–39.

[57] See note 14 above. Articles 9–17 address the need for and requirements of investigations.

[58] *McKerr* paras 100–103, 157–59; *Hugh Jordan* paras 95–97, 142–43; *Kelly* paras 83–86, 136–37; *Shanaghan* paras 77–80, 122–23. On similar investigatory issues see *McShane v United Kingdom* (2002), in which the applicant's husband had been crushed by an army vehicle during a major public disturbance; and *Finucane v United Kingdom* (2003), a case involving a killing by loyalist paramilitaries and possible RUC collusion.

[59] *Makaratzis v Greece* (2004).

[60] *Makaratzis* para 74. Further examples of inadequate investigatory practices include *Karagiannopoulos c Grèce* (2003), in which the applicant had been shot in the head and seriously disabled during a police operation, but the authorities had not carried out a key forensic test, a reconstruction of events, or examined the police officer's holster, from which the applicant was claimed to have seized a pistol. In *Akkum v Turkey* (2005) para 250 the investigation into a number of killings of alleged terrorists by state agents was inadequate due to an absence of elementary forensic and evidential elements, leading the ECtHR to conclude that Turkey had failed to account for its agents' actions. Note also *Yüksel Erdoğan*

to the procedural dimension will also involve considering whether the domestic authorities have considered all aspects of a police operation,[61] and whether or not they have acted in good faith and applied reasonable standards. In that regard a High Contracting Party will not be permitted to benefit from its own mismanagement of an investigation.[62]

In addition to the satisfactoriness of evidence-gathering, an investigation must be adequate in terms of the legal standard applied by the state authorities. In *Nachova*,[63] the Grand Chamber identified inadequacies in the forensic and evidence-gathering aspects of the state's investigation due to its legal scope. Specifying that an Article 2 investigation 'must apply a standard comparable to the "no more than absolutely necessary" standard required' in Article 2(2),[64] the Grand Chamber was critical of the way the investigation had adhered to the unacceptably broad ambit of the national regulations, which (as discussed in Chapter 4) had been found to breach the legal framework dimension of the right to life:

> the investigation into the deaths of Mr Angelov and Mr Petkov assessed the lawfulness of the officers' conduct in the light of the relevant regulations. The fact that the investigation validated the use of force in the circumstances only serves to confirm the fundamentally defective nature of those regulations and their disregard of the right to life. By basing themselves on the strict letter of the regulations, the investigating authorities did not examine relevant matters such as the fact that the victims were known to be unarmed and represented no danger to anyone, still less whether it was appropriate to dispatch a team of heavily armed officers in pursuit of two men whose only offence was to be absent without leave. In short, there was no strict scrutiny of all the material circumstances.[65]

and Others v Turkey (2007) paras 106–16. In *Celniku c Grèce* (2007) paras 64–71, in which the applicants' brother had been killed during an arrest operation in which he kicked a police officer, causing his gun to fire, the police failed to carry out an adequate forensic investigation of the fatal shot.

[61] For example in *Shchiborshch and Kuzmina v Russia* (2014) para 258, the ECtHR found a breach of the duty to investigate because the authorities had not considered the planning and control dimensions of the operation to extract the mentally disturbed victim from his flat by force. In *Perk et Autres c Turquie* (2006) paras 72, 80–81, the applicants' relatives were suspected terrorists shot dead by the police during a raid on a flat. The ECtHR found that the domestic court should have considered whether non-lethal force could have been an option in preparing the operation, which together with the lack of a sketch map of the flat or reconstruction of events, led to a breach of the procedural dimension, even though a substantive breach was not found for the absence of a graduated use of force.

[62] See *Soare et autres c Roumanie* (2011) para 147, in which the applicant had been seriously wounded by a gunshot to the head during an apparent arrest operation by the police in disputed circumstances. The ECtHR noted various failings in the authorities' factual investigation, which meant a clear conclusion about the events was not possible; however, the ECtHR held that the investigatory failings led it to reject the Government's denial of responsibility and to find a breach of Article 2 – to hold otherwise would be to allow the state to benefit from its own shortcomings. Similar issues arose in *Gheorghe Cobzaru c Roumanie* (2013) para 76. See also *Finogenov v Russia* (2012), the Moscow theatre siege case, para 271: 'More specifically, a requirement of "thorough investigation" means that the authorities must always make a serious attempt to find out what happened and should not rely on hasty or ill-founded conclusions to close their investigation or as the basis of their decisions. They must take all reasonable steps available to them to secure the evidence concerning the incident'.

[63] *Nachova and Others v Bulgaria* (2005).

[64] *Nachova* para 113.

[65] *Nachova* para 114. Similarly, in *Wasilewska and Kałucka v Poland* (2010) paras 62–63, the state investigation into the fatal shooting only considered the necessity to use force and not its

The connection between the national legal standard, its compliance with Article 2 and the scope of the investigation was also a point of disagreement in the Grand Chamber decision in *Armani da Silva v United Kingdom* (involving the shooting of Jean Charles de Menezes on the London Underground, considered in Chapter 4).[66] Although there were numerous apparent problems with the police operation in the circumstances, the applicant based her case solely on the procedural dimension of Article 2. Her argument was that the UK investigation was insufficiently rigorous in its examination of the facts, because the test for self-defence under domestic law that was applied focused solely on 'honest belief', which she argued was lower than the standard required by the absolute necessity test under Article 2(2) of the ECHR, due to its apparent requirement of an objective component.[67] Refuted by the Government but supported by the UK Equality and Human Rights Commission in its third party intervention,[68] the applicant's case was rejected by a thirteen to four majority of the Grand Chamber, which (as indicated in Chapter 4) emphasised the subjective dimension of the absolute necessity test.[69]

Ultimately, the adequacy element of the duty to investigate focuses on the potential of the High Contracting Party's domestic procedure. This was made clear in the first ECtHR decision on Article 2 in a case of lethal force after the 1998 reforms, *Oğur v Turkey*, in which case the applicant's son had been killed in an operation by security forces.[70] Finding a breach of the procedural dimension due to forensic inadequacies and a lack of independence (a criterion discussed further below), the Grand Chamber echoed the 1998 cases against Turkey (in Part I above) and held that Article 2 and Article 1 of the ECHR require:

> that there should be some form of effective official investigation when individuals have been killed as a result of the use of force, in particular by agents of the state. This investigation should be capable of leading to the identification and punishment of those responsible.[71]

This capability aspect of investigations, which is echoed in all decisions under the procedural dimension of Article 2, means that sufficient reasonable steps

proportionality in the circumstances, which together with other inadequacies led to a breach of the procedural dimension. In *Ülüfer c Turquie* (2012) paras 76–78, in which the applicant's son had been shot while trying to escape from arrest by gendarmes, the investigation was defective primarily because it was based on the applicable domestic law, which ignored both the necessity and proportionality of the use of force. In contrast, in the Admissibility Decision in *Oláh v Hungary* (2004) 15, the lack of explicit engagement with a proportionality test by the domestic court did not lead to a breach due to general compliance with Article 2 requirements. In *Haász and Szabó v Hungary* (2015) paras 66 and 70–72, the national authorities only considered the state agent's potential criminal liability rather than the absolute necessity of his conduct in terms of Article 2. The ECtHR undertook a broader assessment of the issues, finding a breach of the substantive and procedural dimensions due to the state's narrow approach.

[66] *Armani da Silva v United Kingdom* (2016).

[67] *Armani da Silva* paras 190–94. See also Natasa Mavronicola, 'Taking Life and Liberty Seriously: Reconsidering Criminal Liability Under Article 2 of the ECHR' (2017) 80.6 *Modern Law Review* 1026, 1042.

[68] *Armani da Silva* paras 224–28.

[69] *Armani da Silva* paras 244–56.

[70] *Oğur v Turkey* (1999).

[71] *Oğur* para 88. On similar issues see *Gül v Turkey* (2000) paras 88–95.

should be taken, reasonably well, so that the investigation *could in principle* lead to a finding about responsibility for the death in question. This was summed up in *Ramsahai v Netherlands*, a case involving the fatal shooting by police of a suspected armed robber.[72] Finding a breach of Article 2's procedural dimension due to various inadequacies in the state authorities' investigation into the killing,[73] the ECtHR held that:

> In order to be 'effective' as this expression is to be understood in the context of Article 2 of the Convention, an investigation into a death that engages the responsibility of a Contracting Party under that Article must firstly be adequate. That is, it must be capable of leading to the identification and punishment of those responsible. This is not an obligation of result, but one of means. The authorities must have taken the reasonable steps available to them to secure the evidence concerning the incident. Any deficiency in the investigation which undermines its ability to identify the perpetrator or perpetrators will risk falling foul of this standard …[74]

The ECtHR subsequently qualified the obligation of means, stating in *Giuliani and Gaggio* that an investigation must be 'capable of leading to a determination of whether the force used was or was not justified in the circumstances and of identifying and – if appropriate – punishing those responsible'.[75] This was reiterated in *Armani da Silva*. The applicant's second argument in that case was that the threshold evidential test for prosecutions in England and Wales, requiring 'a realistic prospect of conviction', was too demanding and meant that state agents who used lethal force in circumstances in which a self-defence argument could be raised were not being prosecuted,[76] but the ECtHR held that this did not breach Article 2.[77] While acknowledging the family's frustration at the lack of any individual prosecution, the ECtHR observed that sometimes identifying overall systemic failures was more appropriate than focusing on the responsibility of a specific state agent, and that in this regard the conviction of the Metropolitan Police Service for institutional failings under health and safety law was deemed to be an adequate outcome.[78] Recalling its nuanced restatement of the obligation

[72] *Ramsahai v Netherlands* (2007) paras 14–22.

[73] *Ramsahai* paras 270–71, 326–32. Held by thirteen votes to four: see Joint Partly Dissenting Opinion of Judges Costa, Sir Nicolas Bratza, Lorenzen and Thomassen, who disagreed about the significance of the forensic points identified by the majority.

[74] *Ramsahai* para 324. On obligations of means see Linos-Alexandre Sicilianos, 'Preventing Violations of the Right to Life: Positive Obligations under Article 2 of the ECHR' (2014) 3.2 *Cyprus Human Rights Law Review* 117, 120–21.

[75] *Giuliani and Gaggio* para 301. See also the Admissibility Decision in *Romijn*, in which a decision not to prosecute a police officer for mistakenly shooting the victim was held not to breach the procedural dimension of Article 2 because (p 26) 'it would be perverse to construe Article 2 or any other Article of the Convention as requiring a criminal prosecution even in circumstances where it is apparent that the individual prosecuted is entitled to claim self-defence'.

[76] *Armani da Silva* paras 195–206.

[77] *Armani da Silva* paras 258–64, 265–82. Note paras 259–60 in which the ECtHR indicates its general deference to states with regard to prosecutorial systems.

[78] *Armani da Silva* paras 283–88.

of means in *Giuliani*, the ECtHR held that the duty to investigate duty 'does not entail the right to have third parties prosecuted – or convicted – for a criminal offence'.[79]

Overall, the obligation of means in the procedural dimension of Article 2 highlights key aspects of the ECtHR's understanding of what is necessary to protect that right in democratic society. On that basis the duty to investigate is primarily concerned with ensuring accountability and lesson-learning in line with Article 2's substantive standards, fostering appropriate levels of deterrence in national systems,[80] which cannot be circumvented merely by offering compensation to a victim,[81] as well as establishing acceptable investigatory practices.[82] These aspects reflect the idea of inherent values in democratic society under the rule of law and the ECtHR's teleological establishment of standards for High Contracting Parties under Article 2. Whilst the ECtHR does not specify a model of

[79] *Armani da Silva* paras 233 and 257. This was questioned by the dissentients: *Armani da Silva*, Joint Dissenting Opinion of Judges Karakaş, Wojtyczek and Dedov para 11 and Dissenting Opinion of Judge López Guerra paras 1–11. On the dissenting views note anon, 'Case Comment: Investigation of Police Operations' (2016) 4 *European Human Rights Law Review* 442. Although in para 274 the ECtHR noted the scarcity of prosecutions of police officers for lethal shootings in the United Kingdom, it attributed this to the 'extremely restrictive policy on the use of firearms by State agents' and the overall rarity of weapons being discharged during armed interventions. However, even though a low total number of incidents might correlate with a low number of prosecutions, a restrictive policy does not automatically mean flawless practice.

[80] In *Alikaj et autres c Italie* (2011) paras 100–13, the ECtHR found a procedural breach due partly to insufficient deterrence and an inadequate remedy for the killing, because the domestic ruling found the police officer's conviction for homicide was time barred and no other disciplinary measures were imposed. In *Evrim Öktem c Turquie* (2008) paras 54–57, the applicant had been seriously injured when police fired warning shots while chasing protesters. As the officer responsible had been granted an amnesty, the ECtHR found a procedural breach as the domestic criminal process lacked sufficient rigour and deterrent effect. In *Enukidze and Girgvliani v Georgia* (2011) paras 274–77, in which state agents killed the victim in a way not connected with their official duties, so substantive Article 2 responsibility did not arise, the ECtHR found a procedural breach, stressing the importance of 'particularly stringent scrutiny' to avoid 'instilling a sense of impunity'. This concern with deterrence is, though, restricted in some situations: in the admissibility decision in *McBride v United Kingdom* (2006), the applicant's son had been shot dead by two soldiers in Northern Ireland, who were convicted of murder. After serving their sentence they were not dismissed from the army, an outcome that the applicant claimed breached Article 2. The Chamber held that the investigation and criminal trials had been satisfactory for Article 2 purposes, and that the soldiers' subsequent retention by the army caused no breach (p 10): 'While reference has also been made to the future protection of citizens, presumably through either continued risk of unlawful conduct by the two soldiers or through a deterioration in attitudes or standards in the armed forces generally, this would appear somewhat hypothetical and speculative and certainly remote in consequence as regards any effect on the rights of this applicant. To the extent concerns might arise as to the composition of the armed forces and existence of appropriate disciplinary regulations and machinery, these would appear to be matters of general policy for public and political debate falling outside the scope of Article 2 of the Convention as applicable in this case'.

[81] In *Nikolova and Velichkova v Bulgaria* (2007) police officers beat a man over the head while arresting him, leading to his death. The ECtHR emphasised that a compensation payment could not displace the procedural obligation under Article 2, which was essential to prevent abuse of rights: para 55.

[82] Note also *McKerr* para 113; Fionnuala Ní Aoláin 'Truth Telling, Accountability and the Right to Life in Northern Ireland' (2002) 5 *European Human Rights Law Review* 572, 581.

investigations,[83] its decisions indicate minimum standards, although the ECtHR's evaluation of domestic practices does not always demonstrate clear understanding of their relationship with Article 2.[84] The adequacy limb of the effectiveness test in the procedural dimension of Article 2 is thus particularly important in engaging with the structural aspects of accountability narratives, that is, establishing the elements of fact and human conduct involved in a use of force incident that can then be narratively assessed, and relates to state practices in response to a resultant death.

B. Independence

The second limb of effectiveness concerns independence, in principle and practice. This requires an investigation to be carried out by an authority that is separate from those involved in the incident, in terms of legal structure and hierarchy, as well as actual activity and operational ability.[85] Issues of independence were important factors in the procedural failings found by the ECtHR in the joined Northern Irish cases, in which the same branch of the police implicated in the incidents in question was involved in the investigation thereof.[86] In finding such a lack of independence to be a procedural inadequacy, the ECtHR underlined

[83] For example *McKerr* para 111. On this point note the death in custody case *Velikova v Bulgaria* (2000) para 80 and for example *Mustafa Tunç and Fecire Tunç* para 225. See further Mowbray, 'Duties of Investigation' 438.

[84] For example, although the ECtHR underlined in the joined Northern Irish cases that it was not its role 'to specify in any detail which procedures the authorities should adopt in providing for the proper examination of the circumstances of a killing by State agents' (*McKerr* para 159), it nevertheless made some explicit criticisms of inquest procedures in Northern Ireland as compared with the wider explanatory approach required under Article 2. Note Rainey, Wicks and Ovey, *Jacobs, White & Ovey: The European Convention on Human Rights* 173–74; Christine Bell and Johanna Keenan, 'Lost on the Way Home? The Right to Life in Northern Ireland' (2005) 32.1 *Journal of Law and Society* 68, 71–84; Marny Requa and Gordon Anthony, 'Coroners, Controversial Deaths and Northern Ireland's Past Conflict' (2008) *Public Law* 443; John F Larkin, 'Dialogue at Cross Purposes? The Northern Ireland Inquest and Article 2 of the European Convention on Human Rights' in Early, Austin, Ovey and Chernishova (eds), *The Right to Life under Article 2 of the European Convention on Human Rights* 161. See also Fiona Doherty and Paul Mageean, *Investigating Lethal Force Deaths in Northern Ireland* (Belfast, Northern Ireland Human Rights Commission, 2006). In *Bubbins v United Kingdom* (2005) the ECtHR had found that the investigation into the shooting of a man who pointed a replica firearm at police was generally satisfactory despite some omissions and, even though the Article 2 compatibility of inquests was doubted by the domestic courts, that the inquest process could satisfy the duty to investigate: paras 107–13, 120–25, 153. On inquests in England and Wales and the impact of Article 2 on the need for broad 'narrative verdicts' see David Baker, 'Deaths After Police Contact in England and Wales: The Effects of Article 2 of the European Convention on Human Rights on Coronial Practice' (2016) 12.2 *International Journal of Law in Context* 162 and more generally *Deaths After Police Contact: Constructing Accountability in the 21st Century* (London, Palgrave Macmillan, 2016).

[85] For example, see *Ergi* para 83, on the lack of effective independence between the prosecutor and the police involved in the incident.

[86] *McKerr* paras 112, 157–59; *Hugh Jordan* paras 142–43; *Kelly* paras 136–37; *Shanaghan* paras 122–23.

the importance of making independence apparent in decision-making processes through the giving of reasons, even if independence in practice was not clear.[87] Subsequently in *Ramsahai* the ECtHR held that in addition to adequacy the effectiveness of an investigation depended on its independence:

> Secondly, for the investigation to be 'effective' in this sense it may generally be regarded as necessary for the persons responsible for it and carrying it out to be independent from those implicated in the events. This means not only a lack of hierarchical or institutional connection but also a practical independence ...[88]

On that basis the ECtHR held that a brief delay in arranging independent control of the police investigation meant that there was a procedural breach of Article 2 in this case, even though the materiality of that shortcoming was arguably marginal.[89]

However, in other cases the requirement of independence, albeit fundamental to effectiveness and the goal of impartiality in investigations, has been held not to be unlimited. For example, the Grand Chamber in *Giuliani and Gaggio* did not find a procedural inadequacy where the *carabinieri* carried out aspects of the forensic examination even though members of the same force had been involved in the incident itself, nor where one of the ballistics experts had apparently and publicly already formed a view on the incident in question before completing his tests.[90] Basing this conclusion on the 'technical and objective' nature of the activities involved and the fact that the expert had operated as part of a team, the ECtHR appeared to relax the independence requirement so as not to risk excluding recourse to particular expertise.[91] Moreover, in *Golubeva v Russia* the ECtHR approached this requirement on balance, and held that a lack of independence in one aspect of an investigation will not lead to a breach of the procedural

[87] For example, *Hugh Jordan* para 123.

[88] *Ramsahai* para 325. Mowbray, 'Duties of Investigation' 440 explains practical independence as self-reliance. See also *Guerdner et autres c France* (2014) paras 82–84, in which the investigation into a fatal shooting by a gendarme was undertaken by a different branch of the same force and was found by the ECtHR to be sufficiently independent due to its organisational distinction.

[89] *Ramsahai* paras 333–41. Held by sixteen votes to one: see Partly Dissenting Opinion of Judge Thomassen, who considered that the lack of independence had had no real impact on the investigation in the circumstances. See Maija Pitkänen, 'Fair and Balanced Positive Obligations: Do They Exist?' (2012) 5 *European Human Rights Law Review* 538, 547–50. Note also *Grams* 11, and the question of material effect. In contrast, later the same year in *Brecknell v United Kingdom* (2007) para 76, a case not involving the use of lethal force by the state but the re-investigation of alleged collusion between the RUC and a terrorist group that had carried out a deadly attack, the ECtHR decided that the Police Service of Northern Ireland (PSNI) responsible for the re-investigation was 'institutionally distinct from its predecessor' the RUC, which had carried out the initial investigation, 'even if, necessarily, it inherited officers and resources', despite the fact that when formed in 2001 the PSNI was substantially a continuation of the RUC. However, the RUC's role in the early part of the investigation was found to be a breach of the independence requirement. See also on the same issue *Reavey v United Kingdom* (2007) para 29.

[90] *Giuliani and Gaggio* paras 322–24; Skinner, 'The Right to Life, Democracy and State Responsibility in "Urban Guerilla" Conflict' 574–75.

[91] *Giuliani and Gaggio* para 322.

dimension if there is adequate independence in another aspect.[92] Thus, although independence is a fundamental aspect of fairness, reliability and good practice in investigations, and therefore (as considered in Chapter 6) of credible accountability under the rule of law in democratic society, it is evaluated by the ECtHR in context, allowing some flexibility in state practices. This is partly due to concerns with democratic subsidiarity, and partly so as not to be unfeasibly demanding in pragmatic recognition of the need for proportionate human rights standards to allow for operational leeway.

C. Transparency and Scrutiny

In the procedural dimension of Article 2, the ECtHR has determined that domestic investigations must involve some degree of transparency, by requiring family involvement and more general public scrutiny, but within limits. As discussed further in Chapter 6, these forms of transparency are deemed to be vital in protecting the interests of victims and their families, and supporting the perceived legitimacy of, and public confidence in, the nature and operation of accountability processes.[93] Family involvement is both a specific aspect of public scrutiny, in that the next-of-kin are those most directly and immediately concerned in seeking to understand what has happened, as well as a way of ensuring that the interests of the victim, even if deceased, are somehow represented in the process.

The involvement of the victim's family had been found by the ECtHR to be an essential aspect of the duty to investigate from its early decisions on lethal force under Article 2. Starting an investigation must not be left to the next-of-kin, but once it has started they should be involved, to a reasonable extent. For example, in the *Güleç* case the procedural dimension was breached for various reasons, including the fact that the deceased's father had been excluded from certain stages of the investigation and that he was not informed of key decisions, especially about discontinuing the case against the gendarmes involved in shooting his son.[94] Similarly in *Oğur* the procedural dimension of Article 2 was found to have been breached due to investigatory inadequacies that included a lack of family access, which had had a negative impact on their ability to protect the deceased's and their own interests.[95] These issues were addressed by the ECtHR in the joined cases

[92] In *Golubeva v Russia* (2009) paras 85–86, in which the applicant's husband had been shot dead during a police intervention in a disturbance at a block of flats, a lack of independence in the police internal investigation was offset by a satisfactorily independent parallel criminal investigation. In the Admissibility Decision in *Duggan v United Kingdom* (2017) paras 56–69, the applicants claimed that a failure to prevent a risk of collusion among the police officers involved in a fatal shooting undermined the independence of the investigation, but the ECtHR found that even though this was a shortcoming, the investigation was effective overall.

[93] Mowbray, 'Duties of Investigation' 442–43.

[94] *Güleç* para 82.

[95] *Oğur* para 92.

from Northern Ireland. In *McKerr* for example, the ECtHR stated that in order to maintain public confidence:

> there must be a sufficient element of public scrutiny of the investigation or its results to secure accountability in practice as well as in theory. The degree of public scrutiny required may well vary from case to case. In all cases, however, the next-of-kin of the victim must be involved in the procedure to the extent necessary to safeguard his or her legitimate interests …[96]

However, as a further demonstration of the ECtHR's understanding of democratic society as requiring compromise and balance in the area of human rights, family access is not an unlimited requirement and may be restricted if state concerns with security and pragmatic feasibility are deemed to require it.[97] Thus, the ECtHR held in *McKerr* that:

> As regards the lack of public scrutiny of the police investigations, the Court considers that disclosure or publication of police reports and investigative materials may involve sensitive issues with possible prejudicial effects to private individuals or other investigations and, therefore, cannot be regarded as an automatic requirement under Article 2. The requisite access of the public or the victim's relatives may be provided for in other stages of the available procedures.[98]

Moreover in *Ramsahai*, the ECtHR Grand Chamber decided that family access to an investigation in general is not an all-encompassing or automatic right,[99] a view subsequently confirmed by the Grand Chamber in *Giuliani and Gaggio*,[100] and that public scrutiny needs to be sufficient rather than constant or complete, provided there was enough 'to obviate the danger of any improper cover-up' by the authorities.[101] This view was echoed soon after *Ramsahai* in *Huohvanainen v Finland*, in which no breach of Article 2 was found substantively or procedurally. Concluding that the extent of family involvement was to be determined on the basis of a sufficient protection of interests, the ECtHR stated:

> As for the complainants' investigation requests which were turned down and their criticism of the conduct of the investigation, the Court would note that whilst it is of the utmost importance that a complete and accurate picture emerges of the events leading up to a killing by State agents, the evidence to be gathered to that end must be filtered in accordance with its relevance. What is important for the Court is the fact that the family

[96] *McKerr* para 115. The following year in a death in custody case, *Anguelova v Bulgaria* (2002), the ECtHR combined these points about public confidence in a single statement (para 140) that was then relied on by the Grand Chamber in *Ramsahai* para 321.

[97] See also Sofia Mirandola, 'The Involvement of the Deceased Victim's Next of Kin in Criminal Investigations: An Analysis of the Standards under Article 2 of the Convention and of Directive 2012/29/EU on the Rights of Victims of Crime' in Early, Austin, Ovey and Chernishova (eds), *The Right to Life under Article 2 of the European Convention on Human Rights* 179.

[98] *McKerr* para 129.

[99] *Ramsahai* paras 347–48.

[100] *Giuliani and Gaggio* paras 303, 314–15. A limitation on family involvement was found on balance not to have adversely affected the procedural dimension in *Golubeva* para 91.

[101] *Ramsahai* para 354.

> had at its disposal as much information as was commensurate with the defence of its interests in the national proceedings, namely clarifying the facts surrounding the death of J. [the complainants' deceased relative] and securing the accountability of the police officers involved for any alleged acts and omissions.[102]

Thus, as with other elements of Article 2 protection, in the ECtHR's view this important aspect of the procedural dimension of the right to life is a crucial aspect of state accountability under the rule of law, as well as justice for victims and their families (addressed in Chapter 6), but must still be considered on balance in the context of competing priorities in democratic society.

D. Temporal Aspects

As addressed by Ricoeur, narratives are processes for making sense of experience in relation to the passage of time, and temporal factors are a significant part of the structural factors on which narratives are based. This is particularly evident in the ECtHR's approach to the procedural dimension, with time and timing key elements in the way it evaluates state investigatory practices. Primarily here, due to the importance of Article 2 in democratic societies and the need to ensure its effective protection, the ECtHR has developed the procedural dimension to evaluate state conduct after the events in question, extending the temporal application of the right to life to subsequent investigatory issues. The ECtHR has also held that it is the state's responsibility to initiate the process of investigating a death and has linked that responsibility with questions of temporality in investigations. For example, in the joined cases from Northern Ireland, the ECtHR held that the 'authorities must act of their own motion once the matter has come to their attention' and 'cannot leave it to the initiative of the next-of-kin either to lodge a formal complaint or to take responsibility for the conduct of any investigative procedures'.[103] In evaluating the degree to which a state fulfils that responsibility and provides effective protection of the right to life through the procedural dimension of Article 2, the ECtHR has focused on two related temporal questions. These are the importance of when an investigation starts and how long it lasts, holding that an investigation must be commenced and undertaken by the state without excessive delay, that is, 'a requirement of promptness and reasonable expedition'.[104]

The ECtHR has found that delays in commencing and managing proceedings have contributed to a breach of the procedural dimension of Article 2 in

[102] *Huohvanainen v Finland* (2007) para 111, combining earlier statements in *Bubbins* paras 159, 161.

[103] *McKerr* para 111.

[104] For example *McKerr* para 114. The requirement for promptness was echoed, for example, in *Ramsahai* para 322. The timing issue also recurred in the dissentients' views: see Joint Partly Dissenting Opinion of Judges Costa, Sir Nicolas Bratza, Lorenzen and Thomassen, para 10 and especially Joint Partly Dissenting Opinion of Judges Jočienė and Popović para 9, echoing previous decisions.

several cases,[105] and has approached this requirement strictly. For example, it has found the effectiveness of an investigation to be inadequate even where existing procedures have been followed correctly, resulting in delays, or where new measures supposed to improve human rights protection have been introduced, but have nevertheless caused delays.[106] Even so, the ECtHR has indicated that some allowance can be made for varying and even challenging circumstances,[107] or for explicable delays that have not adversely affected effectiveness.[108]

This requirement of timing, including the need for the state to take the initiative, can partly be understood as being related to the underlying concern with effectiveness and adequacy in investigatory processes. This is because, as the ECtHR recognises, authorities need to act promptly when they become aware of a death so as to gather evidence before it is lost or contaminated.[109] Moreover, as the ECtHR noted in *McKerr*, if a case of lethal force involves a state agent and an issue of his or her potential responsibility is raised, then prompt and expeditious action is required to address legitimate public concerns and maintain public confidence.[110] This can be understood to involve a rationale of public protection, in case the state agents involved are dangerous, as well as fairness, in that a state agent involved may need to be taken off public duties, yet not unfairly affected if no wrongdoing is identified. Importantly (as discussed further in Chapter 6), the ECtHR has recognised the effect of delays in undertaking an investigation on public confidence as an issue distinct from the actual impact of any delay on its effectiveness.[111]

Lastly here, the ECtHR has considered the temporal dimension of ECHR responsibilities by extending its jurisdiction to include events that occurred before the ECHR came into force.[112] Based on the argument that High Contracting

[105] For example *Hugh Jordan* paras 136–40 and *McKerr* paras 152–55, as well as *Collette and Michael Hemsworth v UK* (2013) paras 69–74 and *McCaughey and Others v UK* (2013) paras 130–40. See also the breach of Article 2 for a lack of promptness in other cases of fatal police shootings: *Usta and Others v Turkey* (2008) para 67, *Juozaitienė & Bikulčius v Lithuania* (2008) paras 88–89 and *Gülen v Turkey* (2008) para 44. In *Mocanu and Others v Romania* (2014) para 337 the ECtHR noted that 'the very passage of time is liable not only to undermine an investigation, but also to compromise definitively its chances of being completed'.

[106] Note *Hemsworth* paras 72–74.

[107] See also *Hugh Jordan* para 108 and *Shanaghan* para 91.

[108] For example, in *Bakan c Turquie* (2007) para 60, in which the applicants' husband and father had been killed by a bullet ricocheting from a warning shot fired by a gendarme pursuing an escaping arrestee, the procedural dimension was held not to have been rendered ineffective despite a three-year delay in opening the criminal trial, which was due to the investigation and related legal proceedings. In *Trévalec c Belgique* (2011) paras 92–98, in which the applicant had been shot and seriously injured by police while filming their operations, the ECtHR held that the investigation had been commenced with sufficient rapidity and was satisfactory overall, despite occasional delays.

[109] Compare O'Boyle and Brady, 'Investigatory Powers' 382–83.

[110] *McKerr* para 114.

[111] *Hemsworth* para 69 and *McCaughey* para 130.

[112] Note *Janowiec and Others v Russia* (2013) paras 127–51 and 152–61, in which the applicants claimed a breach of Article 2 in its procedural dimension in relation to an investigation into the 1940 massacre of Polish prisoners of war in the Katyn Forest; and *Mocanu* paras 205–11, in which the

Parties need to conduct investigations into past killings in a manner compatible with Article 2, if such investigations were ongoing when the ECHR became binding on the state in question, this extension of the procedural dimension of the right to life places the importance of the values and protection it represents before the usual temporal limits on international legal obligations. Although such cases have primarily involved killings in the context of past totalitarian repression, or governmentally-backed violence during a transition of power, rather than regular domestic policing and law enforcement operations, they serve to highlight the significance of Article 2 in seeking to secure accountability of the state in democratic society, to which the passage of time may not always be a barrier.

Overall, the ECtHR's development of the procedural dimension of Article 2 in its conjunction with democratic society represents an important extension of the scope of that provision beyond its original textual terms, establishing a positive obligation on the state to investigate killings and threats to life. This is a way of ensuring that High Contracting Parties' investigatory processes are satisfactory in achieving the practical and effective protection of the right to life by law under the ECHR, and in so doing support the ECtHR's practical need for reliable information from states. The procedural dimension of Article 2 is a powerful component of the protection and control provided by the right to life in democratic society, but it nevertheless involves some flexibility in that context in recognition of competing concerns and pressures. Like the ECtHR's approach to the substantive dimension of Article 2, the flexibility involves balancing a high level of protection for the right to life with the interests of the state, respect for subsidiarity and the need to avoid over-burdensome standards that could be counter-productive. As in the discussion in Chapter 4, the ECtHR's case narratives about the procedural dimension demonstrate the inherent tension in Article 2 and its connection with democratic society as the context and value matrix grounding the importance of the right to life, but also requiring its proportionate limitation.

applicants claimed a procedural breach of Article 2 in relation to the use of lethal and life-threatening force during the repression of demonstrations in Bucharest in June 1990. Note also on similar facts to *Mocanu*, relating to the 1989 Timişoara shootings, *Şandru et autres c Roumanie* (2009). See further James Sweeney, 'The Elusive Right to Truth in Transitional Human Rights Jurisprudence' (2018) 67 *International and Comparative Law Quarterly* 353.

6

Purposes and Values in Right to Life Case Law on Lethal Force

This chapter continues the analysis of Article 2 case law on the use of lethal and potentially lethal force in policing and law enforcement situations by reflecting on the purposes and values that underpin ECtHR judgments in this area. As Chapters 3–5 have shown, the tension at the heart of the right to life as set out in Article 2 of the ECHR is equally evident in the ECtHR's interpretation and application of it in conjunction with the concept of democratic society. Constituting the fundamental narrative theme in the case law and the basis for determining the compatibility of state conduct with Article 2, the right to life/democratic society nexus underpins both the importance of that right and its proportionate limits, leading to narrative fluidity. This is apparent in the ways in which the ECtHR's case narratives, which are (necessarily) developed on a case-by-case basis requiring application of Article 2 in differing contexts, always involve consideration of the obligation to respect and protect the right to life whilst also allowing flexibility in state conduct and investigatory practices. Although state duties and the interests of society, as reflected in Article 2 itself, mean that that right cannot be absolute, this contestable narrative fluidity between strict protection and pragmatic leeway, even deference, arguably leaves the core of the right to life uncertain. In other words, in some judgments the flexible application of Article 2 can raise doubts about its degree of importance as a basic value of democratic society, which is not simply a matter of whether or not the ECtHR decides that the right to life has been breached. This chapter therefore considers what the core of the Article 2–democratic society relationship can be understood to include. The outcomes of this analysis provide the bases for the overarching discussion of Article 2 law that follows in Chapter 7.

In the case law, the ECtHR's reasoning has involved the explicit articulation of rationales for developing and limiting Article 2's substantive and procedural dimensions, as well as implicit assumptions about acceptable and desirable state practice. It is suggested here that these explicit and implicit factors can usefully be understood as encompassing two main elements, namely the importance of the rule of law as the keystone in the relationship between the right to life and democratic society (as discussed more generally in Chapter 3); and an understanding that democratic society and the protection of the right to life involve not only concrete legal factors, but also intangible qualitative factors. In terms of Robert

Cover's theory, these two elements are important parts of the narratives that locate and ground the 'nomos' of the judgments, and that build 'relations between the normative and the material universe, between the constraints of reality and the demands of an ethic'.[1] They constitute essential parts of the broader narratives that give Article 2 judgments 'explanation and purpose', a 'prescriptive point' or moral, linking the legal decision with 'social constructions of reality' based on historically-shaped and currently significant values.[2] These issues of wider narratives of value are also apparent in Ricoeur's theoretical model, and the ways in which the 'world of action' that provides the raw material of narrative representation encompasses the symbolic dimensions of conduct.[3] This refers to the thicker cultural significance of forms of conduct, the wider questions about systemic values that an element of fact or action can be seen to raise, giving it a 'readability' in terms of fundamental norms of social conduct within a system. In this respect, ECtHR judgments take account of the symbolic and cultural dimensions of state conduct by recognising how they relate to the ideological foundations and socio-political processes of democratic society. By bringing to light key narrative threads from within selected cases, this chapter argues that a set of values and purposes is apparent in Article 2 case law, even if it is not always at the forefront of the ECtHR's proportionality- and subsidiarity-based reasoning. To that end, Part I addresses some essential aspects and purposes of the rule of law as a fundamental value in, and symbolic dimension of case law on the right to life and uses of force, and Part II turns to some essential qualitative and cultural factors identifiable in ECtHR judgments.

I. Article 2 and Democratic Society: The Rule of Law

As discussed in Chapter 3, the bedrock of democratic society in the Council of Europe consists of political pluralism and freedom, supported by human rights under the rule of law. Essentially concerned with the prevention of arbitrariness and the controlled exercise of power, the concept of the rule of law lies at the heart of the ECHR and of the ECtHR's understanding of rights protection and accountability, in terms of both substance and procedure. This section considers how the ECtHR's focus on the rule of law is apparent in Article 2 case law on state uses of lethal and potentially lethal force by examining three interlinked interpretations. These are the importance of the rule of law as a value providing the fundamental orientation of the case law since the *McCann* ruling; the nature of the rule of law in democratic society as a symbolic dimension of judgments that demonstrates the

[1] Robert M Cover, 'Foreword: Nomos and Narrative' (1983) 97 *Harvard Law Review* 4, 9.
[2] Cover, 'Foreword: Nomos and Narrative' 4–5, 9–10.
[3] Paul Ricoeur (Kathleen McLaughlin and David Pellauer, trans), *Time and Narrative, Volume 1* (Chicago, University of Chicago Press, 1984) 54, 57–58.

linkage between the right to life's application and its ideological roots in opposition to totalitarianism; and the rule of law as a prescriptive and protective concept that requires and entails an understanding of the socio-political order of democratic society as being rooted in normativity, or a functional adherence to and dependency on law.

A. Controlling the State as a Fundamental Purpose

The rule of law is fundamental to the ECHR, as a declared foundational value in the Preamble, as an inherent dimension of all articles of the ECHR,[4] and in practice because the system of rights protection through the ECHR depends on law and judicial controls. It is also a practical necessity, due to the stark reality that the cases giving rise to actions under the right to life predominantly involve death or serious physical harm which cannot be undone. The emphasis on pre-emptive legal controls and responsive accountability under the rule of law are therefore the only effective ways to address state conduct, by determining past compliance to guide future action, by holding the state to account, and by giving applicants a last chance to be heard at the ECtHR level and achieve some sort of justice. However, the outcomes of this process depend on how the ECtHR approaches it, that is, how it narratively constructs and positions its analysis, as shaped by its understanding of the nature and purpose of the rule of law in relation to human rights protection. As noted above, the tension inherent in Article 2 and in the ECtHR's reliance on the concept of democratic society is similarly apparent in the concept of the rule of law itself, because, as Geranne Lautenbach notes, the 'aim of the rule of law – to provide law and order – may be in tension with its aim to protect the individual from arbitrary governmental power'.[5] This issue is explored here by considering the core rationale in *McCann*, not in terms of the decision about whether Article 2 was breached, but the underlying sense of the purpose of the right to life and the rule of law in democratic society.

In *McCann*, as discussed in Chapter 4, the judgment represented the issues in the case in terms of a fundamental dilemma for the UK, involving the need to protect citizens and security personnel, whilst also respecting the right to life of the suspects, who were known terrorists.[6] Anchoring the analysis of Article 2 in its conjunction with democratic society at the outset of a judgment about the state's use of lethal force against terrorists was a powerful way of emphasising the conflicting interests at stake, as well as the principal systemic values that

[4] Note European Commission for Democracy through Law, *Report on the Rule of Law*, adopted by the Venice Commission at its 86th plenary session (Venice, 25–26 March 2011) Study no 512/2009, CDL-AD (2011)003rev (Strasbourg, Council of Europe, 2011) 6, para 23.

[5] Geranne Lautenbach, *The Concept of the Rule of Law and the European Court of Human Rights* (Oxford, Oxford University Press, 2013) 23.

[6] *McCann and Others v United Kingdom* (1995) paras 192–94.

were in question. Underlining the importance of the right whilst also making allowances for state conduct, ultimately the ECtHR found that the United Kingdom had breached the planning and control aspect of Article 2 by one vote (the dissentients on that point agreed with the findings of no breach regarding the provision's other aspects). What is of interest here is to consider the case narrative's implicit significance in light of the explicit reasoning in the dissentients' configuration of their 'counter-narrative'.

The dissenting opinion in *McCann* highlighted a different view on the fundamental tension involved in determining appropriate protection for the right to life in relation to terrorist threats, and thereby on the meaning of rights protection under the rule of law. On this point the dissentients' key argument appeared in their opening statement:

> … the need for the authorities to act within the constraints of the law, while the suspects were operating in a state of mind in which members of the security forces were regarded as legitimate targets and incidental death or injury to civilians as of little consequence, would inevitably give the suspects a tactical advantage which should not be allowed to prevail. The consequences of the explosion of a large bomb in the centre of Gibraltar might well be so devastating that the authorities could not responsibly risk giving the suspects the opportunity to set in train the detonation of such a bomb. Of course the obligation of the United Kingdom under Article 2 para. 1 … of the Convention extended to the lives of the suspects as well as to the lives of all the many others, civilian and military, who were present in Gibraltar at the time. But, quite unlike those others, the purpose of the presence of the suspects in Gibraltar was the furtherance of a criminal enterprise which could be expected to have resulted in the loss of many innocent lives if it had been successful. They had chosen to place themselves in a situation where there was a grave danger that an irreconcilable conflict between the two duties might arise.[7]

On the face of it similar to the preliminary point made by the majority about the dilemma facing the UK, the dissentients stressed two key points. The first was the idea that the law can constrain state action. While the concept of the rule of law is intended both to ground and circumscribe what the state can do, the dissenting opinion focused on what is in principle the main challenge to – or even weakness of – liberal democracies in facing threats to their security, that is the need to respect the rule of law as a foundational value that may in fact curtail their ability to protect themselves. The point about needing to act within the constraints of the law seemed to indicate a sense of disadvantage when compared with the terrorists' position.[8] Even though in many ways liberal democracies have treated the rule of law flexibly in the areas of political crime, internal security and national

[7] *McCann*, Joint Dissenting Opinion of Judges Ryssdal, Bernhardt, Thór Vilhjálmsson, Gölcüklü, Palm, Pekkanen, Freeland, Baka and Jambrek, para 9.

[8] The semantic implication of the dissentients' expression of this point appears to differ from the definition of the rule of law in terms of constraint included in, for example, Venice Commission, *Report on the Rule of Law* 4, para 12 and 8, para 31.

defence, the rule of law nevertheless represents a primordial definitional attribute of democracy that grounds state power and protects against its misuse, even though it may also (at least in principle) limit its freedom of action. The view of the minority in *McCann* on this point underlined the concern about the state's ability to respond to a threat being curtailed by the law and almost appeared to suggest that in a case like *McCann* the rule of law should be different to make sure that the state did not lose the tactical advantage.[9]

The second point is that the dissentients' opinion underlined the view that although individual rights are important and should be respected, and that even the terrorists had a right to life, they were nevertheless terrorists set on a course of murderous criminal action and had put themselves in a situation of conflict with the state. In that sense, the dissentients appeared to suggest that the terrorists had compromised (or qualified) their right to life, if they had not forfeited it, by their chosen course of action to the extent that its curtailment by the state when they were deemed to represent an immediate danger to life should be understandable and permissible, even justifiable in the full sense of that term as indicating the rightness of action. In other words, they appeared to adopt a different understanding of equality of rights protection under the rule of law and to conflate the victims' conduct and moral position with the Article 2 test for a permissible use of lethal force. Consequently, the dissentients in *McCann* disagreed not only with the factual bases of the majority's findings in relation to the planning and control dimension, but also apparently the entire orientation of its approach to human rights. Given that it would not have been permissible under Article 2 for the UK to execute the terrorists on this basis had they been tried and convicted of an offence due to the prohibition on the death penalty, this sort of reasoning about their conduct should not creep into discussion of the permissible deprivation of life by state agents during a law enforcement operation.

This different, dissenting counter-narrative within the *McCann* ruling serves to illustrate the core tension between the right to life as a basic value and the competing priorities of democratic society. It also indicates the divergent orientations that

[9] This was particularly criticised by Axelle Reiter-Korkmaz, 'Droit à la vie et répression du terrorisme' (1996) 26 *Revue Trimestrielle des Droits de l'Homme* 252, 264: 'the claimed necessity of not letting the [IRA active service unit] have a tactical advantage resulting automatically from its lack of respect for the law remains the most fanciful argument. The minority judges thus advocate the annihilation of one of the most fundamental rules of human rights and place a state under the rule of law on an equal footing with a terrorist organisation!' [author's translation]. Stephanie Palmer asked the crucial question in 'Death on the Rock and the European Convention on Human Rights' (1996) 55.1 *The Cambridge Law Journal* 1, 3: 'According to [the dissentients], terrorists would have an unacceptable tactical advantage if the authorities were required to act within the constraints of the law when dealing with such activity. Yet, one might ask, are they really suggesting that the rule of law should have a different operation for members of law enforcement bodies from that which it has for others?' Sarah Joseph, 'Denouement of the Deaths on the Rock: The Right to Life of Terrorists' (1996) 14.1 *Netherlands Quarterly of Human Rights* 5, 22, similarly concluded that the 'UK counterterrorist authorities must subscribe to the rule of law, lest they lower themselves to the level of disregard of human life of the terrorist'. A more favourable view on the dissenting opinion is indicated by John Andrews, 'Right to Life in Gibraltar' (1996) 21.4 *European Law Review* 333, 335.

are possible in understanding the rule of law and its role in state accountability and the control of state power. In that regard, the theme and purpose of the majority narrative in *McCann* can be seen to have been configured – but only just – around a sense of democratic society that was prepared to countenance restraint of state action in favour of human rights, that is, an appropriate restriction of state power within the scope of the ECHR and the rule of law.[10] In other words, even though concern with proportionate balancing in the democratic context entailed flexible leeway for state action, and only one substantive aspect of state conduct was narrowly found to breach Article 2, in principle the descriptive and idealised sense of democratic society and the fundamental importance of protecting the right to life through law were dominant rationales. This has been confirmed in subsequent judgments and needs to be retained as the essential purpose of Article 2, even in difficult cases.[11]

B. The Right to Life and the Rule of Law in the Post-Totalitarian Context

The starting point of all ECtHR judgments on the use of lethal and potentially lethal force under Article 2 is the importance of that provision in democratic society, and in many decisions the ECtHR focuses in that regard on preventing arbitrariness, with reference to other international law measures on the right to life and the use of force. As discussed in Chapter 3, the prevention of arbitrariness is based specifically on Article 6 ICCPR and refers to the use of unbridled and unjustified force by the state. The issue of arbitrariness can be seen as the opposite of appropriate conduct by a democratic state under the rule of law and adhering to the ECHR,[12] and so to represent the sort of unchecked repressive action by the state that the ECHR (as well as the UDHR before it) was introduced to prevent, with regard to both pre- and post-1945 forms of totalitarianism. This aspect of the interpretation of the right to life in Article 2 ECHR can thus be directly associated with the historical and political narratives of democratic identity, construction and protection through rights and the rule of law in which it originated. The contrast between democratic and 'anti-democratic' totalitarian

[10] As observed by Joseph, 'Denouement of the Deaths on the Rock', 22 'The case upholds the right to life of terrorists, thereby fulfilling one of the most important mandates of the guardians of international human rights: upholding the rights of those perceived to be the "least deserving" in society. It is these people whose rights are most likely to be infringed without domestic remedy or outcry'.

[11] As noted more recently in *Tagayeva and Others v Russia* (2017) para 497, 'The Court has also fully acknowledged the difficulties faced by the Russian Federation in combating illegal militant groups in the North Caucasus who have recourse to the most audacious terrorist methods. It therefore understands the need to set up an efficient system capable of counteracting them, and maintaining law and order in this much-suffering region. Nevertheless, the confines of a democratic society governed by the rule of law cannot allow this system to operate in conditions of guaranteed impunity for its agents'.

[12] Note Venice Commission, *Report on the Rule of Law* 11, para 52.

societies in the use of force and protection of rights by law, and the importance of these issues in the ECtHR's narratives of the right to life and its connections with the rule of law, can be clearly illustrated by reference to a landmark judgment on Communist state violence.

The German Democratic Republic (GDR, the former East Germany) border guards case, *Streletz, Kessler and Krenz v Germany*[13] (henceforth *Streletz*) concerned the validity of three convictions of GDR officials for their roles in numerous killings of people trying to cross the border and leave East Germany between 1971 and 1989. Brought under Article 7 (the non-retroactivity of criminal sanction), the case also provided important perspectives on Article 2. Focusing on the fact that those killed were unarmed and did not represent a threat to anyone, the ECtHR held that the use of lethal force against them (including firearms and anti-personnel mines), whilst ordered by the GDR authorities, breached both domestic law and international protection of the right to life to which GDR law purportedly adhered.[14] The ECtHR thus held that state practice in killing people seeking to cross the national border without authorisation meant that both the right to life and the rule of law itself had been breached:

> The Court considers that a State practice such as the GDR's border-policing policy, which flagrantly infringes human rights and above all the right to life, the supreme value in the international hierarchy of human rights, cannot be covered by the protection of Article 7(1) of the Convention. That practice, which emptied of its substance the legislation on which it was supposed to be based, and which was imposed on all organs of the GDR, including its judicial bodies, cannot be described as 'law' within the meaning of Article 7 of the Convention.[15]

Stressing the significance of the rule of law as a fundamental value in the ECHR and the importance of protecting the right to life in principle and in practice, the ECtHR in *Streletz* underlined the connections between these concepts in controlling the state, and how the rule of law involves substantive and qualitative dimensions, that is, its content and its attributes as a normative order. The most important point to note here is that the *Streletz* case points to the foundations of the connection between the ECHR and the rule of law, by illustrating the sort

[13] *Streletz, Kessler and Krenz v Germany* (2001). See Chapter 3 Part I.C on this case in relation to the paramountcy of the right to life. This judgment has been described as 'a tremendously paradigmatic judgment which shows the direction to be followed in the interpretation of many other regimes which, directly or indirectly, touch upon the right to life': Christian Tomuschat, 'The Right to Life – Legal and Political Foundations' in Christian Tomuschat, Evelyne Lagrange and Stefan Oeter (eds), *The Right to Life* (Leiden, Martinus Nijhoff, 2010) 3, 12. See also John A Andrews, 'Case Comment – Article 7: No Punishment Without Law' (2002) 27 *European Law Review* 176–78; Leo Zwaak, 'Council of Europe' case comment section, (2001) 19.3 *Netherlands Quarterly of Human Rights* 317–19. The Article 7 aspect of the judgment was critically received by Jörg Arnold, Nora Karsten and Helmut Kreicker, 'The German Border Guard Cases before the European Court of Human Rights' (2003) 11.1 *European Journal of Crime, Criminal Law and Criminal Justice* 67, note 79–80 on retroactivity and the rule of law and 76 on the right to life.

[14] *Streletz, Kessler and Krenz* paras 22, 29, 62–64.

[15] *Streletz, Kessler and Krenz* para 87.

of totalitarian and repressive violence that the Council of Europe and the ECHR were established to reject and prevent, and that stood as the antithetical point of reference in the early years of European human rights law's development. Looking further back, it also implicitly echoed the longer history of the ECHR and the right to life in the eighteenth-century development of legal protection for rights in the face of other forms of state oppression. It is thus a case that can be seen to highlight the relevance of the origins and legitimating narratives of the ECHR as a whole and the right to life in particular.

With regard to the rule of law in practice, the *Streletz* case demonstrates the destructive consequences of the sort of disconnection from purported values that might occur in a state when other ideological aims outweigh respect for legality and protective norms, not only nominally and rhetorically but also in terms of their realisation. By underlining the unjustifiability of the GDR authorities' actions against those killed in the situations giving rise to the *Streletz* case, the ECtHR shows what arbitrary and indiscriminate state killing looks like, thereby affirming the importance of restraining the state and respecting the value of life through the right to life and strictly proportionate controls over the use of force in achieving that restraint. In the case of *Streletz* therefore, there was no doubt about what the ECtHR thought the appropriate scope of state action and the essence of the rule of law should be. Although an exceptional case covering extreme facts, the *Streletz* case's analysis of a 'worst case' scenario gives a clear sense of the essential values and purposes underpinning Article 2. As such it can be seen as a case confirming the combination of factors set out in the ECHR Preamble, namely the interdependency of democracy, the rule of law and human rights and, as discussed in Part II below, the need for a combination of normative and behavioural standards to embed these factors in society and ensure effective protection of the right to life.

C. The Rule of Law as a Connective and Protective Mechanism

The ECtHR indicated the vital importance of the rule of law as a connective mechanism for protecting the right to life in democratic society in its important judgments in *Makaratzis v Greece*[16] and *Nachova and Others v Bulgaria*.[17] As discussed in Chapter 4, in these rulings the ECtHR found breaches of the right to life on grounds of the states' non-compliance with that provision in their domestic legal and regulatory frameworks, in terms of substantive compatibility with Article 2 and respect for the rule of law. Focusing on the 'level of protection "by law" of the right to life that is required in present-day democratic societies in Europe',

[16] *Makaratzis v Greece* (2004).
[17] *Nachova and Others v Bulgaria* (2005).

a key purpose of the ECtHR narratives in those cases was to underline the ways in which appropriate law could tie together state obligations under the ECHR, state agents' training, preparation for operations, operational conduct and resort to force. In that sense the rule of law was understood by the ECtHR to constitute a connective, or integrating and cohesive mechanism, supporting and protecting the right to life under Article 2(1). These issues were also addressed and the same principle conveyed more recently in, for example, *Soare et autres c Roumanie*,[18] in which the lack of an adequate legal framework was the root problem from which other failings were deemed to flow, and *Guerdner et autres c France*,[19] in which an albeit imperfect legal and regulatory framework was found to be compatible with Article 2 and to have sufficiently filtered through into the gendarme's training and conduct.

As indicated in *Streletz* by reference to a context from the other end of the scale from democratic society, the underlying rationale in these cases was that democratic society under the rule of law required and entailed the pervasiveness of law, as well as institutional practice within its limits, so as to prevent arbitrariness, and especially arbitrary killing. In the ECtHR's narrative, law must be evident and active in democratic society, the democratic nature of which is diminished, if not negated, when the opposite prevails, namely a 'vacuum' in which state agents operate at will[20] or with excessive autonomy involving the taking of 'unconsidered initiatives'.[21] As noted in Chapter 3, the ECtHR's reference to the concept of 'democratic *society*' suggests that it understands a functioning democratic order to involve socially embedded and interconnected rules and values, including the rule of law.[22] The law protecting the right to life and the legal framework generally should not just be something superimposed on a society, but an inherent part of its organisation and functioning, including acceptance and internalisation by its members and by agents of the state. Consequently, the rule of law, and Article 2-compatible domestic law, can be effective only to the extent that they achieve the self-regulation of conduct. The negative vacuum of unregulated conduct must be prevented by a framework that achieves control without stifling discretion completely or in potentially counter-productive ways. Ultimately, the Article 2 case narratives reflect the deeper cultural significance of law, which takes the form of a profound confidence in normativity, that is, the acceptance of

[18] *Soare et autres c Roumanie* (2011) para 135.

[19] *Guerdner et autres c France* (2014) paras 67–68.

[20] *Makaratzis* para 59.

[21] *Soare* para 135.

[22] Mikael Rask Madsen and Gert Verschraegen, 'Making Human Rights Intelligible: An Introduction to a Sociology of Human Rights' in Mikael Rask Madsen and Gert Verschraegen (eds), *Making Human Rights Intelligible: Towards a Sociology of Human Rights* (Oxford, Hart, 2013) 1, 9: 'Rights have to be seen as more than legal norms discerned by judges trained in legal reasoning. For human rights to have social meaning, they must become institutionalised socially and become embedded in people's mindsets as well as in the day-to-day workings of societal institutions such as the judiciary, the schooling system, health care and the family'.

and reliance on law-based modes of social organisation and regulation. In that regard, normativity gives law both a special status in the organisation of society and a real impact on human conduct through obedience to law. As Paul Kahn argues:

> The rule of law is a social practice: it is a way of being in the world. To live under the rule of law is to maintain a set of beliefs about the self and community, time and space, authority and representation. It is to understand the actions of others and the possible actions of the self as expressions of these beliefs. Without these beliefs, the rule of law appears as just another form of coercive governmental authority.[23]

In these case narratives, a key purpose appears to be to indicate that although law cannot resurrect a victim or physically stop a bullet or fatal blow, as a value and a cultural phenomenon in the right socio-political context the rule of law should be able to prevent such force from being used inappropriately or, at the very least, to ensure that the state is accountable for it. In that regard, accountability is a core purpose of the duty to investigate. The ECtHR justified its extended interpretation of Article 2 ECHR to require this duty in *McCann* and subsequent cases on the basis of the right to life's importance and the need to give it a concomitant degree of practical and effective protection in procedural terms (as discussed in Chapter 5).[24] Protection of the right to life by law in democratic society thus involves the substantive dimension of Article 2 regarding the use of force, as well as the process by which state conduct in relation to that provision can be evaluated and accounted for. This partly echoes in historical terms the long common law and constitutional rights heritage of due process and procedural propriety as ways of locking state power into a system that can (potentially) restrain it, not only in terms of what the system requires in its rules and rights, but also how it implements and protects them, in order to ensure that the imbalance of power between state and individual is not exploited to the latter's detriment. The ECtHR specified the aims of the procedural dimension (the duty to investigate) in the joined Northern Irish cases:

> The essential purpose of such an investigation is to secure the effective implementation of the domestic laws which protect the right to life and, in those cases involving State agents or bodies, to ensure their accountability for deaths occurring under their responsibility.[25]

As both a means and an end in itself, ensuring accountability in the democratic context requires particular conditions of possibility, as covered by the criteria of the duty to investigate (accurate evidence, access to the system, impartiality,

[23] Paul W Kahn, *The Cultural Study of Law: Reconstructing Legal Scholarship* (Chicago, The University of Chicago Press, 1999) 36–37. See also Part II.A below.

[24] *McCann* para 161.

[25] For example, *McKerr v United Kingdom* (2001) para 111. Note Juliet Chevalier-Watts, 'Effective Investigations under Article 2 of the European Convention on Human Rights: Securing the Right to Life or an Onerous Burden on a State?' (2010) 21.3 *European Journal of International Law* 701, 711.

appropriate timescales). Accountability is thus not only important for the applicants in a right to life case as a potential way of achieving answers and some sense of justice, but also for democratic society more generally as a bridge between rule of law legality and legitimacy, linking the concrete aspects of evidence gathering and legal standards with intangible aspects of public confidence in the state in political terms (discussed in more detail in Part II below).[26] The importance of accountability in the ECtHR's case law on Article 2 is apparent in the status of the procedural dimension. Even though the ECtHR has made allowances in relation to the substantive dimension of Article 2 and the specificities of the duty to investigate in some situations, it has been consistently clear that difficult circumstances cannot displace the procedural dimension under Article 2.[27] As such it constitutes a significant 'red line' that should not be crossed in Article 2 cases. This means that if a death has occurred, and the right to life has therefore not been completely protected by law, that right's importance in democratic society and under the rule of law mean that protection of the right must at least fall back to an investigatory and accountability process, no matter how challenging an incident or a state's domestic context might be. This demonstrates the ECtHR's core concern with constancy and consistency under the right to life. This right and its procedural dimension must be constant in the sense that, as noted in the discussion above with regard to the substantive legal framework, there must be no vacuum in their applicability, and the application of the duty to investigate under the right to life must be consistent in that irrespective of local conditions or difficulties, this right must be procedurally protected in essentially similar ways. The ECtHR's aim of ensuring procedural protection of minimum standards under the right to life in democratic societies across the Council of Europe overrides potential concerns about differences in the operational circumstances faced by states due to their domestic context.[28]

II. Article 2 and Democratic Society: Qualitative and Contextual Aspects

In Part I of this chapter, the discussion of each point about the rule of law brought the analysis back to essential cultural factors on which that concept ultimately relies, namely normativity, the relationship between value and practice, the acceptance of rules and obedience to law, the state's acceptance of limits on its power, and the socio-political context of democratic society. In reading Article 2

[26] See also David Baker, *Deaths After Police Contact: Constructing Accountability in the 21st Century* (London, Palgrave Macmillan, 2016) 167–183.

[27] As stated early on by the ECtHR in its judgment in *Kaya v Turkey* (1998) para 91 and indicated more recently in *Tagayeva and Others v Russia* (2017) para 497.

[28] Contrast the concerns about disparity in Chevalier-Watts, 'Effective Investigations under Article 2 of the European Convention on Human Rights'.

case narratives it is apparent that the ECtHR is aware, explicitly and implicitly, of these underlying qualitative and behavioural factors and pre-requisites that underpin the substantive and procedural dimensions of the right to life. While there is no fixed, a priori meaning of democratic society, the ECtHR is alert to its social dimension and the interaction of the ECHR normative order with socio-political conditions, which are arguably key aspects of ensuring that protection of the right to life is approached in a practical and effective way and not merely abstractly. In other words, awareness of intangible factors is important in making that right more tangible. These issues are explored here in three stages: qualitative standards and the significance of an attitudinal predisposition in respecting human rights; the place of the legal order and accountability in the socio-political context of democratic society; and the values of compassion and sensitivity that Article 2 case law acknowledges and supports.

A. Qualitative Standards and Behavioural Expectations

The ECtHR's approach to the rule of law and its concern with preventing arbitrary uses of lethal and potentially lethal force involve not only its interpretation of the substantive dimension of Article 2, but also its identification of qualitative standards and behavioural expectations. Underpinning and shaping its evaluation of the concrete, substantive aspects of the right to life, the ECtHR has referred to forms of conduct to be expected from state agents in democratic society, thus arguably adding a significant intangible dimension to what it envisages democratic society to entail. To a certain extent the substantive aspects of Article 2 in and of themselves set behavioural standards in the sense of compliance with domestic rules that are compatible with the spirit of Article 2. That is, permissible action that satisfies the tests of necessity and proportionality established under Article 2(2) should therefore in and of itself meet that right's minimum threshold of protection. However, it is argued here that the ECtHR's analysis of these elements also establishes requirements for state agents' conduct, perhaps more precisely their attitude, that are intended to underpin compliance with the substantive aspects of the right to life.

An apparent behavioural standard was first indicated by the ECtHR in *McCann* in terms of a 'degree of caution in the use of firearms', to which the Court referred when considering the planning and conduct dimension of the security operation in that case and the soldiers' conduct.[29] Here the ECtHR stated:

> Their reflex action in this vital respect lacks the degree of caution in the use of firearms to be expected from law enforcement personnel in a democratic society, even when dealing with dangerous terrorist suspects, and stands in marked contrast to the standard of care reflected in the instructions in the use of firearms by the police which had

[29] *McCann* para 212.

> been drawn to their attention and which emphasised the legal responsibilities of the individual officer in the light of conditions prevailing at the moment of engagement [...] This failure by the authorities also suggests a lack of appropriate care in the control and organisation of the arrest operation.[30]

Advancing a qualitative and behavioural norm relating to the conduct of security forces, this aspect of the ECtHR's decision appears to support the fundamental importance of the right to life as a basic value and to situate it in relation to democratic society by interpreting the latter as requiring certain sorts of conduct from law enforcement officials. In this sense as well, the ECtHR draws on its earlier construction of the state's dilemma of protecting against terrorists whilst respecting their right to life, by suggesting that in the Gibraltar operation the balance went too far towards the former. The requirement of caution is thus presented as a key principle in guiding how such state action should be implemented where recourse to lethal force is an operational possibility. While a state agent's conduct will stand or fall under Article 2(2) in terms of its absolute necessity, the ECtHR indicates that a use of force should not just be a technical matter of measuring threat and response, albeit at times an instinctive or emotional matter based on perception in the heat of the moment,[31] but also an engagement with a situation that requires behaviour predicated on awareness of and an attitude of respect for the value of the other's life.

However, the statement nevertheless appears to rest on fine – and problematic – distinctions with regard to earlier aspects of the judgment. The ECtHR had already found that the use of force did not breach Article 2, due to its acceptance of the soldiers' 'honest mistake for good reasons' in their perception of the apparent threat, so its focus here seems to be on the SAS soldiers' training and how they were deployed in this particular operation.[32] Although it had earlier rejected the argument that there was a premeditated plan for the soldiers to 'shoot to kill',[33] it nevertheless controversially suggested that their training caused them to do so automatically. Yet the dissentients in *McCann* particularly criticised the idea that training to respond rapidly was the same as a reflex action, and they rejected the possibility that shooting to wound was a realistic option. Indeed, the latter point is supported by research into the practicalities and limits of police use of firearms and reflected in armed police tactics of aiming at the torso and 'shooting to stop' (completely incapacitate) in certain circumstances, which with modern firearms and non-combat (ie expanding or soft tipped) ammunition usually means causing life-threatening trauma or death.[34]

[30] *McCann* para 212.

[31] Note Randall Collins, 'Entering and Leaving the Tunnel of Violence' (2012) 61.2 *Current Sociology* 132.

[32] *McCann* para 212. See also Joseph, 'Denouement of the Deaths on the Rock' 19–20.

[33] *McCann* para 180.

[34] PAJ Waddington, '"Overkill" or "Minimum Force"?' (1990) *Criminal Law Review* 695; Joseph, 'Denouement of the Deaths on the Rock' 19–20. See also Peter Squires and Peter Kennison, *Shooting to Kill? Policing, Firearms and Armed Response* (Chichester, Wiley-Blackwell, 2010) 7–8.

Moreover, the narrow majority in the ECtHR criticised the instructions and commands given to the soldiers about how to carry out their duties, and how they in fact did so, even though it had previously observed that 'it was only natural' for the UK to 'resort to the skill and experience' of a specialist anti-terrorist unit like the SAS 'in order to deal with the threat in the safest and most informed manner possible'.[35] Thus the selection and deployment of the SAS was acceptable, and their ultimate use of force due to a mistake not unacceptable, but the majority's assessment that the soldiers were too hasty in using their weapons in a way that would be lethal partly grounded a finding that the planning and control of the operation fell below the Article 2 standard. The analysis thus gives a mixed message that lies at the problematic junction of concerns with subsidiarity, practicality and democratic standards of conduct for state agents.

Despite these difficulties the same behavioural standard has been referred to by the ECtHR in later decisions about the use of force in policing operations. For example, in *Shchiborshch and Kuzmina v Russia*, a police intervention to carry out the involuntary hospitalisation of a mentally disturbed individual resulted in his death.[36] Even though the cause of death could not be clearly established, the police action was found to have breached Article 2. This was because, the ECtHR held, it was 'conducted in an uncontrolled and unconsidered manner', and because 'the measures taken by the police lacked the degree of caution to be expected from law-enforcement officers in a democratic society'.[37]

Moreover, similar qualitative and behavioural standards have been indicated by the ECtHR in relation to the domestic legal framework aspect of Article 2. For example, in *Nachova*, linking the importance of an Article 2-compatible domestic legal and regulatory framework with the training of state agents, the ECtHR set out what such training ought to involve with regard to the right to life:

> … the national law regulating policing operations must secure a system of adequate and effective safeguards against arbitrariness and abuse of force and even against avoidable accident (see *Makaratzis*). In particular, law enforcement agents must be trained to assess whether or not there is an absolute necessity to use firearms, not only on the basis of the letter of the relevant regulations, but also with due regard to the pre-eminence of respect for human life as a fundamental value.[38]

[35] *McCann* para 183.

[36] *Shchiborshch and Kuzmina v Russia* (2014).

[37] *Shchiborshch and Kuzmina* para 240. Compare *Boukrourou et autres c France* (2017) paras 59–62, which involved a police intervention to arrest a disturbed individual, but in this case the victim was deemed to be under the officers' control at the time force was used. While there was a causal link between the force used and the unintended death, that death was unforeseeable due to the victim's unknown heart defect. Although technically a custody case and so outside the scope of this study, it is informative to note here that the ECtHR held that a state agent's responsibility under Article 2 depended on his ability to determine the victim's condition and the degree of caution needed in the use of force in the circumstances. Article 2 was not breached on that basis, but Article 3 was.

[38] *Nachova* para 97.

This indicates that training must involve Article 2 compatibility in terms of not only the substantive aspects of domestic law on the resort to force, but also caution, restraint and the spirit of the right to life, that is the qualitative, intangible dimension of respect for it.[39] In that regard, the ECtHR in *Nachova* concluded that 'the manner in which the operation was planned and controlled betrayed a deplorable disregard for the pre-eminence of the right to life'.[40] Subsequently echoed in similar terms in other decisions,[41] it is apparent that these qualitative aspects are an essential part of the ECtHR's evaluation of the substantive dimensions of Article 2 and that transforming state agents' conduct is one of the ECtHR's teleological aims in the democratic context in seeking to give practical effect to Article 2's protective intention.

Consequently, the qualitative aspect of the right to life in democratic society goes beyond mere obedience to law and its technical terms. While behaving in a way that complies with law is in part a question of subordinating instinct and reaction to reason and reflection, it also involves an element of desire or willingness, in the sense of a choice to accept law's authority and, more fundamentally, its purposes. Respect for the right to life could thus be said to require a particular attitude towards others and society, that is, a way of perceiving them and being ready to behave towards them, that embraces human rights norms as both rules and indicators of a way of being. In the ECtHR's view, therefore, the importance of the right to life in democratic society encompasses protection of that right as a matter of both law and social conduct.[42]

[39] On these points ECHR law echoes international law: see the UN Basic Principles on the Use of Force and Firearms by Law Enforcement Officials, para 5: 'Whenever the lawful use of force and firearms is unavoidable, law enforcement officials shall: (a) Exercise restraint in such use and act in proportion to the seriousness of the offence and the legitimate objective to be achieved; (b) Minimize damage and injury, and respect and preserve human life' and Principle 20: 'In the training of law enforcement officials, Governments and law enforcement agencies shall give special attention to issues of police ethics and human rights …'. These build on the UN Code of Conduct for Law Enforcement Officials, Article 2: 'In the performance of their duty, law enforcement officials shall respect and protect human dignity and maintain and uphold the human rights of all persons'. In these respects, international law on the use of force in law enforcement is said to be grounded on the twin principles of caution and precaution. Note also Jim Murdoch and Ralph Roche, *The European Convention on Human Rights and Policing: A Handbook for Police Officers and Other Law Enforcement Officials* (Strasbourg, Council of Europe Publishing, 2013) 24–25.

[40] *Nachova* para 105. This requirement to demonstrate respect for the value of life extends to the need to ensure that medical treatment for the wounded is provided promptly: see Jan Arno Hessbruegge, *Human Rights and Personal Self-Defense in International Law* (Oxford, Oxford University Press, 2017) 203–204.

[41] For example, *Leonidis v Greece* (2009) para 57, *Golubeva v Russia* (2009) paras 107–11, 110, *Vasil Sashov Petrov v Bulgaria* (2010) para 45, *Alikaj et autres c Italie* (2011) paras 74–75, and *Guerdner et autres c. France* (2014) para 64. Zidaru, 'Încălcarea art. 2 din Convenţia Europeană a Drepturilor Omului' 178–79 discusses with reference to *Soare et autres c Roumanie* (2011) and the Romanian context the importance of legal standards and training in changing legislators' and agents' mentalities.

[42] Vivian Grosswald Curran, 'Law's Past and Europe's Future' (2005) 6.2 *German Law Journal* 483, 489–90, 512 warns against 'irrational faith' in the power of law and the need for 'vigilance in other socio-cultural areas': in that sense, a combined focus on rules, judicial protection and the need for strong cultural and behavioural foundations is vitally important.

B. Public Confidence and Legitimacy

The purpose of the procedural dimension of Article 2 in the ECtHR's understanding is, like the above behavioural aspect, connected with its qualitative socio-political context. This is because, as noted in Part I, protection of the right to life and accountability under the rule of law through the duty to investigate involve issues of legality and legitimacy, with the latter relating to questions of public confidence in and perception of the state's exercise of power in democratic society.[43] In considering the procedural dimension of Article 2, the ECtHR explicitly acknowledges this aspect of investigatory processes in its rationales.

This was especially apparent in *Ramsahai v Netherlands*, where the ECtHR observed, 'What is at stake here is nothing less than public confidence in the State's monopoly on the use of force'.[44] Showing awareness of (Weberian) social theory and the functions of the state, the ECtHR pointed to the connections between investigatory due process and its role in democracy of holding the state to account to the demos in whose name power is exercised, thereby contributing to public opinion about whether or not a use of force is perceived to be legitimate.[45] In the democratic context, it is not enough for a use of force to be lawful and circumstantially permissible, it must also be seen to be appropriate state action by those to whom the state is in principle answerable, and who (again in principle) consent to its police powers. In that vein, throughout its judgments on the procedural dimension of Article 2, the ECtHR has justified its decisions on what the duty to investigate should involve in terms of the values on which it is based and why it matters, with regard to its effect on public perception and understanding. In the ECtHR's case narratives, the procedural dimension thus partly reflects the ECtHR's endeavour to make the protection of Article 2 practical and effective, as well as its understanding of the wider functional significance of this right and related processes in democratic society.

In *McKerr*, for example, the ECtHR explicitly linked the requirement of a prompt response and public scrutiny with the maintenance of public confidence:

> … a prompt response by the authorities in investigating a use of lethal force may generally be regarded as essential in maintaining public confidence in their adherence to the

[43] Note Fionnuala Ní Aoláin, 'The Evolving Jurisprudence of the European Convention Concerning the Right to Life' (2001) 19.1 *Netherlands Quarterly of Human Rights* 21, 34–35; Paul Ponsaers, 'Is Legitimacy Police Property?' in Gorazd Meško and Justice Tankebe (eds), *Trust and Legitimacy in Criminal Justice: European Perspectives* (Cham, Springer, 2015) 93, 94–96. Note also Jonathan Jackson, Mike Hough, Ben Bradford and Jouni Kuha, 'Empirical Legitimacy as Two Connected Psychological States' in ibid 137, 138–39.

[44] *Ramsahai v Netherlands* (2007) para 325.

[45] Note the Chamber's view in *Ramsahai v Netherlands* (2005) para 422: 'where it is decided that a person vested with public authority at whose hands a human being has died should not face criminal proceedings, Article 2 requires the decision to be open to public scrutiny', citing *Finucane v United Kingdom* (2003) para 79. This was emphasised in *Ramsahai* (2007), Partly Dissenting Opinion of Judges Jočienė and Popović, para 6.

> rule of law and in preventing any appearance of collusion in or tolerance of unlawful acts …
>
> For the same reasons, there must be a sufficient element of public scrutiny of the investigation or its results to secure accountability in practice as well as in theory.[46]

The ECtHR also noted in *Hugh Jordan* that public confidence was related to public perception, with active measures needed to meet concerns about the investigatory process even if actual practice might not be problematic:

> The Court does not doubt the independence of the [Director of Public Prosecutions]. However, where the police investigation procedure is itself open to doubts of a lack of independence and is not amenable to public scrutiny, it is of increased importance that the officer who decides whether or not to prosecute also gives an appearance of independence in his decision-making. Where no reasons are given in a controversial incident involving the use of lethal force, this may in itself not be conducive to public confidence. It also denies the family of the victim access to information about a matter of crucial importance to them and prevents any legal challenge of the decision.[47]

Similarly, the ECtHR noted in *McKerr* that, even though delays in the examination of the officers' weapons and the handling of their interviews were not 'a matter of serious prejudice to the investigation as a whole', the effect on public confidence needed to be acknowledged. As the ECtHR stated, the investigatory irregularities did 'lend weight to assertions that investigations into the use of lethal force by police officers give the appearance of being qualitatively different from those concerning civilian suspects'.[48]

A related issue was also raised in *Armani da Silva*, in which the applicant argued that the evidentiary test used in English prosecutorial practice breached Article 2 because 'the threshold was set too high to maintain public confidence, to ensure adherence to the rule of law and to prevent any appearance of tolerance of or collusion in unlawful acts'.[49] However, although the ECtHR agreed that 'public confidence in both the law enforcement agencies and the prosecution service could be undermined if State agents were not seen to be held accountable for the unjustifiable use of lethal force',[50] it held that this did not entail an obligation to prosecute in all cases, as that could also undermine public confidence.[51]

Significantly, the joined cases from Northern Ireland, in addition to the applicants' similar claims, shared an origin in a divided society that had long suffered

[46] *McKerr* paras 114–15. Due to these concerns with supporting public confidence the requirement for prompt action may become more important in sensitive cases, such as those involving a racial motivation. Although not involving state lethal force but a police investigation into a homicide, note on this issue *Menson and Others v United Kingdom* (2003) 13–14.
[47] *Hugh Jordan v United Kingdom* (2001) para 123.
[48] *McKerr* para 126.
[49] *Armani da Silva v United Kingdom* (2016) para 199, and see also the argument in para 201.
[50] *Armani da Silva* para 273.
[51] *Armani da Silva* para 273.

from violent conflict among terrorist groups and the state.[52] In particular, all the cases raised issues relating to an intense controversy about an alleged 'shoot to kill' policy on the part of the UK's security forces, that is, an apparently deliberate strategy of summarily using lethal force without justification.[53] The applicants claimed that the ineffective investigations demonstrated the authorities' tolerance of the use of unlawful lethal force.[54] In this context, as well as establishing specific requirements for satisfying the duty to investigate under Article 2, the ECtHR emphasised the object and purpose of the procedural dimension in terms of public confidence and democratic accountability:[55]

> The Court would observe that the shortcomings in transparency and effectiveness identified [in the case] run counter to the purpose identified by the domestic courts of allaying suspicions and rumour. Proper procedures for ensuring the accountability of agents of the State are indispensable in maintaining public confidence and meeting the legitimate concerns that might arise from the use of lethal force. A lack of such procedures will only add fuel to fears of sinister motivations, as is illustrated, *inter alia*, by the submissions made by the applicant concerning the alleged shoot-to-kill policy.[56]

When the state kills, maintaining or restoring public confidence in the authorities, in official control procedures, and in the law itself, are fundamental purposes of accountability processes, but are at the same time complex challenges. In democratic societies, which at least theoretically function on a basis of consensual government and public confidence in the legitimacy of its authority, these processes are essential. Where the democratic society has been divided, and trust in the state rocked, such processes become focal points of socio-political and legal concerns. As Fionnuala Ní Aoláin has observed:

> In a fraught communal context such as that in Northern Ireland, law functions paradoxically. It both upholds the established order but must call that order to account when it fails to protect all citizens equally. If pivotal legal institutions are perceived to fail in that endeavour, then the legitimacy of the legal order itself is threatened.[57]

[52] See further Fionnuala Ní Aoláin, *The Politics of Force: Conflict Management and State Violence in Northern Ireland* (Belfast, Blackstaff Press, 2000) and 'Truth Telling, Accountability and the Right to Life in Northern Ireland' (2002) 5 *European Human Rights Law Review* 572; also Brice Dickson, *The European Convention on Human Rights and the Conflict in Northern Ireland* (Oxford, Oxford University Press, 2010) 1–22, 248–65.

[53] Ní Aoláin, *The Politics of Force* 48, 55 and 'Truth Telling' 572; Hannah Russell, *The Use of Force and Article 2 of the ECHR in Light of European Conflicts* (Oxford, Hart, 2017) 30–31; Christopher K Connolly, 'Seeking the Final Court of Justice: The European Court of Human Rights and Accountability for State Violence in Northern Ireland' (2007) 9 *San Diego International Law Journal* 81, 89; and Kader Asmal, *Shoot to Kill: International Lawyers' Inquiry into the Use of Lethal Firearms by the Security Forces in Northern Ireland* (Cork and Dublin, The Mercier Press, 1985). See *McKerr* paras 21–34.

[54] Dickson, *The European Convention on Human Rights and the Conflict in Northern Ireland* 268–75.

[55] Chevalier-Watts, 'Effective Investigations' 714.

[56] For example, *McKerr* para 160.

[57] Ní Aoláin, 'Truth Telling' 584. See also for example *Yaşa v Turkey* (1998) para 104 on the importance of public confidence in circumstances of acute public tension. These issues are not unique to Europe and have been the focus of much attention in the USA in recent years: note for example Zach Newman, '"Hands Up, Don't Shoot": Policing, Fatal Force, and Equal Protection in the Age of

The ECtHR's awareness of the socio-political dimension of public confidence in relation to the procedural dimension of Article 2 is therefore an important qualitative aspect of its case narratives, linking the right to life with democratic society in a contextually-attentive way. This raises an important caveat, however, as well as an important point of principle. With regard to the caveat, the complexity of some social contexts, such as a country or region disrupted by internal conflict, means that ECHR law is only one aspect of public confidence and the need for accountability, which indicates that as important as the ECtHR's awareness and its role are, Article 2 law can only offer an incomplete perspective. As noted by Günter Frankenberg, human rights law can never provide the 'whole story',[58] and as indicated by Cover, legal prescription is located in an array of narratives, including wider public perceptions.[59]

For example, in Northern Ireland, Brice Dickson has shown that Article 2 and related case law developments only came to play a significant role in the later years of the conflict, and that the ECHR in general terms 'was very largely irrelevant both to the way the conflict was managed while it was raging and to the way it was largely resolved'.[60] With regard to the same issues, Ní Aoláin has argued that there is a need for 'multiple narratives … in order to come to terms with the complexity of a prolonged internal conflict',[61] including its layers of cultural meaning[62] and the interaction of law and politics in the state's management of it,[63] which fall beyond the usual scope of human rights cases.[64] In other contexts as well, the issues of

Colorblindness' (2015) 43.1 *Hastings Constitutional Law Quarterly* 117; Jon Swaine, Oliver Laughland and Jamiles Lartey, 'Shoot to Kill: A US Horror Story' *The Guardian* (2 June 2015); Matthieu Écoiffier, 'À Ferguson, la "plaie" toujours vive' *Libération* (28–29 May 2016) 2–4; and Stuart Casey-Maslen and Sean Connolly, *Police Use of Force under International Law* (Cambridge, Cambridge University Press, 2017) 210–17. Similar issues were discussed over 30 years previously: for example, Robert Berkley Harper, 'Accountability of Law Enforcement Officers in the Use of Deadly Force' (1983) 26 *Howard Law Journal* 119 and Edward J Littlejohn, Geneva Smitherman and Alida Quick, 'Deadly Force and its Effects on Police-Community Relations' (1984) 27 *Howard Law Journal* 1131. The latter argued that reforming rules on the use of lethal force would send an important message to the community that 'all life is important', 1177. For a broader comparative perspective on police misuse of force in India and the USA see Jyoti Belur, *Permission to Shoot? Police Use of Deadly Force in Democracies* (New York, Springer, 2010).

[58] Günter Frankenberg, *Comparative Law as Critique* (Cheltenham, Edward Elgar, 2016) 176–77.

[59] Cover, 'Foreword: Nomos and Narrative' 7. Note also David Baker, *Deaths After Police Contact: Constructing Accountability in the 21st Century* (London, Palgrave Macmillan, 2016) 24.

[60] Dickson, *The European Convention on Human Rights and the Conflict in Northern Ireland* 225 and 362.

[61] Ní Aoláin, *The Politics of Force* 10–11, 246.

[62] Ní Aoláin, *The Politics of Force* 87.

[63] Ní Aoláin, *The Politics of Force* 247.

[64] On the construction of Article 2 narratives compared with political memory narratives see Kris Brown, 'Rights and Victims, Martyrs and Memories: The European Court of Human Rights and Political Transition in Northern Ireland' in Antoine Buyse and Michael Hamilton (eds), *Transitional Jurisprudence and the ECHR: Justice, Politics and Rights* (Cambridge, Cambridge University Press, 2011) 52–80. On wider narrative perspectives see for example, Kirk Simpson, *Truth Recovery in Northern Ireland: Critically Interpreting the Past* (Manchester, Manchester University Press, 2009) and Marie Smyth and Marie-Therese Fay (eds), *Personal Accounts from Northern Ireland's Troubles: Public Conflict,*

public confidence and public perception of the state's use of lethal force have not been entirely addressed through a domestic investigation found to be compatible with Article 2 and an ECtHR judgment. For example, the long-running controversies about the *Giuliani and Gaggio v Italy* case,[65] the De Menezes shooting that led to the above-mentioned *Armani da Silva* case,[66] and other incidents such as the shooting of Mark Duggan in London in 2011,[67] have all involved serious problems of public confidence despite an ECHR element in each case. Consequently, judgments about the right to life and its procedural dimension cannot address all public concerns and there is an inevitable gap between them and broader public opinion, as well as representations of public opinion, in some situations.[68]

Nevertheless, the key point of principle in terms of Article 2 law is that the ECtHR is aware of the function of the right to life and its procedural dimension in their wider socio-political context, and that it is guided by the rationale of contributing to the maintenance of public confidence in the state in democratic society, in its uses of force and in the rule of law. As such, this qualitative dimension of

Private Loss (London, Pluto Press, 2000). See also the Northern Ireland Human Rights Commission, *Dealing with Northern Ireland's Past: Towards a Transitional Justice Approach* (Belfast, NIHRC, 2013).

[65] *Giuliani and Gaggio v Italy* (2009) and (2011). On the range of narratives about this case see Duncan McDonnell, 'The Genoa G8 and the Death of Carlo Giuliani' in Stephen Gundle and Lucia Rinaldi (eds), *Assassinations and Murder in Modern Italy: Transformations in Society and Culture* (Basingstoke, Palgrave Macmillan, 2007) 73, situating the shooting in a longer cultural experience of politically-charged public deaths; Genoa Social Forum, *Genova: Il Libro Bianco* (Milan, Nuova Iniziativa Editoriale, 2002) 80–91, situating it in its volatile context of protest and anti-establishment contestation; and Melody Niwot, 'Narrating Genoa: Documentaries of the Italian G8 Protests of 2001 and the Persistence and Politics of Memory' (2011) 23.2 *History and Memory* 66, 68–71, on the range of civil and media perspectives on the shooting, its wider context and impact – Niwot concludes that 'the struggle over narrating Genoa and determining the *meaning* and *memory* of those events remains a raw and open wound'.

[66] See for example Alan Norrie, 'The Problem of Mistaken Self-Defense: Citizenship, Chiasmus and Legal Form' (2010) 13.2 *New Criminal Law Review* 357, 377; and Maurice Punch, Ralph Crawshaw and Geoffrey Markham, 'Democratic Principles and Police Fatal Force: Avoidance of Debate, Unresolved Accountability and Human Rights' (2016) 46 *International Journal of Law, Crime and Justice* 2, 2–4.

[67] *Duggan v United Kingdom* (2017) (admissibility decision). In this incident Mark Duggan was shot by a police officer who mistakenly thought the victim was holding a gun. Interestingly, but perhaps only due to a drafting oversight, in this decision the ECtHR states twice in paras 49 and 65 that 'what is at stake here is nothing less than public confidence in the State's monopoly on the use of force'. On community concerns about the case see www.theguardian.com/uk-news/2016/aug/06/mark-duggan-death-fifth-anniversary-march (consulted 28 August 2018).

[68] On the issue of wider public concerns and perspectives in this context see Baker, *Deaths After Police Contact* (on England and Wales) and in broader theoretical terms Ian Loader, 'The Cultural Lives of Security and Rights' in Benjamin J Goold and Liora Lazarus (eds), *Security and Human Rights* (Oxford, Hart, 2007) 27–43 at 28. Note also on the 'vernacular' and Geertzian cultural dimensions of social discourse on issues of law and order Lucia Zedner, 'In Pursuit of the Vernacular: Comparing Law and Order Discourse in Britain and Germany' (1995) 4 *Social and Legal Studies* 517, 518. Work on media portrayals of police uses of lethal force in the US context has pointed to problematic variations in the representation and interpretation of parties' conduct: Paul J Hirschfield and Daniella Simon, 'Legitimating Police Violence: Newspaper Narratives of Deadly Force' (2010) 14.2 *Theoretical Criminology* 155. Other work on media representations of human rights questions in more general terms similarly points to difficulties in the way they are portrayed for popular audiences: Eric Heinze and Rosa Freedman, 'Public Awareness of Human Rights: Distortions in the Mass Media' (2010) 14.4 *International Journal of Human Rights* 491.

the ECtHR's case narratives acknowledges how protection of the right to life by law in concrete ways is linked with democratic society's intangible requirements of legitimacy. Even though the ECtHR approaches this on balance, due to the need for proportionate mediation between the demands of rights protection and competing interests and pressures, the case narratives reflect the thick significance of accountability under the rule of law, linking the control of state power through formal processes with the social base that accountability procedures are meant to respect and protect, and the political dimension of democracy on which they are founded.

C. Humanity and Sensitivity

In the ECtHR's judgments on the procedural dimension of Article 2, there is a more implicit set of values at work in the case narratives that can be interpreted as forming another intangible and qualitative aspect of the essential connection between Article 2 and democratic society as understood by the ECtHR. In its decisions on transparency and public scrutiny in the procedural dimension of Article 2, the ECtHR has consistently emphasised, within certain limits, the requirement for family involvement in investigations. This has partly been an important aspect of procedural transparency relating to public confidence, but it is also arguably an indication of the values associated with the right to life in the context of democratic society due to the cultural significance of death, and especially sudden and violent death.[69] As a concomitant of respecting and protecting the right to life per se, there is a recognition in the ECtHR's judgments that when human life is lost or seriously endangered the next-of-kin will be negatively affected emotionally, and so respect for dignity and humanity requires them to have access to the investigation.[70] This reflects a cultural respect for death and its impact on the living (as discussed further in Chapter 7), especially family members, and thereby acknowledgement of the need of bereaved relatives to seek the truth about what happened, perhaps even to achieve some sort of 'closure' as part of the grieving process.[71] This can be seen to raise issues similar to the

[69] Note Mary Bradbury, *Representations of Death: A Social Psychological Perspective* (London, Routledge, 1999) 159–60 and Glennys Howarth, *Death and Dying: A Sociological Introduction* (Cambridge, Polity, 2007) 155.

[70] A concern with humanity and sensitivity is explicit in Article 3 case law, where the ECtHR considers a failure to investigate a disappearance as inhuman treatment: Anja Seibert-Fohr, *Prosecuting Serious Human Rights Violations* (Oxford, Oxford University Press, 2009) 132; see also Eva Brems, 'Procedural Protection: An Examination of Procedural Safeguards Read into Substantive Convention Rights' in Eva Brems and Janneke Gerards (eds), *Shaping Rights in the ECHR* (Cambridge, Cambridge University Press, 2013) 137, 156 on 'inhuman procedural shortcomings' in such cases.

[71] Compare Sam McIntosh, 'Taken Lives Matter: Open Justice and Recognition in Inquests into Deaths at the Hands of the State' (2016) 12.2 *International Journal of Law in Context* 141: focusing on inquests in England and Wales, McIntosh discusses the moral foundations for a claim that a deceased's family and the public 'have legitimate and important interests in learning about the circumstances

behavioural standard of respect for the value of life in the substantive dimensions of Article 2, by pointing to qualities of conduct towards others and how these matters might be incorporated into official procedures.

These aspects of humanity and sensitivity can be seen in relation to the ECtHR's approach to the temporal aspects of investigations as well. The ECtHR has addressed the temporal dimension of investigations in terms of the need for a prompt initiation by the state and reasonable expedition in the way the procedure progresses. As key aspects of state responsibility, adequate investigation and the maintenance of public confidence, these questions of timing serve practical aims in the establishment of standards under Article 2 and reflect the socio-political underpinnings of the rule of law in relation to public confidence, as addressed above. Yet such temporal aspects also arguably reflect the ECtHR's awareness of the acute need for information and answers when human life is ended (or endangered), on the part of the family and public, which is amplified in situations in which an individual life is affected by force used in the name of society, or worse still in circumstances of repression.[72] In recognising the need for promptness and expedition, the ECtHR implicitly acknowledges the need for awareness of, and sensitivity to, these family and public concerns. In these ways the case narratives can be seen to involve an underlying purpose of respecting the human dimension of Article 2 cases and the need for appropriate responses to state uses of lethal or potentially lethal force by, to some extent, acknowledging their emotional significance.[73]

To conclude, in its interpretation and application of Article 2 the ECtHR has constructed its analytical narratives around the fundamental importance of the right to life in democratic society, as well as the proportionate management of that right in the social context. Yet, despite fluidity in the ways in which the ECtHR's case narratives have reflected the resulting tensions in protecting and restricting the right to life, those narratives can be seen to indicate some underlying purposes and values, primarily involving the rule of law, as well as qualitative and behavioural standards for state agents' conduct. These purposes and values arguably indicate some of the main narrative meanings arising from

behind use-of-force deaths at the hands of the state through public accountability'. See also Olga Chernishova, 'Right to the Truth in the Case-Law of the European Court of Human Rights' in Lawrence Early, Anna Austin, Clare Ovey and Olga Chernishova (eds), *The Right to Life under Article 2 of the European Convention on Human Rights: Twenty Years of Legal Developments since McCann v The United Kingdom* (Oisterwijk, Wolf Legal Publishers, 2016) 145 and James Sweeney, 'The Elusive Right to Truth in Transitional Human Rights Jurisprudence' (2018) 67 *International and Comparative Law Quarterly* 353.

[72] See the discussion of *Streletz* above and note *Şandru et Autres c Roumanie* (2009) para 79 on the importance of a prompt investigation given public concern about the 1989 Timişoara shootings.

[73] As Hessbruegge notes, the emotional impact of such incidents extends to the state agents themselves, for whom care provisions should also be made by the state: Hessbruegge, *Human Rights and Personal Self-Defense in International Law* 203–204.

the cases and can usefully supplement their technical specificities, to orient critical engagement with them and guide their development. Although in case-by-case decisions caught between the poles of the right to life as a basic value of democratic societies in the Council of Europe and the need for subsidiary and proportionate interpretation of its scope it can at times seem that Article 2's fundamental democratic values and goals are overlooked, this chapter has sought to underline their immanence in the case law as a foundation for a clearer focus on this right's underlying ethos.

7

Narratives of Death and Democracy

This chapter builds on the previous chapters' analyses of the right to life in Article 2 and the ECtHR's interpretation and application of it, in order to reflect on how Article 2 case law produces meaning about democratic society in relation to lethal and potentially lethal force. As Robert Cover observed, no legal prescription 'exists apart from the narratives that locate it and give it meaning' and law has the capacity 'to imbue action with significance'.[1] Similarly, for Ricoeur the 'world of action' is dynamically configured through narrative to produce and communicate meaning about it.[2] The particular problem here is to consider how ECtHR judgments configure meaning from death and serious harm, aspects of experience that lie at the limits of comprehension and expression, and imbue them and the conduct that causes them with significance in terms of a politico-legal order – democratic society – that itself encompasses a contestable matrix of actual and potential meanings. Yet the ECtHR can be seen to do so, not only in the form of specific points of Article 2 law and their application, but also in broader terms of overarching values and principles that reflect core aspects of democratic virtue and identity. In the context of the right to life and the use of lethal and potentially lethal force, this requires a two-stage reflection.

To begin with, the chapter addresses the question of how judgments that stem from death, life-threatening harm or the danger of death can produce meaning about the right to life and democratic society. This requires exploring in theoretical terms the meaning-making function of legal narrative with regard to its subject matter, the use of coercive force against the human body by agents of the state, which involves forms of conduct and experience that challenge the capacity of human understanding and represent the limits not only of the relationship between individual and community, but also of existence itself when death results. In this regard the chapter argues that by giving death and life-threatening harm meaning in terms of rights and democracy by classifying forms of experience, a key function of Article 2 law is to demarcate democracy's interpretive and constitutive boundary between (unacceptable) violence and (acceptable) force.

[1] Robert M Cover, 'Foreword: Nomos and Narrative' (1983) 97 *Harvard Law Review* 4, 8 and 4.

[2] Paul Ricoeur (Kathleen McLaughlin and David Pellauer, trans), *Time and Narrative, Volume 1* (Chicago, University of Chicago Press, 1984) 70–71.

The chapter then turns to discuss what overarching meaning about democratic society can be derived from the body of case law on Article 2. Here the chapter focusses not on the technical detail of the cases, but on the implications of their connective values and purposes, as indicated in previous chapters (especially Chapter 6). As these values and purposes can be understood to be essential to achieving strong protection for the right to life due to its status in the ECHR and in the democratic societies making up the Council of Europe, they can also be understood to indicate what is essential in the concept of democratic society itself. Reading the case law inductively and cumulatively, with reference to theoretical connections between narrative and the formation of identity, the chapter argues that by joining these threads together, the case narratives can be understood to produce an outline of the nature of democratic society in terms of key attributes. Although predominantly abstract and aspirational, it is suggested here that these attributes are significant in that they can provide a clear sense of direction in Article 2 law and a counterweight in terms of fundamental systemic values to the pressures of subsidiarity and deference.

I. Lethal Force and Legal Narrative

This book began with the shooting of the terrorist suspects in the *McCann* case and has discussed several ECtHR judgments about the state's use of lethal and potentially lethal force. Here the discussion returns to that starting point and the root of all these cases on the right to life under Article 2 ECHR: the use of coercive and destructive force and its human impact. In the theories of Robert Cover and Paul Ricoeur, the significance of that specific context, the use of force, in expressive and interpretive terms represents a significant obstacle to the making of meaning through narrative, a point that becomes particularly important with regard to law that is intended to provide universal and authoritative standards that can be accepted and adhered to across a community. Yet, it is argued here, the nature of ECtHR case narratives and ECHR law can be seen to circumvent that obstacle and in so doing indicate key aspects of their function in democratic society's normative framework.

In his discussion of 'Nomos and Narrative', Cover makes some important observations that are relevant to the relationship between the use of force and legal narrative. Noting that some legal provisions, which in his example came from US constitutional law, purport to convey a common meaning to structure a community but are contested through different (political) interpretations, he observed that 'there is a radical dichotomy between the social organization of law as power and the organization of law as meaning'.[3] In that sense, Cover sought

[3] Cover, 'Foreword: Nomos and Narrative' 18.

to show that while a law might be intended to have one meaning as an expression of power, law's meaning when interpreted by its intended community may be manifold. If law depends on narrative for making meaning, then (as Ricoeur observed) its configuration might not necessarily result in the communication of a singular message. Focusing on the potential of contested legal meaning in society and opposition to the state as a source of inspiration for legal change, Cover argued that different normative worlds and their narratives might inform each other, in that law as a realm of argumentation and differing interpretive perspectives can produce meaning from disagreement, which can result in change at any level of society. He then concluded his article by observing that 'Legal meaning is a challenging enrichment of social life, a potential restraint on arbitrary power and violence'.[4] The key point in his discussion was therefore that the meaning generated through law and the narratives that locate it can affect understanding and conduct to the extent that even state power may be limited.

However, further reflection on that potentially positive interaction between narrative and power through law led Cover to express an important reservation in another influential article published two years later. In 'Violence and the Word', Cover famously observed that:

> Legal interpretation takes place in a field of pain and death. This is true in several senses. Legal interpretive acts signal and occasion the imposition of violence upon others: A judge articulates her understanding of a text, and as a result, somebody loses his freedom, his property, his children, even his life. Interpretations in law also constitute justifications for violence which has already occurred or which is about to occur. When interpreters have finished their work, they frequently leave behind victims whose lives have been torn apart by these organized, social practices of violence. Neither legal interpretation nor the violence it occasions may be properly understood apart from one another.[5]

Cover's main aim in this argument was to return to the 'radical dichotomy' in law[6] that he had previously noted, and to clarify the problem it represented, namely 'the essential tension' between 'the elaboration of legal meaning and the exercise of or resistance to the violence of social control'.[7] In other words, having earlier addressed the making of meaning in law through the narratives that locate legal prescription, in 'Violence and the Word' Cover sought to address the special nature of law and legal interpretation in 'the context of the organised social practice of violence'.[8] If interpretation means 'a social construction of an interpersonal reality through language' then it meets its limits in pain and death, which destroy

[4] Cover, 'Foreword: Nomos and Narrative' 68; see also 49–50 on narratives of resistance reshaping law and justice.
[5] Robert Cover, 'Violence and the Word' (1985) 95 *Yale Law Journal* 1601.
[6] Cover, 'Violence and the Word' 1602 fn 2 and 'Nomos and Narrative' 18.
[7] Cover, 'Violence and the Word' 1602 fn 2.
[8] Cover, 'Violence and the Word' 1602 fn 2.

language, prevent communication and challenge the possibility of shared or shareable meaning-making.[9]

Cover's main concern was with the role of courts in the US as part of 'the social organization of law as power', especially in the field of criminal law with regard to punishment and above all the death penalty.[10] In that sense, therefore, his discussion was contextually specific, and critically engaged with the literary turn in jurisprudence that seemed to concentrate on abstract interpretive dimensions of law, ignoring its harsh realities. Where the law and judges applying it are implementing the state's monopoly of (legitimate) force then the law is itself an instrument of coercion. The meaning conveyed through that law and the narratives locating it will be blocked by the impact of coercive force and the resulting contestation of meaning. Although Cover's theoretical reflection on the relationship between legal meaning and the 'field of pain and death' was developed with these particular concerns in mind, it nevertheless raises relevant questions for this book's analysis of Article 2 ECHR in relation to lethal and potentially lethal force for two main reasons.

One reason is that Cover's reminder of the need to recognise that legal interpretation takes place in a context of force and violence, which he interpreted literally and metaphorically, is similarly important in Article 2 law due to its subject matter as addressed here, namely the use of coercive force in policing and law enforcement. This needs to be considered with regard to both the extent to which pain and death are acknowledged in the law on the right to life and the challenges they represent in narrative terms for making sense of experience and constructing legal meaning.[11] This relates to what Cover addressed as the disruptive effect of pain on language, and echoes Ricoeur's reflection on the difficulty of constructing a narrative that can adequately encompass death and express meaning in relation to it. The other reason is that whereas Cover's concern was with the application of law that involves the implementation of state power and its implications for developing shareable meaning, Article 2 law is not itself a direct application of state power, but involves its evaluation at the transnational level, above state systems and importantly without coercive aims. In that light, the first section below situates Article 2 narratives in their field of pain and death, to acknowledge their engagement with it and their limits in doing so. The second section considers how the case law circumvents those limits, addressing the case narratives' function of determining the permissibility of a deprivation of life or a

[9] Cover, 'Violence and the Word' 1602–1603 referring to Elaine Scarry, *The Body in Pain: The Making and Unmaking of the World* (New York, Oxford University Press, 1985) on the impossibility of expressing an experience of pain. Also note Stephen Skinner, 'Stories of Pain and the Pursuit of Justice: Law, Violence, Experience and Jurisprudence' (2009) 5 *Law, Culture and the Humanities* 131, 146, 151–52.

[10] Cover, 'Violence and the Word' 1602, 1607, 1618, 1622, 1628–29.

[11] See also Austin Sarat, 'Introduction: On Pain and Death as Facts of Legal Life' in Austin Sarat (ed), *Pain, Death and the Law* (Ann Arbor, University of Michigan Press, 2001) 1–9, 6: 'If we are adequately to theorize law, we must think about law in relation to death'.

nearly fatal threat to life by displacing attention from the field of pain and death to the field of legal accountability and legal classification.

A. Article 2 and the Field of Pain and Death

Protection of the right to life by law under Article 2 is motivated by a concern with limiting deprivation of life, and the case law on lethal and potentially lethal force stems from and responds to death or life-threatening harm. These cases record and represent the fragility of life and the devastating impact of physical force and modern weaponry on human flesh and bone, as well as its effects for others. This can usefully be illustrated by recalling some examples, in order to reconnect the theoretical and legal analysis with the harsh reality of the use of force in policing and law enforcement.

In *McCann and Others v United Kingdom* the incident that triggered the landmark judgment stemmed from the moment of confrontation between the soldiers and the suspects, which was described as follows:

> He opened fire on Farrell. He deemed that McCann was in a threatening position and was unable to see his hands and switched fire to McCann. Then he turned back to Farrell and continued firing until he was certain that she was no longer a threat, namely, her hands away from her body. He fired a total of seven shots. … D fired nine rounds at rapid rate, initially aiming into the centre of Savage's body, with the last two at his head. Savage corkscrewed as he fell. D acknowledged that it was possible that Savage's head was inches away from the ground as he finished firing. He kept firing until Savage was motionless on the ground and his hands were away from his body.[12]

In *Gül v Turkey*, the finding of an unnecessary and disproportionate use of force was based on these facts:

> The intensity of the firing destroyed fingers on Mehmet Gül's right hand and inflicted numerous wounds. As he turned away from the door, a bullet struck him in the back inflicting a fatal injury. He staggered back up the corridor, leaving blood stains against the wall … he was transferred to an ambulance which took him to Şanliurfa hospital. He died however prior to his arrival. His body was taken to the morgue.[13]

The decision in *McShane v United Kingdom* to extend the meaning of a use of force to any conduct by state agents that resulted in death or harm resulted from this situation:

> Dermot McShane fell underneath the hoarding over which the APC [Armoured Personnel Carrier] advanced. The circumstances in which the APC struck the hoarding, its speed, and the length of time which it remained on the hoarding are subject to dispute … RUC officers reached Dermot McShane and arranged for his transfer by ambulance to hospital where he died a short time later. According to the pathologist

[12] *McCann v United Kingdom* (1995) paras 62 and 78–79.
[13] *Gül v Turkey* (2000) paras 23–24.

> who carried out the post mortem examination, his injuries were consistent with having been run over by the wheels of a vehicle while lying underneath a sheet of hoarding.[14]

The finding of a breach of Article 2 in *Timus and Tarus v Moldova* resulted from a sudden and fatal encounter on a staircase in a residential block of flats:

> Two police officers rushed after Alexei Vlasi, who started to run back up the stairs. They apprehended him on the fifth floor. Shortly afterwards, one of the police officers shot him in the back of the head at very close range. He died instantly.[15]

Similarly, the judgment in *Shchiborshch and Kuzmina v Russia* about a police intervention to take a mentally disturbed man from his apartment to hospital resulted in terrifying fatal injuries:

> After trying unsuccessfully to negotiate with him, [the police unit] decided to 'storm' the kitchen. Mr Shchiborshch ran to the balcony and cried for help while the police officers continued trying to apprehend him. When he fell on the balcony floor, they handcuffed him and put him on the kitchen floor. … Mr Shchiborshch was taken to hospital no. 7 with multiple wounds and in a coma. He died without regaining consciousness, having sustained craniocerebral trauma, brain oedema, concussion, and slash wounds to the head, body and extremities, several fractured ribs and a ruptured jugular vein.[16]

Every case report contains a similar outline of the contested incident, couched in the same sort of professionally detached terms.[17] This is how law responds to trauma, through the neutral recording of fact and its evaluation in terms of applicable rules and norms. Similarly, the experience and feelings of a victim's relatives, who have standing to bring a claim under Article 2 in the name of the victim through the right to individual petition, are indirectly and directly acknowledged in the case law. Relatives' experience and emotions are indirectly apparent in the 'Procedure' section of case reports, which notes the identities of applicants:[18] names of parents, grandparents, spouses, children, and brothers and sisters, who are bringing cases about the death of their child, grandchild, husband or wife, parent or sibling. They are also directly acknowledged in the next-of-kin's entitlement to be included in the investigatory process[19] and in the assessment of damages, which sometimes notes the applicants' distress.[20]

Although Article 2 case law, and the narratives it constructs, are thus connected with the field of pain and death from which the narratives stem and

[14] *McShane v United Kingdom* (2002) paras 12–13.

[15] *Timus and Tarus v Republic of Moldova* (2013) para 9.

[16] *Shchiborshch and Kuzmina v Russia* (2014) paras 9–10.

[17] For examples of life-threatening force note *Vasil Sashov Petrov v Bulgaria* (2010) paras 6–8 and *Soare et autres c Roumanie* (2011) paras 11–12, 23 and 25–28 on the victim's potentially lethal injuries; compare *Haász and Szabó v Hungary* (2015) para 11 on a potentially fatal near miss with a firearm.

[18] For example, *Kakoulli v Turkey* (2005) paras 1–3, *Ramsahai and Others v The Netherlands* (2007) paras 1–3; *Huohvanainen v Finland* (2007) paras 1–3; and *Gheorghe Cobzaru c Roumanie* (2013) paras 1–3.

[19] See the discussion in Chapter 5.

[20] For example, *McKerr v United Kingdom* (2001) para 181.

seek to make meaning, they are nevertheless limited and incomplete.[21] As recognised theoretically by Cover, the experiential dimensions of pain, suffering and death fall beyond the scope of the law, partly it must be noted because it is not law's purpose to try to express and address them fully, but mainly because of their ineffability.[22] Moreover, as considered by Ricoeur, the human construction of narrative to make sense of experience, especially with regard to its temporality, cannot adequately do so when the experience relates to or involves death, due to a profound existential difficulty in understanding the nature of life as a finite phenomenon in relation to its end, and the nature of death as the end point of life and the end of sensory and cognitive capability.[23] In Ricoeur's philosophical reflection, narratives can only indirectly address and make sense of death and in that regard are always insufficient.[24] Although Ricoeur focused on literary and historical narratives, the same can be said for legal narratives. Whereas in Article 2 law it is not the inevitability of human death and the inexorable passage of life that are problematic, but the untimeliness of sudden death – the unexpected, forceful abbreviation of the victim's lifetime and the hastening of its end[25] – death is noted as the origin of a case but is not otherwise directly addressed. As noted in Chapter 4, attention shifts from the outcome of a use of force to its circumstances.

Lastly, this incompleteness is also apparent in the way that Article 2 case narratives only partially engage with the field of pain and death in its extension beyond the scope of individual judgments on the right to life. While the case law addresses some connections among cases to a certain extent, it leaves aside

[21] AT Williams, 'Human Rights and Law: Between Sufferance and Insufferability' (2007) 123.1 *Law Quarterly Review* 133, 137–39; see also Scott Veitch, *Law and Irresponsibility: On the Legitimation of Human Suffering* (Oxford, Routledge-Cavendish, 2007) 92–93.

[22] Cover, 'Violence and the Word' 1602–1603. See also Austin Sarat, 'Situating Law Between the Realities of Violence and the Claims of Justice: An Introduction' in Austin Sarat (ed), *Law, Violence and the Possibility of Justice* (Princeton, Princeton University Press, 2001) 3–16; Desmond Manderson, 'Introduction: Tales from the Crypt – A Metaphor, An Image, A Story' in Desmond Manderson (ed) *Courting Death: The Law of Mortality* (London, Pluto Press, 1999) 1–2 and Peter Fitzpatrick, 'Death as the Horizon of the Law' in Manderson (ed) *Courting Death* 19.

[23] Ricoeur, *Time and Narrative, Volume 1* 85–87, 110–11; Paul Ricoeur (Kathleen Blamey and David Pellauer, trans), *Time and Narrative, Volume 3* (Chicago, University of Chicago Press, 1988) 92–93; Hans Kellner, '"As Real as it Gets" – Ricoeur and Narrativity' in David E Klemm and William Schweiker (eds), *Meanings in Texts and Actions: Questioning Paul Ricoeur* (Charlottesville, University Press of Virginia, 1993) 51–52. In this regard Ricoeur was influenced by Martin Heidegger's work on the concept of *Dasein*, or 'being' (literally 'being there'), according to which life essentially involves an ineluctable process over time of existing 'towards death'. See Martin Heidegger (John MacQuarrie and Edward Robinson, trans), *Being and Time* (Oxford, Blackwell, 1962). Note also Ted Honderich (ed), *The Oxford Companion to Philosophy*, 2nd edn (Oxford, Oxford University Press, 2005) 373 and James M Demske, *Being, Man and Death: A Key to Heidegger* (Lexington, University Press of Kentucky, 1970) 10–73. On the ways of determining death as the end of life see P-L Chau and Jonathan Herring, 'The Meaning of Death' in Belinda Brooks-Gordon, Fatemeh Ebtehaj, Jonathan Herring and Martin Johnson (eds), *Death Rites and Rights* (Oxford, Hart, 2007) 13.

[24] Ricoeur, *Time and Narrative, Volume 1* 110–11; Kellner, '"As Real as it Gets"' 58.

[25] Glennys Howarth, *Death and Dying: A Sociological Introduction* (Cambridge, Polity, 2007) 155.

the aggregate effect of uses of lethal and potentially lethal force more generally.[26] While Article 2 judgments respond to particular incidents, they do not address wider issues of quantity, frequency and patterns in uses of lethal and potentially lethal force within individual states and across the Council of Europe.[27] As a result, the relationship between the right to life and democratic society that can be understood from reading a particular case, or a body of systemically related cases together, is but part of the broader reality of uses of force, their impact on that relationship and the lived experience of democracy.

In terms of the narrative theories of Cover and Ricoeur, it is thus important to recall that the configuration of meaning about the right to life and democratic society in Article 2 case law stems from pain and death, which are partly acknowledged in the law but which also leave a problematic experiential and interpretive shadow at its edges. While this indicates a limit on the expressive capacity of legal narratives, their operation under Article 2 to locate and configure meaning about the right to life demonstrates their primary transformative function, that is, to make meaning through legal analysis from that which resists expression, interpreting the boundaries of acceptable force, and giving sense to pain and death in the name of democratic society and its recognised legitimate objectives.

B. Article 2 Narratives and the Transformative Function of Law

As noted above, whereas Cover's theoretical concern with the dichotomy between the elaboration of meaning through law and the exercise of social control was based on forms of law applying state power and giving rise to pain and death, Article 2 law is about the accountability of state power in their aftermath. The right to life should be protected so as to minimise the risk of death and ideally avoid it, but legal action can be triggered to determine compliance with the right when death, a risk

[26] Some forms of connection among similar cases are considered by the ECtHR such as, for example, its approach to the joined cases from Northern Ireland and its cross references in legal framework cases involving Greece, Bulgaria, Romania and Turkey (noted in Chapters 4 and 5). The pilot judgment procedure introduced under Protocol 14, in force since 2010 and amending Rule 61 of the Rules of the ECtHR, allows a collective perspective on similar cases in some circumstances: see Hannah Russell, *The Use of Force and Article 2 of the ECHR in Light of European Conflicts* (Oxford, Hart, 2017) 212–24. However, overall aggregate issues of the use of force in more general terms within and across systems are not currently part of the ECtHR's remit.

[27] Note on this issue in the context of Northern Ireland Fionnuala Ní Aoláin, *The Politics of Force: Conflict Management and State Violence in Northern Ireland* (Belfast, Blackstaff Press, 2000) 63–64, 107, 247 and 'Truth Telling, Accountability and the Right to Life in Northern Ireland' (2002) 5 *European Human Rights Law Review* 572, 588. See also Christine Bell and Johanna Keenan, 'Lost on the Way Home? The Right to Life in Northern Ireland' (2005) 32.1 *Journal of Law and Society* 68, 72; and Brice Dickson, *The European Convention on Human Rights and the Conflict in Northern Ireland* (Oxford, Oxford University Press, 2010) 27–28, 225. On the need for broader quantitative and comparative analyses of lethal force internationally see Anneke Osse and Ignacio Cano, 'Police Deadly Use of Firearms: An International Comparison' (2017) 21.5 *The International Journal of Human Rights* 629.

of death or serious life-threatening harm occur. Even though Article 2 law's subject matter involves experiential limits on communication due to the ineffability of pain and death, judicial narratives of the right to life are rooted in a representation of the relationship between that universal right and democratic society, reflecting and constructing meaning (as discussed in Chapter 3) from a basis in actually, purportedly and prospectively shared democratic values and concerns about why lethal or potentially lethal force and their impact matter. Article 2 case narratives thus evaluate, and communicate meaning about, state power, law and force, rather than implement it. Although the narratives in some cases produce meaning that endorses and legitimates an exercise of state power, in others they criticise and censure it, and in all cases are produced at a transnational level separate from state systems themselves. In this regard, Article 2 case narratives can be seen to displace attention from pain and death to the configuration of meaning through a legal frame of reference about state conduct that produced them or resulted from them (the use of force, its planning and control, and its investigation by the state).[28] In this way rather than being obstructed by the experiential gulf generated by pain and death, Article 2 law circumvents it.

Right to life cases on lethal and potentially lethal force are predominantly determined in the absence of the victim, the person killed or seriously injured.[29] Due to the overriding importance of the right to life as a basic value of democratic society, Article 2 law overcomes the absence of the right holder by requiring others, namely the applicants and state government via their legal teams, to provide accounts of the events and circumstances that led to the victim's death or injury.[30] Although as noted in Chapter 4 the turn from the death to the use of force appears to leave unanswered questions about the rightness of the end of a victim's life, in terms of individual justice and moral desert, this turn avoids the experiential (even existential) problems of a narrative engagement with death by addressing instead the state's conduct and its public significance in the democratic order. In that way in Article 2 law, the death or harm that marks the end of an individual's life time, either completely or in a drastically changed way as the result of severe injury, leads to the beginning of a period of collective or public time, in which the case narrative seeks to make sense of how the death or harm

[28] Veitch, *Law and Irresponsibility* 76–77; Günter Frankenberg, *Comparative Law as Critique* (Cheltenham, Edward Elgar, 2016) 176–77.

[29] Even if they survive, they may be seriously incapacitated: for example, *Soare* paras 25–28. The absence of the victim is also addressed by David Baker, *Deaths After Police Contact: Constructing Accountability in the 21st Century* (London, Palgrave Macmillan, 2016) 139.

[30] As Cheryl L Hughes, 'Reconstructing the Subject of Human Rights' (1999) 25.2 *Philosophy and Social Criticism* 47, 52 observes, we cannot make sense of our own deaths (as or after they occur) through narrative, so only third-person narratives such as legal accounts can to some extent endeavour to do so: 'stories of my death will belong to those who survive me'. On the deceased's body and death as sites of interpretive contestation see Elizabeth Hallam, Jenny Hockey and Glennys Howarth, *Beyond the Body: Death and Social Identity* (London, Routledge, 1999) 88, a point discussed by Baker, *Deaths After Police Contact* 139.

happened in terms of the right to life and to derive from it meaning for others, the next-of-kin and society.

The function of Article 2 case narratives is thus to determine whether or not a use of force was permissible, or as Cover put it, to configure 'the justifications for violence that has already occurred'.[31] If violence is understood not just as contested hurting but, in its prima facie negative sense, as illegitimate and unacceptable hurting or injury, then in the area of state uses of force human rights law is one of its principal determinants.[32] Just as Article 2(2) itself makes allowances for a 'use of *force*' against 'unlawful *violence*', so the ECtHR must decide on the difference between them, constructing a narrative to justify whether or not a state's coercive action is within the bounds of Article 2 or a contested killing or hurting that falls beyond its scope, and is therefore unacceptable in democratic society.[33]

As noted in Chapter 1, and referred to by the ECtHR itself,[34] in fundamental theoretical terms Article 2 law on lethal or life-threatening force involves the most serious aspects of the state's monopoly of force. By establishing the distinction between acceptable and unacceptable uses of such force, Article 2 law provides an authoritative determination of whether or not the state's exercise of that monopoly is permissible and so legitimate in ECHR terms (although as noted in Chapter 6, legitimacy and public confidence are also matters of perception that may only partially be informed by a legal application of the right to life).[35] In this regard, Article 2 case law illustrates the transformational power of legal interpretation, configuring the representation of events to impose order on them and produce meaning from them, not only about the scope and effect of applicable norms, but also about the legally authorised classification and understanding of the events themselves.[36] Linking this classification with the concept of democratic society shows that the meaning of that concept itself reflects the problematic co-existence of potential force and potential violence, and depends on the contingent distinction between them.[37]

[31] Cover, 'Violence and the Word' 1601.

[32] Paul Mahoney and Fredrik Sundberg, 'The European Convention on Human Rights: A Case Study of the International Law Response to Violence' in Kathleen E Mahoney and Paul Mahoney (eds), *Human Rights in the Twenty-First Century: A Global Challenge* (Dordrecht, Martinus Nijhoff Publishers, 1993) 361, 362, 375; Skinner, 'Stories of Pain' 146–51.

[33] Note Frankenberg, *Comparative Law as Critique* 172 on human rights narratives and the justification of violence. See also James B Brady and Newton Garver, 'Introduction to the Issues' in James B Brady and Newton Garver (eds), *Justice, Law and Violence* (Philadelphia, Temple University Press, 1991) 1. Compare Hallam et al, *Beyond the Body* 88.

[34] *Ramsahai v Netherlands* (2005) para 325. See Chapter 5.

[35] See also John Ladd, 'Ideological Components of the Concepts of Collective Violence, Human Rights, and Solidarity' in Mahoney and Mahoney, *Human Rights in the Twenty-First Century* 223, 230; Jan Narveson, 'Force, Violence and Law' in Brady and Garver (eds), *Justice, Law and Violence* 149–69. Note David Held, 'Central Perspectives on the Modern State' in Gregor McLennan, David Held and Stuart Hall (eds), *The Idea of the Modern State* (Milton Keynes, Open University Press, 1984) 29, 62–63.

[36] Baker, *Deaths After Police Contact* 147, 157–59.

[37] Peter Squires and Peter Kennison, *Shooting to Kill? Policing, Firearms and Armed Response* (Chichester, Wiley-Blackwell, 2010) 50; Jonathan Kuttab, 'Overt Forms of State Violence' in

II. Article 2 Narratives and Democratic Society

Drawing together the main points addressed in the previous chapters, this section turns to discuss the overarching meaning of democratic society that can be derived from the body of Article 2 law on the use of lethal and potentially lethal force. This involves moving from the variable configuration of meaning in individual case narratives around the theme of the right to life and its connection with democratic society, to consider how a sense of the underlying ethos of Article 2 law can be identified from the ECtHR's analyses by reading the case law transversally. On that basis, this section outlines what the thematic connections among judgments can be understood to constitute together, in terms of the main systemic attributes of democratic society appertaining to the protection of the right to life and the use of force.

A. Towards an Overarching Meaning: Reading the Article 2 Case Narratives

Individual judgments by the ECtHR give the definitive statement about whether or not a state has complied with ECHR law on the facts of a case and provide specific practical guidance on the concrete measures needed to achieve compliance with Article 2. Such concrete measures could be seen to be not only a necessary, but also a sufficient focus of inquiry in ECHR legal analysis, as a crucial step in clarifying the scope of Article 2.[38] Yet in addition to identifying the specifics of what must be done to comply with that provision, it is also important to be aware of why it must be done, that is, according to which values, principles, standards and rationales. The narratives of democratic society apparent in Article 2 law, the values they reflect and the meanings they construct, can arguably play an essential role in providing a cohesive purpose to the legal analysis, tying together the legal technicalities of what are often highly detailed judgments and supporting consistency in the specifics and spirit of the right to life.[39]

Where the state is involved in causing death or a serious threat to life, right to life narratives raise the deepest questions about the values at stake, as well as connections among the individual, the community, and the state. Democracy and democratic society are more than a set of institutions and mechanical processes,

Mahoney and Mahoney, *Human Rights in the Twenty-First Century* 241, 241–42; Michael McClintock, 'Establishing Accountability for State Violence' in Mahoney and Mahoney, *Human Rights in the Twenty-First Century* 247, 248.

[38] See especially the important contribution to these ends in Russell, *The Use of Force and Article 2 of the ECHR in Light of European Conflicts* 1, 9–10, 17–22.

[39] On the relevance and contribution of general 'regulatory principles' in shaping and guiding reform processes, specifically with regard to policing, see the discussion in Ian Loader, 'In Search of Civic Policing: Recasting the "Peelian" Principles' (2016) 10 *Criminal Law and Philosophy* 427, 432–33.

and their essence is to be found in the ways their values and practices intersect.[40] The purposive direction and meaning of case narratives[41] produced at the highest level of European human rights adjudication, the ECtHR, about what states do and what they should do when using force, evaluated in relation to the right to life, are vital indicators of the core values and nature of democratic society itself, which it is the ECtHR's role to protect.[42] In that regard, the aim here is to revitalise the cohesive rationale stated by the ECtHR at the outset of all of its judgments in this area, but which is at times obscured by the apparently restricted scope of Article 2's protection in some cases. Underlining the value matrix that provides the contextual theme in this area of law, it is suggested here, has three main applications.

One is to encourage the ECtHR to make the connection between the right to life and democratic society more central to its reasoning and adjudication processes, and to recognise it more clearly, especially when hard cases draw it onto a more precarious, deferential path.[43] Upholding the fundamental relationship between protection of the right to life and democratic society has to involve more than a concern with subsidiarity, and the ECtHR's own strong indications of the importance and potential of that relationship in some judgments could usefully become a more robust part of its analysis. Another reason, along similar lines, is that strengthening the core relationship between Article 2 and democratic society in case law could enhance the communicative role of ECtHR judgments, including the dialogic and educative aspects of the interaction between ECHR law and states noted in Chapter 2. Disseminating a sense of the essential connection between the protection of the right to life in the context of policing and systemic values is a key part of the socialisation role of ECHR law in the Council of Europe,[44] and a clearer narrative of values could provide an important counterweight to the growing predominance of the security paradigm. As discussed in the following section, although maintaining security is a core requirement and preserve of national sovereignty, security must not be seen in isolation from the values that make it worthwhile. A third reason lies in Article 2's broader socio-political appeal. In some contexts, the limited influence of ECtHR judgments

[40] See also Conor Gearty, *Liberty and Security* (Cambridge, Polity Press, 2013) 113–16.

[41] Cover, 'Foreword: Nomos and Narrative' 4–5; Ricoeur, *Time and Narrative, Volume 1* 64–67.

[42] Sir Nicolas Bratza, 'Living Instrument or Dead Letter – The Future of the European Convention on Human Rights' (2014) 2 *European Human Rights Law Review* 116, 128 on the importance of the ECHR and ECtHR in preserving the ideals of democracy.

[43] Stephen Skinner, 'Deference, Proportionality and the Margin of Appreciation in Lethal Force Case Law under Article 2 ECHR' (2014) 1 *European Human Rights Law Review* 32, 37–38.

[44] According to Jeffrey T Checkel, a socialisation process is a distinctive feature of European organisations and involves 'a process of inducting actors into the norms and rules of a given community', resulting in compliance with them. This may involve merely formal compliance with the normative framework ('playing a role') or fully adopting that framework ('normative suasion' or internalisation): 'International Institutions and Socialization in Europe: Introduction and Framework' (2005) 59 *International Organization* 801, 804, 811–812.

on some High Contracting Parties[45] means that the provisions and principles of ECHR law take on a different form of significance through campaigning in other socio-political fora. In that regard, political pressure, critical debate and activism in civil society can provide significant leverage on state practice, using ECHR law in ways that are not necessarily dependent on its enforcement within the Council of Europe.[46]

As shown in previous chapters through the analysis of the longer-term and twentieth-century history of the right to life, as well as the ways in which the case law manages the inherent tension in Article 2, the key points of the case narratives discussed here are partly explicit and partly implicit. Reflecting on the overarching significance of Article 2 law in terms of narrative theory thus involves what Cover referred to as 'jurisgenesis', or the creation of legal meaning through engagement with the narratives that locate it,[47] and Ricoeur's discussion of narrative communication and reception ($mimesis_3$).[48] For both of these theoretical perspectives, narrative meaning is partly what is intended by a narrator, but may also be interpreted separately from that intention. In that sense, the discussion here does not seek to attribute a particular model of democratic society solely to an active process of construction by the ECtHR, but to interpret that model as an implication of the ECtHR's decisions.

This discussion also draws indirectly on Cover's and Ricoeur's theoretical connections between narrative and the formation of identity. For Cover, narratives form the world in which people live and are plotted on their imaginations, and as such narratives can be seen to situate and to be inherently linked with people's sense of who they are.[49] For Ricoeur, narrative has important connections with identity, in that the process of identifying an actor or agent in a fictional or historical account requires a narrative process of establishing and designating that actor or agent (an individual or a community) in a way that allows them to

[45] As Juliet Chevalier-Watts has observed, 'the Court will always be subject to constraints in its ability to enforce or demand regime change in a liberal democracy': 'Effective Investigations under Article 2 of the European Convention on Human Rights: Securing the Right to Life or an Onerous Burden on a State?' (2010) 21.3 *European Journal of International Law* 701, 721. States' responsiveness to ECtHR rulings has been linked to the degree of development in domestic legal and governmental systems: Dia Anagnostou and Alina Mungiu-Pippidi, 'Domestic Implementation of Human Rights Judgments in Europe: Legal Infrastructure and Government Effectiveness Matter' (2014) 25.1 *European Journal of International Law* 205, but see also on their data analysis Erik Voeten, 'Domestic Implementation of Human Rights Judgments in Europe: Legal Infrastructure and Government Effectiveness Matter: A Reply to Dia Anagnostou and Alina Mungiu-Pippidi' (2014) 25.1 *European Journal of International Law* 229. On the relationship between perceived legitimacy and compliance see also Thomas Franck, *The Power of Legitimacy among Nations* (Oxford, Oxford University Press, 1990) 24.

[46] Bell and Keenan, 'Lost on the Way Home?' 88–89; Chevalier-Watts, 'Effective Investigations' 715, 718. Note also more generally Cover, 'Foreword: Nomos and Narrative' 68 and Amartya Sen, 'Human Rights and the Limits of Law' (2006) 27.6 *Cardozo Law Review* 2913, 2920–21.

[47] Cover, 'Foreword: Nomos and Narrative' 4, 9, 11, 68. A useful parallel discussion is provided by Paul P Linden-Retek, 'Cosmopolitan Law and Time: Toward a Theory of Constitutionalism and Solidarity in Transition' (2015) 4.2 *Global Constitutionalism* 157, 178–79.

[48] Ricoeur, *Time and Narrative, Volume 1* 70–71.

[49] Cover, 'Foreword: Nomos and Narrative' 4, 5, 9.

be recognisable as the same over time and through processes of change.[50] For Ricoeur, the key aspect of narrative identity over time lies not in a static concept of 'being the same (*idem*)' but a fluid concept of 'oneself as self-same (*ipse*)'.[51] In other words, identity in a narrative sense does not require or entail homogeneity or immutability, but a way of maintaining consistency with the values and attributes that make a person or community distinct.

However, these aspects of narrative theory in this context need to be approached with some caution. Cover assumes a connection between legal narrative and a general sense of identity. The ECtHR represents and protects the interests of democratic societies in the Council of Europe, so the ECtHR's indications of societal attributes in the democratic context reflect its understanding of them, but that does not necessarily indicate a wider intersection between the ECtHR's perception and that of societies themselves. Moreover, Ricoeur's theory relates to the process of actor identification in particular forms of narrative, whereas in the present discussion the focus is on the meaning of democratic society that can be discerned in judgments about the right to life. In that sense, as discussed in narrative terms in the previous chapters, democratic society primarily appears in the Article 2 case law as a contextual theme that refers to the nature of the system in which force is used by a state, rather than as an actor per se. This is though not always clear cut, in that the ECtHR's evaluation of conduct by a state agent or state authorities as actors is by implication an evaluation of the conduct of a system which may or may not be called a democratic society.

Nevertheless, there is a useful parallel between this analysis of Article 2 law and the narrative theory with regard to identity, in that by establishing standards under Article 2 in relation to that right's importance in democratic society, the ECtHR shows what it understands democratic society to be, thereby developing an authoritative transnational and normative sense of democratic society's identity from the perspective of the principal ECHR institution.[52] Given the development of the ECHR over time as a living instrument, the ECtHR's references to 'democratic societies' in the plural, and its aim of recognising a diversity of approaches

[50] Ricoeur, *Time and Narrative, Volume 3* 244–47, 'L'identité narrative' (1988) 140–141 *Esprit* 295 and 'L'identité narrative' (1991) 95.221 *Revue des Sciences Humaines* 35; note also on a related point 'Who Is the Subject of Rights?' in Paul Ricoeur (David Pellauer, trans), *The Just* (Chicago, University of Chicago Press, 2000) 1, 3. See the commentary in Hughes, 'Reconstructing the Subject of Human Rights' 47–60 and Bernard P Dauenhauer, 'Ricoeur and Political Identity' in Morny Joy (ed), *Paul Ricoeur and Narrative: Context and Contestation* (Alberta, University of Calgary Press, 1997) 129, 131–32.

[51] Ricoeur, *Time and Narrative, Volume 3* 246–47; 'L'identité narrative' (1988) 296.

[52] Compare in the European Union context Linden-Retek, 'Cosmopolitan Law and Time' 178–85. See also Paul W Kahn, 'Freedom, Autonomy, and the Cultural Study of Law' (2001) 13 *Yale Journal of Law and the Humanities* 141 and his argument that law is 'constitutive of the self-understanding of individuals and communities'. However, note the cautious approach to the idea of European identity (specifically in relation to the European Union) in Alessandro Ferrara, *The Force of the Example: Explorations in the Paradigm of Judgment* (New York, Columbia University Press, 2008) 164–65 and on competing perspectives in identity formation Jiří Přibáň, *Legal Symbolism: On Law, Time and European Identity* (Aldershot, Ashgate, 2007) 138.

across the Council of Europe, that identity is not, in Ricoeur's terms, understandable in an '*idem*' sense of uniformity but, due to the fundamental importance of the right to life as a basic value in the post-war era, more an '*ipse*' sense of a common core of European democracy as post- and non-totalitarian, operating under the rule of law, upholding human rights and conducting itself in particular ways that reflect and support those other elements.

To address these issues of narrative meaning, and to explore their implications, the Article 2 case law is considered here through an inductive and cumulative reading. Although inductive reasoning is a contested approach to the establishment of general principles from the observation of fact or other specific objects of analysis, it is considered to be justifiable here because it involves extrapolating from the (express or implied) rationales and purposive interpretation of the ECtHR in case law, rather than seeking to produce broad scientific claims from specific empirical evidence.[53] The inductive analysis of Article 2 narratives is also considered cumulatively, in order to go beyond the case narratives' details and distil from them a broader interpretation (in other words, this is a process of 'joining up the dots'). This reading brings to light a set of key attributes of democratic society in the context of Article 2.

B. The Right to Life and the Attributes of Democratic Society

Whereas the discussion of 'democratic society' and 'democratic societies' in Chapter 3 sought to address the scope of these concepts as referred to by the ECtHR, the discussion here shows what the concept of democratic society can be understood to encompass in terms of systemic attributes identifiable through the case law. As with the discussion in Chapter 3, the attributes outlined here are partly descriptive and partly normative. They are descriptive to the extent that they are identifiable in the conduct of High Contracting Parties that comply with Article 2, and normative to the extent that they reflect minimal goals for High Contracting Parties that do not meet the Article 2 standard in the ECtHR's interpretation. However, given that compliance with Article 2 sometimes raises questions about the rigour of the standards applied, it is the normative, teleological potential of these attributes that is more significant.

It is argued here that an inductive and cumulative reading of the ECtHR's rulings on the substantive and procedural dimensions of Article 2 in the context of the state's use of lethal and potentially lethal force can be seen to reveal three main interconnected and ideal attributes of democratic societies in the Council of Europe, as restrained, responsible and reflective systems. These attributes,

[53] On this point note Honderich (ed), *The Oxford Companion to Philosophy*, 432. Compare on inductive reasoning in relation to the ECHR Alain Zysset, 'Searching for the Legitimacy of the European Court of Human Rights: The Neglected Role of 'Democratic Society'' (2016) 5.1 *Global Constitutionalism* 16, 19.

although abstract and general, encapsulate the key minimum standards and qualitative aspects associated with democratic societies in the Article 2 case narratives, and which states in the Council of Europe should demonstrate in relation to the use of force.

The first attribute of a democratic society, and the state within it, is that it must be restrained. This is the principal aim of the right to life and, where it is complied with, what should be its consequence, namely protection of the right through a minimal resort to force and a minimisation of risks to life. A concern with restraining the state through the prescriptive and protective power of law was fundamental to the eighteenth-century developments in rights protection through constitutional law. Restraining the state was also one of the original driving forces behind twentieth-century universal human rights, including the ECHR and Article 2, and as discussed in Chapter 4 is central to international law on the use of force in policing and law enforcement. Such a concern has been a core element of the interpretive narratives developed by the ECtHR, as discussed in Chapter 6, in relation to the purpose of the rule of law and the avoidance of arbitrary killing.

The attribute of restraint reflects the problematic tension at the heart of Article 2 law between the need to use force and the need to limit it. As addressed in Chapter 3, in democratic societies the use of force is a necessary, sometimes even essential, element of policing, law enforcement and the maintenance of order and security.[54] Democratic societies, even when they espouse and adhere to principles of liberalism, rights and minimal force in domestic policing, do not necessarily have to tolerate disorder or violence within and against them, and need to be able to protect themselves and their members.[55] The idea of militant democracy even allows such societies to be proactive in securing their own protection, within the limits of their value systems. The right to life, despite its foundational status and paramount importance, cannot therefore be absolute, in the sense of a guarantee for all lives and a completely binding fetter on state action, but it must limit what the state can do, and the democratic state must limit what it does with regard to that right if its protection is to be meaningful. The strength of Article 2 ECHR thus depends on the scope of its exceptions and the degree of flexibility within them, and the extent to which their limiting effects are respected by state agents and upheld by judges. The attribute of restraint in democratic society therefore requires legal restraint of the state, through its own regulatory frameworks, implementing and supported by international law, together with a clear awareness of the democratic objective of ensuring the limitation and restraint of state power under the rule of law, as well as – crucially – self-restraint by the state in its operational conduct.

[54] Note also Fionnuala Ní Aoláin, 'The Evolving Jurisprudence of the European Convention Concerning the Right to Life' (2001) 19.1 *Netherlands Quarterly of Human Rights* 21, 42.

[55] Recall from Chapter 1 Egon Bittner, *The Functions of the Police in Modern Society – A Review of Background Factors, Current Practices, and Possible Role Models* (New York, Jason Aronson, 1975) 46–47.

As discussed in Chapter 6, this internal, behavioural aspect of restraint is an essential element in giving law and the rule of law practical significance, and in ensuring that force is only used in appropriate and proportionate ways.[56]

The second attribute is responsibility. This encompasses the well-known idea of the state accepting and assuming its positive and negative obligations towards individuals, as required by Article 1 ECHR.[57] In substantive terms, the positive and negative obligations under Article 2 require the state and its agents to protect the right to life, to implement adequate regulatory frameworks, and in so doing to be reliable, professional and trustworthy in carrying out their duties including the resort to force.[58] As discussed in Chapter 6, responsibility (like restraint) is a question of regulation and culture, at both institutional and individual behavioural levels. In procedural terms, a responsible democratic state must take the required investigatory steps in the aftermath of uses of force, acting promptly and of its own motion rather than ignoring or covering up what has happened, and adhering to related values of humanity and sensitivity. In that regard, a responsible democratic society must be responsive, in the sense that it must demonstrate a readiness to recognise that its actions have had fatal or nearly fatal consequences and that it must deal with them, by complying at least with the minimum standards of the duty to investigate under Article 2. As Fionnuala Ní Aoláin has argued in relation to lethal force, given that recourse to force is often necessary in contemporary democratic societies, what a state claims about protecting the right to life is sometimes less important than what it actually does when it kills:

> the most meaningful and genuine test of a State's commitment to protect life is *how and by what means it responds to the taking of life by one of its own agents*. This means that the process of accounting for the taking of life has become as significant as the theoretical value of the right itself [emphasis added].[59]

Above all regarding this attribute of responsibility, as reflected in the ECtHR's engagement with the rule of law and the behavioural aspects of Article 2 narratives discussed in the previous chapter, a responsible democratic society must also be respectful of human rights. This requires not only respect in principle but also in practice, and therefore not just compliance with rules but also a qualitatively a priori respect for human rights and human dignity.[60] This raises requirements

[56] Compare Peter Squires and Peter Kennison, *Shooting to Kill? Policing, Firearms and Armed Response* (Chichester, Wiley-Blackwell, 2010) 1 who discuss what they call a 'restraint paradigm' in the context of British policing and its long-standing ethos of minimal force.

[57] Note AR Mowbray, *The Development of Positive Obligations under the European Convention on Human Rights by the European Court of Human Rights* (Oxford, Hart, 2004) 225.

[58] On positive obligations and the requirement for professional standards in policing see Mowbray, *The Development of Positive Obligations* 13. Note also *Makaratzis v Greece* (2004) paras 57–59 on the need for effective control over police personnel and the discussion in Chapter 6.

[59] Ní Aoláin, 'The Evolving Jurisprudence of the European Convention Concerning the Right to Life' 21, 42.

[60] For related international observations note Quirine Eijkman, 'A Socio-Legal Perspective on Human Rights and Policing' (2007) 25.1 *Netherlands Quarterly of Human Rights* 5, 10, 19 and specifically on

in the areas of regulation and training, and the need for the state to provide and support appropriate institutional cultures.[61] Respect for human rights, not only under Article 2 but more broadly across the range of ECHR rights and other national and international commitments, means that a democratic society accepts the value of all individuals, their worthiness of rights, and that respecting human rights is important as a universal social good, rather than an inconvenient obstacle to state conduct.

Thirdly, the most significant defining attribute of democratic society and the democratic state that can be identified in Article 2 case narratives is reflectiveness. As the ECtHR made clear in *McCann* when first shaping and justifying the implied procedural dimension of the right to life, the whole point of an investigation under Article 2 is for the state to review and learn from what has happened.[62] In that sense, a restrained and responsible democratic society and state can be said to be reflective where they are open to a process of inquiry and reform, recognising when necessary their own limits and fallibility, as well as their need and ability to learn and evolve, especially when state agents have caused death or endangered life.[63] Legal accountability through human rights law in the democratic context is not only about retrospective inquiry, apportionment of responsibility and liability, but also prospective information gathering and preparation for improvement, as well as the inherent systemic value per se of holding the state to account.[64] Notably, not only is this attribute identifiable through the Article 2 case narratives, but is also itself an inherently narrative process, as addressed in Chapter 2, through adjudication and accountability, and more generally in democratic society's processes of political reflection and discussion.

The argument that reflectiveness is essential to democratic society as a descriptive and teleological concept can be supported by Günter Frankenberg's theory of the 'learning sovereign'.[65] Frankenberg's concept of the sovereign in this context refers to 'the people' as the ultimate holders of sovereignty in democratic constitutionalism. He emphasises that the learning sovereign needs to be understood in two senses, as one who both *must* and who *can* learn, both of which

the UK see the discussion of police culture in Jane Gordon, 'A Developing Human Rights Culture in the UK? Case Studies of Policing' (2010) 6 *European Human Rights Law Review* 609, 610–13, 615, 619–20.

[61] Challenging questions arise in this regard in relation to, inter alia, tactics and the use of potentially dehumanising language to discuss operational objectives: for example, on the militarisation of policing and its potential effects see Squires and Kennison, *Shooting to Kill?* 196–97.

[62] *McCann* para 161.

[63] The importance of reflection in relation to force was stressed by Simone Weil (Mary McArthy, trans), 'The Iliad, or the Poem of Force' (1965 [1940]) 18.2 *Chicago Review* 5: 'The man who is the possessor of force seems to walk through a non-resistant element; in the human substance that surrounds him nothing has the power to interpose, between the impulse and the act, the tiny interval that is reflection. Where there is no room for reflection, there is none either for justice or prudence'.

[64] On accountability and learning in relation to Article 2 see also Baker, *Deaths After Police Contact* 41–43, 170–75.

[65] Günter Frankenberg, 'The Learning Sovereign' in András Sajó (ed), *Militant Democracy* (Utrecht, Eleven International Publishing, 2004) 113–32, 115–16.

can equally be applied here to the concept of democratic society in relation to Article 2.

In the first sense, the idea that democratic society must learn needs in part to be understood in terms of a rejection of its antithesis in the European context, that is, the range of anti-democratic, Fascist, Communist and other totalitarian and authoritarian regimes that haunted its pre-war, world war and Cold War past. These regimes were not 'obliged to learn'[66] by any systemic restraint, or generally even inclined to learn due to their ideological self-perception of supremacy, unless it was in their immediate interests to do so – the Führer, Duce or General Secretary of the Politbureau was always right. In contrast, Frankenberg argues that democracy is defined by its 'self-constraint', processes of political communication across sectors of society, accountability and transparency, due to the absence of an assumption that the sovereign power knows everything; as such, a democracy *must* learn.[67] In the European context, as discussed in Chapter 3, the post-war construction of the Council of Europe, the ECHR (and other European organisations) was essentially based on the sense of an obligation to learn in the aftermath of totalitarianism and conflict, 'never again' to return to that past and to ensure that its own potential weakness does not cause it to regress or allow past horrors to recur.[68]

In the second sense, a democratic society *can* learn in that it has the capability and capacity to learn, with processes for addressing experience and drawing from it for the future. In this regard Frankenberg relates lesson-learning to legitimation, suggesting that the ways in which 'learning experiences lead to practical consequences' can confer legitimacy on the application of rules.[69] Here it is perhaps important to add to Frankenberg's outline that a capability and a capacity to learn presuppose a willingness to do so as the result of any learning process that it must undertake,[70] and require a degree of flexibility in seeking to learn, as well as resilience in managing any resultant change. Extrapolating from Frankenberg's abstract constitutional argument to the human rights sphere, this points to the ways in which rights norms can enable democratic societies to learn through accountability processes, in which ECHR law and Article 2's procedural dimension are essential elements, and in so doing support the legitimacy of both the norms that justify the learning[71] and the state power that is thereby restrained and ideally improved as a result.[72]

[66] Frankenberg, 'The Learning Sovereign' 115.

[67] Frankenberg, 'The Learning Sovereign' 115.

[68] On these points see further the discussion in Catherine Dupré, *The Age of Dignity: Human Rights and Constitutionalism in Europe* (Oxford, Hart, 2015) 179, 183.

[69] Frankenberg, 'The Learning Sovereign' 115.

[70] Compare Baker, *Deaths After Police Contact* 175.

[71] Mark Tushnet, 'Critical Legal Studies and the Rule of Law' (7 March 2018) in Martin Loughlin and Jens Meierhenrich (eds), *Cambridge Companion to the Rule of Law* (Cambridge, Cambridge University Press, forthcoming), Harvard Public Law Working Paper No 18-14: https://ssrn.com/abstract=3135903.

[72] Dupré, *The Age of Dignity* 179–80.

By extension, both of these senses indicate that democratic society *needs* to learn, in that it is neither perfect (it can get things wrong), nor fully accomplished yet (it can get better). In the area of Article 2 law, this is the main aim of the procedural dimension, as first indicated by the ECtHR in *McCann*. This understanding of democratic society as a 'work in progress' is apparent in the teleological aspect of Article 2 narratives in which 'democratic society' is an aspirational concept for the improvement of High Contracting Parties' compliance with ECHR standards.[73] Democracy in this regard is not static but arguably always a process of democratisation, or the development and enhancement of democratic practices and qualities, which is not only applicable to systems moving away from a non-democratic past.[74]

The reflective attribute of democratic society also relates to the narrative concept of jurisgenesis in Cover's theory of nomos and narrative, and Ricoeur's element of narrative communication, as outlined above. To be reflective and to be able to learn, a democratic society needs to be deliberative and discursive, to have systems in place to foster learning through responsive democratic processes. Under Article 2, this means investigative procedures that can identify what needs to be learned, institutions (government, police and military) that can learn, as well as a court structure – including access to the ECtHR – for supporting the investigation, accountability and reflection processes. Yet taking this further, a democratic society cannot only be effectively reflective in one domain, and arguably needs to embrace a wider culture of learning. In that sense, narratives under Article 2 and alternative socio-political narratives about the issues involved need to be able to find a space to encounter one another at the intersection of concerns with legality and legitimacy, for jurisgenesis to occur through the meeting of narratives,[75] and cross-narrative communication among different sectors of civil society to inform democratic reflection. In the democratic context, narrative communication and dialogue in human rights law should not only be the preserve of governments and courts.[76]

At a time when violent crime and the threat of terrorism dominate political debate about domestic policing and law enforcement, the relevance of these issues

[73] See also Pierre Rosanvallon (Arthur Goldhammer, trans), *Democratic Legitimacy: Impartiality, Reflexivity, Proximity* (Princeton, Princeton University Press, 2011) 226: 'Democracy then points towards a social organization that is still a work in progress, which cannot claim to have been fully achieved anywhere'.

[74] Dupré, *The Age of Dignity* 183–85.

[75] Cover, 'Foreword: Nomos and Narrative' 68; Michael Ryan, 'Meaning and Alternity' in Martha Minow, Michael Ryan and Austin Sarat (eds), *Narrative, Violence and the Law: The Essays of Robert Cover* (Ann Arbor, The University of Michigan Press, 1995) 267, 271; Linden-Retek, 'Cosmopolitan Law and Time' 178; Julen Etxabe, 'The Legal Universe after Robert Cover' (2010) 4.1 *Law and Humanities* 115, 147.

[76] Recall the discussion of the significance of core values in Article 2 law for civil society in II.A above and the discussion of public confidence in the state's monopoly of force in Chapter 6, II.B. Note on England and Wales Baker, *Deaths After Police Contact* 173–92 on accountability relationships and the roles of different actors and audiences.

of narrative meanings and the attributes of democratic society in relation to the state's use of force could be called into question. In cruder terms, it might be asked, what use is a narrative of democratic society against an armed robber, a knife attack, a riot or a terrorist? Perhaps a blunt response here would be, 'not much'. When the AK-47s are blazing, it is important to know that the police can shoot back to protect those at risk, and that agents of the state are not required to let themselves become easy targets in the name of liberal values, or let passers-by die while contemplating politico-legal identity. When tackling organised and violent crime, dealing with serious disorder, or responding to terrorist attacks, thinking about how a narrative might seek to make sense of the state's response, and to situate it in relation to European history or human rights standards, might seem a low priority. In a time of crisis, it may be argued, human rights and theories of democracy must give way to a robust response to threats, unfettered by conceptual niceties. When a democratic society needs to protect itself, the argument might run (as indeed it did for the dissentients in *McCann*), the law must facilitate and not hinder.

And yet, it is argued here, the way that we understand and make sense of responses to such situations, and thereby how responses should be prepared and managed, is essential to the construction and conservation of the concept and reality of democratic society, in the name of which those responses are made. As famously noted by Aharon Barak, President of the Supreme Court of Israel:

> This is the destiny of democracy, as not all means are acceptable to it, and not all practices employed by its enemies are open before it. Although a democracy must often fight with one hand tied behind its back, it nonetheless has the upper hand. Preserving the Rule of Law and recognition of an individual's liberty constitutes an important component in its understanding of security. At the end of the day, they strengthen its spirit and its strength and allow it to overcome its difficulties.[77]

Democratic society may need, or even be obliged, to take action to preserve itself, and a narrative of its attributes and values is an essential part of acknowledging and conserving the core that it seeks to protect.[78] Although balancing legal protection of human rights with operational demands is always a challenge, especially in the area of the state's use of force in domestic policing and law enforcement,

[77] HCJ 5100/94, *Public Committee against Torture in Israel v The State of Israel* (6 September 1999) para 39. See also Aharon Barak, *The Judge in a Democracy* (Princeton, Princeton University Press, 2006) 283–87 and 'On Judging' in Martin Scheinin, Helle Krunke and Marina Aksenova (eds), *Judges as Guardians of Constitutionalism and Human Rights* (Cheltenham, Edward Elgar, 2016) 27, 32–35; and Tom Bingham, *The Rule of Law* (London, Allen Lane, 2010) 158–59. On similar arguments relating to the issue of targeted killing note HCJ 769/02, *The Public Committee against Torture in Israel v The Government of Israel* (11 December 2005) paras 61–64 and the discussions of legality, legitimacy and the right to life in Nils Melzer, *Targeted Killing in International Law* (Oxford, Oxford University Press, 2009) 433–34 and Mary Ellen O'Connell, 'The Law on Lethal Force Begins with the Right to Life' (2016) 3.2 *Journal on the Use of Force and International Law* 205.

[78] Compare Conor Gearty, 'Is the Human Rights Era Drawing to a Close?' (2017) 5 *European Human Rights Law Review* 425, 431. See also Ian Loader and Neil Walker, *Civilizing Security* (Cambridge, Cambridge University Press, 2007) 4, 7–29.

as Barak observes the rule of law, liberty and security need to be understood as interconnected rather than opposites in the democratic context.[79]

In conclusion, this chapter has addressed the outcomes and implications of the analyses of Article 2 and related cases in the areas of lethal and potentially lethal force in policing and law enforcement activities that were set out in the previous chapters. It has considered the impact of the use of force in relation to meaning-making about it through human rights law, and the narrative function under Article 2 of differentiating between acceptable force and unacceptable violence. The chapter has then shown how, through a cumulative and inductive reading of the case law, core attributes of democratic society and the democratic state can be delineated, which can support the development and maintenance of clear standards in the policing and law enforcement context. In a time of change, doubt and political fragility, it is argued that reflecting on the attributes of democratic society and the democratic state that can be seen to flow from Article 2 judgments is a vital part of maintaining a clear focus on core values, by the ECtHR, states and in wider democratic society, even in the face of threats, and as sources of strength in preparing for and overcoming them.

[79] Linos-Alexandre Sicilianos has argued in 'The European Court of Human Rights at a Time of Crisis in Europe' (2016) 2 *European Human Rights Law Review* 121, 134 that the ECtHR 'refuses to enter into the dilemma of the false choice between liberty and security. It advocates both liberty and security at the same time'.

8

Conclusion

> '"I will start with a question which I address chiefly to myself," said Don Fernando. "What does it mean to be against death?"'[1]

The aim of this book has been to explore the possible connections between the right to life under Article 2 ECHR and democratic society in the context of the use of lethal and potentially lethal force by the state. The book's starting points were the foundational declarations by the ECtHR in its landmark judgment in the case of *McCann and Others v United Kingdom*,[2] in which it said that Article 2 on the right to life enshrines a basic value of the democratic societies making up the Council of Europe, and as such is an important provision requiring 'most careful scrutiny'. To question why and how the ECtHR linked the right to life with democratic society and what the implications of this interconnection might be, the book has developed a dual analysis of Article 2 law on the state's use of force. It has thus sought to contribute to understanding of this area of ECHR law in doctrinal terms by examining the specificities of Article 2 law and the ECtHR's reasoning, and to develop a critical reflection on the right to life in relation to democratic society and state uses of force by drawing on theories of narrative. The main objective overall has been to highlight that the right to life's connections with democratic society, as apparent in Article 2 law, can be understood as a source of values and a basis for a sense of identity that could serve to strengthen Article 2's normative thrust.

The book's narrative analysis of Article 2 law has built on antecedent work in legal theory and human rights law, based on the argument that narrative is a fundamental human mode of understanding and making sense of experience, which is equally apparent in law. It has been developed by drawing specifically on the work of Robert Cover, whose seminal contribution to jurisprudence situated law in relation to wider social, political and cultural narratives of meaning, and Paul Ricoeur, whose hermeneutic analysis of narrative in fictional and historiographical texts elucidated their processes of representation and interpretation. Observing the relevance of narrative to human rights law, given the nature of rights

[1] Antonio Tabucchi (JC Patrick, trans), *The Missing Head of Damasceno Monteiro* (New York, New Directions Publishing, 1999 [1997]) 164.
[2] *McCann and Others v United Kingdom* (1995) paras 147 and 150.

and the processes of adjudication, justification and accountability they involve, especially in the complex context of the ECHR, the book has used these theorists' engagement with narrative to guide the discussion and identify key aspects of meaning-making and meaning-contingency in Article 2 law. This has involved an endeavour to engage with the layers of theoretical, historical and socio-political significance encapsulated in the right to life and its connections with democratic society as responses to state uses of force, and to reflect on how ECtHR judgments themselves constitute narratives. In that sense the book has considered the function of judgments in making meaning from experience – which in the area of Article 2 law involves death or serious harm and the state conduct that caused it – by configuring interpretations of fact and law to determine state compliance with the right to life as understood in relation to democratic society. In so doing, judgments as narratives communicate meaning about the scope of that right and thereby the nature of democratic society itself.

The book has shown how the concept of democratic society as referred to by the ECtHR can be understood to have three main meanings. One is a purportedly descriptive meaning, which is meant to reflect the actual practices and identities of Member States in the Council of Europe, whilst also reflecting an idealised version of their history and values. Another meaning is more of a term of art in the ECHR system, which encapsulates the ECtHR's approach to contextually-informed proportionate compromise or balance in determining the scope and application of rights. A third meaning is normative, which indicates the ECtHR's purposive or teleological approach to fostering and enhancing democratic values and standards. Through its narratively configured connection between the right to life and democratic society, the ECtHR has on one hand underlined the importance of that right and the need to protect it through high standards, and on the other made allowances for balance and restriction in the protection that right affords, in the name of state interests and competing needs. Interpreting Article 2 to include substantive dimensions (covering the use of force itself, the domestic legal and regulatory framework, and state planning and control measures) and procedural dimensions (the duty to investigate), the ECtHR has established a sophisticated set of legal mechanisms for controlling the use of force and state responses to it. Yet while these have led to the development of extensive criteria for evaluating state compliance with the right to life, they have not always communicated a clear sense of standards, with proportionality and subsidiarity at times appearing to prevail over the expression of normative benchmarks.

In that light, the book has sought to identify some core purposes and values associated with the concept of democratic society that it argues run through these decisions on the right to life and the state's use of force. These include an understanding of the rule of law as a basis for controlling state power; the right to life under the rule of law as a distinguishing feature of democratic systems in contrast with the experience of totalitarian orders; and the rule of law as a connective and protective mechanism underpinning democratic society. In addition to these, the case law points to core qualitative and behavioural requirements relating to state conduct that provide an essential human, and social, adjunct to the systemic representation of human rights and their protection by law. Of particular importance in this regard is the need for a culture of adherence to human rights norms, not only in terms of compliance with rules, but also an attitudinal predisposition to respect human life. In addition, in socio-political terms, the case law underlines the need for awareness of the purpose and effect of Article 2 law in relation to public confidence in the state. Lastly here, Article 2 law points to requirements of humanity in the treatment of all those affected by the use of force.

In its final chapter, the book discussed the challenge of producing what Robert Cover referred to as common meanings through the interpretation and application of law in the context of coercive force and its impact on the human body. Focusing on the right to life and taking the analysis back to its starting point in the deprivation of life or infliction of serious harm, the chapter considered how such matters represent theoretical challenges to law and the extent to which judgments on Article 2 addresses them. Here the book reflected on the classificatory role of human rights law in distinguishing between unacceptable violence and acceptable force exercised in the name of democratic society. Death or life-threatening harm cannot be reversed, but the ways in which the conduct causing them is authoritatively interpreted in terms of the matrix of values in relation to which state and society operate and define themselves can result in that conduct and its consequences being classified as legitimate or illegitimate.

Taking the core elements of the case law together and working inductively from the meanings and values developed across the case narratives, the book has argued that the overarching significance of this body of law on Article 2 is to outline a set of attributes that a democratic society, and within it a democratic state, should have, according to the understanding of the ECtHR. This has resulted in an outline of democratic society as a restrained, responsible and reflective system. Although general and abstract, these attributes have been used to propose a normative core for democratic society as both restrained by law and self-restraining; responsible in its adherence to human rights and its legal obligations to protect them, as well as being responsive when it has or may have interfered with them and respectful in its treatment of individuals and their inherent worth; and reflective in its need and willingness to learn, in order to improve its practices and as an essential manifestation of democracy's deliberative foundations. These normative attributes can serve to crystallise and underline the purposive thrust of Article 2 law and the right to life – democratic society nexus. Whilst it is hoped that this could support the elaboration of firmer standards in ECtHR judgments themselves, given the political constraints on what that institution can achieve, and is willing to address, these attributes are perhaps primarily significant at the level of civil society and in critical engagement with the content and potential of ECHR law. This analysis of the implications of the right to life and related case law on lethal and potentially lethal force, it is argued, brings to light the normative foundations and the potential that are immanent within the ECtHR's treatment of Article 2, in order to complement the extensive and technical criteria it has developed with guiding rationales.

This analysis of the right to life and democratic society through the lens of narrative is just a beginning, however, and raises various possibilities for future development.[3] As explained in the Introduction, the book has concentrated on one part of Article 2 law, and it is envisaged that this discussion of narratives and democratic society could also be extended to the areas of deaths in custody or the care of the state, disappearances, and other uses of force, including the scope of Article 3 and techniques of (supposedly) non-lethal or less-lethal coercion. Similarly, the wider perspectives on public confidence and the parallel socio-political narratives around the state's use of force, its legitimacy and relationships of accountability, could also be explored in more detail through narrative theory, to address the intersections and gaps between human rights law and vernacular or cultural frameworks of understanding. In that respect, the wider relevance of uses of lethal and potentially lethal force in democratic society raises the question of differing perspectives on what state agents can lawfully do, and whether there is a clear correspondence among popular understanding of, and expectations about, policing powers (especially the use of firearms), what the law allows and requires, and what training encompasses.

Ongoing engagement with these issues of rights, state power and the reflection and protection of core values through law is essential. At the time of writing, democratic society in Europe seems to be more fragile than ever before. Populism, scepticism and resentment directed at transnational organisations, security crises and terrorism, economic uncertainty, xenophobic claims about protecting national or European culture, and threats to the rule of law seem to be undermining the meaning of democracy and European cohesion around it. In such volatile conditions, recognising the core values in ECtHR narratives about the right to life, the most fundamental human right in the ECHR, and its connections with democratic society, is acutely important, as a step towards not only developing clear and consistent standards for protecting that right but also, it is to be hoped at least, communicating and reinforcing what democratic society itself entails. Judgments on state uses of lethal and potentially lethal force hold a mirror to Member States of the Council of Europe, focusing attention on their values and their practices in the most extreme situations, in which the most basic right is at its most vulnerable. Through their actions and reactions, the nature of states becomes apparent. It is essential to recall that death cannot be undone, while democracy can be. The value of life and the values of democracy therefore depend on the respect and protection they are given. This book's analysis of Article 2 law has shown that the right to life, state uses of force, and the nature of democratic society are interconnected. The narratives that represent this interconnection and why it matters are ultimately narratives of democratic society's very identity.

[3] As Rainer Forst has argued, developing a critical theory should be 'an activity that also reflects back on itself and its own blind spots and exclusions in a self-critical manner': see *Justification and Critique: Towards a Critical Theory of Politics* (Cambridge, Polity Press, 2014) 8.

BIBLIOGRAPHY

Alder, John, 'Robert Cover's "Nomos and Narrative": The Court as Philosopher King or Pontius Pilate?' (2006) 6 *Issues in Legal Scholarship* (article 4; no page numbers)

Almog, Shulamit, 'As I Read, I Weep – In Praise of Judicial Narrative' (2001) 26.2 *Oklahoma City University Law Review* 471

Alston, Philip (ed), *The EU and Human Rights* (Oxford, Oxford University Press, 1999)

Altman, Rick, *A Theory of Narrative* (New York, Columbia University Press, 2008)

Amsterdam, Anthony G and Bruner, Jerome, *Minding the Law* (Cambridge, Mass, Harvard University Press, 2000)

Anagnostou, Dia and Mungiu-Pippidi, Alina, 'Domestic Implementation of Human Rights Judgments in Europe: Legal Infrastructure and Government Effectiveness Matter' (2014) 25.1 *European Journal of International Law* 205

Andrews, John, 'Right to Life in Gibraltar' (1996) 21.4 *European Law Review* 333

—— 'Case Comment – Article 7: No Punishment Without Law' (2002) 27 *European Law Review* 176

Arai-Takahashi, Yutaka, *The Margin of Appreciation Doctrine and the Principle of Proportionality in the Jurisprudence of the ECHR* (Antwerp, Intersentia, 2002)

Arnold, Jörg, Karsten, Nora and Kreicker, Helmut, 'The German Border Guard Cases before the European Court of Human Rights' (2003) 11.1 *European Journal of Crime, Criminal Law and Criminal Justice* 67

Asmal, Kader, *Shoot to Kill: International Lawyers' Inquiry into the Lethal Use of Firearms by the Security Forces in Northern Ireland* (Cork and Dublin, The Mercier Press, 1985)

Axtmann, Roland, *Democracy: Problems and Perspectives* (Edinburgh, Edinburgh University Press, 2007)

Bailyn, Bernard, *The Ideological Origins of the American Revolution* (Cambridge, Mass, Harvard University Press, 1967)

Baker, David, *Deaths After Police Contact: Constructing Accountability in the 21st Century* (London, Palgrave Macmillan, 2016)

—— 'Deaths After Police Contact in England and Wales: The Effects of Article 2 of the European Convention on Human Rights on Coronial Practice' (2016) 12.2 *International Journal of Law in Context* 162

Baker, Keith Michael, 'The Idea of a Declaration of Rights' in Dale Van Kley (ed), *The French Idea of Freedom: The Old Regime and the Declaration of Rights of 1789* (Stanford, Stanford University Press, 1994) 154

Bakircioglu, Onder and Dickson, Brice, 'The European Convention in Conflicted Societies: The Experience of Northern Ireland and Turkey' (2017) 66 *International and Comparative Law Quarterly* 263

Balkin, JM, 'Understanding Legal Understanding: The Legal Subject and the Problem of Legal Coherence' (1993) 103 *Yale Law Journal* 105

Banakar, Reza (ed), *Rights in Context: Law and Justice in Late Modern Society* (Farnham, Ashgate, 2012)

Barak, Aharon, *The Judge in a Democracy* (Princeton, Princeton University Press, 2006)

—— 'On Judging' in Martin Scheinin, Helle Krunke and Marina Aksenova (eds), *Judges as Guardians of Constitutionalism and Human Rights* (Cheltenham, Edward Elgar, 2016) 27–49

Baron, Jane B and Epstein, Julia, 'Is Law Narrative?' (1997) 45 *Buffalo Law Review* 141

Barthes, Roland (Lionel Duisit, trans), 'An Introduction to the Structural Analysis of Narrative' (1975) 6.2 *New Literary History* 237

Bates, Ed, *The Evolution of the European Court of Human Rights: From its Inception to the Creation of a Permanent Court of Human Rights* (Oxford, Oxford University Press, 2010)
Beetham, David, *Democracy and Human Rights* (Cambridge, Polity Press, 1999)
Beitz, Charles, *The Idea of Human Rights* (Oxford, Oxford University Press, 2009)
Bell, Christine and Keenan, Johanna, 'Lost on the Way Home? The Right to Life in Northern Ireland' (2005) 32.1 *Journal of Law and Society* 68
Belur, Jyoti, *Permission to Shoot? Police Use of Deadly Force in Democracies* (New York, Springer, 2010)
Benedek, Wolfgang, Isak, Hubert and Kicker, Renate (eds), *Development and Developing International and European Law* (Frankfurt am Main, Peter Lang, 1999)
Benveniste, Émile (Mary E Meek, trans), *Problems in General Linguistics* (Coral Gables, University of Miami Press, 1971)
Besson, Samantha, 'Human Rights: Ethical, Political ... or Legal? First Steps in a Legal Theory of Human Rights' in Donald Earl Childress, III (ed), *The Role of Ethics in International Law* (Cambridge, Cambridge University Press, 2011) 211
Bianchi, Andrea and Keller, Alexis with Barela, Steven J (eds), *Counterterrorism: Democracy's Challenge* (Oxford, Hart, 2008)
Binder, Guyora and Weisberg, Robert, *Literary Criticisms of Law* (Princeton, Princeton University Press, 2000)
Bingham, Tom, *The Rule of Law* (London, Allen Lane, 2010)
Bittner, Egon, *The Functions of the Police in Modern Society* (New York, Jason Aronson, 1975)
Björgvinsson, David Thór, 'The Role of Judges of the European Court of Human Rights as Guardians of Fundamental Rights of the Individual' in Martin Scheinin, Helle Krunke and Marina Aksenova (eds), *Judges as Guardians of Constitutionalism and Human Rights* (Cheltenham, Edward Elgar, 2016) 329
Blackstone, William, *Commentaries on the Laws of England* (Oxford, Clarendon Press, 1765)
Blanke, Hermann-Josef and Mangiameli, Stelio (eds), *The European Union After Lisbon: Constitutional Basis, Economic Order and External Action* (Berlin, Springer, 2012)
Bottoms, Anthony E and Tankebe, Justice, 'Police Legitimacy and the Authority of the State' in Antje du Bois-Pedain, Magnus Ulväng and Petter Asp (eds), *Criminal Law and the Authority of the State* (Oxford, Hart, 2017) 47
Bovens, Mark, 'Analysing and Assessing Accountability: A Conceptual Framework' (2007) 13.4 *European Law Journal* 447
—— 'Two Concepts of Accountability: Accountability as a Virtue and as a Mechanism' (2010) 33.5 *West European Politics* 946
Bovens, Mark, Goodin, Robert E and Schillemans, Thomas (eds), *The Oxford Handbook of Public Accountability* (Oxford, Oxford University Press, 2014)
Bovens, Mark, Schillemans, Thomas and Goodin, Robert E, 'Public Accountability' in Mark Bovens, Robert E Goodin and Thomas Schillemans (eds), *The Oxford Handbook of Public Accountability* (Oxford, Oxford University Press, 2014) 1
Boyle, CK, 'The Concept of Arbitrary Deprivation of Life' in BG Ramcharan (ed), *The Right to Life in International Law* (Dordrecht, Martinus Nijhoff, 1985) 221
Bradbury, Mary, *Representations of Death: A Social Psychological Perspective* (London, Routledge, 1999)
Brady, James B and Garver, Newton (eds), *Justice, Law and Violence* (Philadelphia, Temple University Press, 1991)
—— 'Introduction to the Issues' in Brady, James B and Garver, Newton (eds), *Justice, Law and Violence* (Philadelphia, Temple University Press, 1991) 1
Brannan, James, 'Coming to Terms with the Supranational: Translating for the European Court of Human Rights' (2013) 26.4 *International Journal for the Semiotics of Law* 909–925
Bratza, Sir Nicolas, 'Living Instrument or Dead Letter – The Future of the European Convention on Human Rights (2014) 2 *European Human Rights Law Review* 116
Brems, Eva, 'Procedural Protection: An Examination of Procedural Safeguards Read into Substantive Convention Rights' in Eva Brems and Janneke Gerards (eds), *Shaping Rights in the ECHR* (Cambridge, Cambridge University Press, 2013) 137

Brems, Eva and Gerards, Janneke (eds), *Shaping Rights in the ECHR: The Role of the European Court of Human Rights in Determining the Scope of Human Rights* (Cambridge, Cambridge University Press, 2013)

British Irish Rights Watch, the Committee on the Administration of Justice, Inquest and Liberty (the National Council for Civil Liberties), joint Third Party Intervention in the case of *McCann and Others v United Kingdom* (November 1994)

Brodeur, Jean-Paul, 'Police et coercition' (1994) 35 *Revue française de sociologie* 457

Brooks, Peter, 'Narrativity of the Law' (2002) 14.1 *Law and Literature* 1

—— 'Narrative Transactions – Does the Law Need a Narratology?' (2006) 18.1 *Yale Journal of Law and the Humanities* 1

Brooks, Peter and Gewirtz, Paul (eds), *Law's Stories: Narrative and Rhetoric in the Law*, (New Haven, Yale University Press, 1996)

Brooks, Thom, 'Let a Thousand Nomoi Bloom? Four Problems with Robert Cover's "Nomos and Narrative"' (2006) 6 *Issues in Legal Scholarship* (article 5; no page numbers)

Brooks-Gordon, Belinda, Ebtehaj, Fatemeh, Herring, Jonathan and Johnson, Martin (eds), *Death Rites and Rights* (Oxford, Hart, 2007)

Brown, Kris, 'Rights and Victims, Martyrs and Memories: The European Court of Human Rights and Political Transition in Northern Ireland' in Antoine Buyse and Michael Hamilton (eds), *Transitional Jurisprudence and the ECHR: Justice, Politics and Rights* (Cambridge, Cambridge University Press, 2011) 52

Buchanan, Allen, 'Human Rights and the Legitimacy of the International Order' (2008) 14.1 *Legal Theory* 39

—— *The Heart of Human Rights* (Oxford, Oxford University Press, 2013)

Buckley, Carla, 'The European Convention on Human Rights and the Right to Life in Turkey' (2001) 1.1 *Human Rights Law Review* 35

Buyse, Antoine and Hamilton, Michael (eds), *Transitional Jurisprudence and the ECHR: Justice, Politics and Rights* (Cambridge, Cambridge University Press, 2011)

Çali, Başak, 'Balancing Human Rights? Methodological Problems with Weights, Scales and Proportions' (2007) 29 *Human Rights Quarterly* 251

Campbell, Tom, Ewing, KD and Tomkins, Adam (eds), *Sceptical Essays on Human Rights* (Oxford, Oxford University Press, 2001)

Caranti, Luigi, 'Kant's Theory of Human Rights' in Thomas Cushman (ed), *Handbook of Human Rights* (Abingdon, Routledge, 2014) 35

'Case Comment: Investigation of Police Operations' (2016) 4 *European Human Rights Law Review* 442

'Case Comment: Terrorist Hostage Taking and Rescue Missions' (2017) 4 *European Human Rights Law Review* 400

Casey-Maslen, Stuart (ed), *Weapons Under International Human Rights Law* (Cambridge, Cambridge University Press, 2014)

—— 'The Use of Firearms in Law Enforcement' in Stuart Casey-Maslen (ed), *Weapons Under International Human Rights Law* (Cambridge, Cambridge University Press, 2014) 3

Casey-Maslen, Stuart and Connolly, Sean, *Police Use of Force under International Law* (Cambridge, Cambridge University Press, 2017)

Chau, P-L and Herring, Jonathan, 'The Meaning of Death' in Belinda Brooks-Gordon, Fatemeh Ebtehaj, Jonathan Herring and Martin Johnson (eds), *Death Rites and Rights* (Oxford, Hart, 2007) 13

Checkel, Jeffrey T, 'International Institutions and Socialization in Europe: Introduction and Framework' (2005) 59 *International Organization* 801

Chernishova, Olga, 'Right to the Truth in the Case-Law of the European Court of Human Rights' in Lawrence Early, Anna Austin, Clare Ovey and Olga Chernishova (eds), *The Right to Life under Article 2 of the European Convention on Human Rights: Twenty Years of Legal Developments since McCann v The United Kingdom* (Oisterwijk, Wolf Legal Publishers, 2016) 145

Chevalier-Watts, Juliet, 'A Rock and a Hard Place: Has the European Court of Human Rights Permitted Discrepancies to Evolve in their Scrutiny of Right to Life Cases?' (2010) 14.2 *The International Journal of Human Rights* 300

—— 'Effective Investigations under Article 2 of the European Convention on Human Rights: Securing the Right to Life or an Onerous Burden on a State?' (2010) 21.3 *European Journal of International Law* 701

Childress, Donald Earl, III (ed), *The Role of Ethics in International Law* (Cambridge, Cambridge University Press, 2011)

Cohen, Samy (ed), *Democracies at War against Terrorism: A Comparative Perspective* (Basingstoke, Palgrave Macmillan, 2008)

—— 'Introduction: Dilemmas in the War against Terrorism' in Samy Cohen (ed), *Democracies at War against Terrorism: A Comparative Perspective* (Basingstoke, Palgrave Macmillan, 2008) 1

Coles, Deborah, Inquest, 'European Court of Human Rights – family to challenge UK government failure to prosecute police officers: background briefing on the broader context of the shooting of Jean Charles de Menezes' (4 June 2015)

Collins, Randall, 'Entering and Leaving the Tunnel of Violence' (2012) 61.2 *Current Sociology* 132

Connolly, Christopher K, 'Seeking the Final Court of Justice: The European Court of Human Rights and Accountability for State Violence in Northern Ireland' (2007) 9 *San Diego International Law Journal* 81

Costa, Jean-Paul, 'On the Legitimacy of the European Court of Human Rights' Judgments' (2011) 7.2 *European Constitutional Law Review* 173

Costa, Pietro and Zolo, Danilo, *The Rule of Law: History, Theory and Criticism* (Berlin, Springer, 2007)

Council of Europe, *Collected Edition of the Travaux Préparatoires of the European Convention on Human Rights* (The Hague, Martinus Nijhoff, 1975–1985)

—— 'Explanatory Report to Protocol No. 11 to the Convention for the Protection of Human Rights and Fundamental Freedoms, restructuring the control machinery established thereby', European Treaty Series no 155 (11 May 1994)

—— Warsaw Declaration, 17 May 2005

Cover, Robert M, 'Foreword: Nomos and Narrative' (1983) 97 *Harvard Law Review* 4

—— 'Violence and the Word' (1985) 95 *Yale Law Journal* 1601

Craig, Paul P, 'Formal and Substantive Conceptions of the Rule of Law: An Analytical Framework' (1997) *Public Law* 467

Crawford, James, 'Democracy and International Law' (1993) 64 *British Yearbook of International Law* 113

Crawshaw, Ralph, 'International Standards on the Right to Life and the Use of Force by Police' (1999) 3.4 *International Journal of Human Rights* 67

Crawshaw, Ralph, Devlin, Barry and Williamson, Tom, *Human Rights and Policing: Standards for Good Behaviour and a Strategy for Change* (The Hague, Kluwer Law International, 1998)

Croce, Mariano, 'La Democrazia come Reciproco Processo di Apprendimento: Procedure Giuridiche e Diritti Umani' (2005) 24 *Ragion Pratica* 281

Cruft, Rowan, Liao, S Matthew and Renzo, Massimo (eds), *Philosophical Foundations of Human Rights* (Oxford, Oxford University Press, 2015)

Curran, Vivian Grosswald, 'Law's Past and Europe's Future' (2005) 6.2 *German Law Journal* 483

Cushman, Thomas (ed), *Handbook of Human Rights* (Abingdon, Routledge, 2014)

Dahl, Robert A, 'Can International Organizations be Democratic? A Skeptic's View' in Ian Shapiro and Casiano Hacker-Cordón (eds), *Democracy's Edges* (Cambridge, Cambridge University Press, 1999) 19

Dauenhauer, Bernard P, 'Ricoeur and Political Identity' in Morny Joy (ed) *Paul Ricoeur and Narrative: Context and Contestation* (Alberta, University of Calgary Press, 1997) 129

De Sanctis, Francesco, 'What Duties do States have with Regard to the Rules of Engagement and the Training of Security Forces under Article 2 of the European Convention on Human Rights?' (2006) 10.1 *International Journal of Human Rights* 31

De Stefani, Paolo, 'Il Diritto alla vita e la sua tutela internazionale' in Paolo De Stefani and Francisco Leita (eds), *La Tutela Giuridica Internazionale dei Diritti Umani* (Padova, CEDAM, 1997) 9

De Stefani, Paolo and Leita, Francisco (eds), *La Tutela Giuridica Internazionale dei Diritti Umani* (Padova, CEDAM, 1997)

De Than, Claire, 'Mistaken Belief in Self-Defence May Justify Use of Lethal Force' (2001) 65 *Journal of Criminal Law* 417

Decaux, Emmanuel, 'Les États parties et leurs engagements' in Louis-Edmond Pettiti, Emmanuel Decaux and Pierre-Henri Imbert (eds), *La Convention Européenne des Droits de l'Homme* (Paris, Economica, 1999) 3

Delgado, Richard, 'Storytelling for Oppositionists and Others: A Plea for Narrative' (1989) 87.8 *Michigan Law Review* 2411

Delmas-Marty, Mireille (ed), (Christine Chodkiewicz, trans), *The European Convention for the Protection of Human Rights: International Protection versus National Restrictions* (Dordrecht, Martinus Nijhoff Publishers, 1992)

—— 'The Richness of Underlying Legal Reasoning' in Delmas-Marty, Mireille (Christine Chodkiewicz, trans), *The European Convention for the Protection of Human Rights: International Protection versus National Restrictions* (Dordrecht, Martinus Nijhoff Publishers, 1992) 319

Dembour, Marie-Bénédicte, *Who Believes in Human Rights? Reflections on the European Convention* (Cambridge, Cambridge University Press, 2006)

Demske, James M, *Being, Man and Death: A Key to Heidegger* (Lexington, University Press of Kentucky, 1970)

Dicey, Albert Venn, *Lectures Introductory to the Study of the Law of the Constitution* (London, Macmillan & Co., 1885)

Dickson, Brice, *The European Convention on Human Rights and the Conflict in Northern Ireland* (Oxford, Oxford University Press, 2010)

—— 'The Planning and Control of Operations Involving the Use of Lethal Force' in Lawrence Early, Anna Austin, Clare Ovey and Olga Chernishova (eds), *The Right to Life under Article 2 of the European Convention on Human Rights: Twenty Years of Legal Developments since McCann v the United Kingdom* (Oisterwijk, Wolf Legal Publishers, 2016) 47

Dinstein, Yoram, 'The Right to Life, Physical Integrity, and Liberty' in Louis Henkin, *The International Bill of Rights: The Covenant on Civil and Political Rights* (New York, Columbia University Press, 1981) 114

Dogliani, Mario, 'I Diritti dell'uomo: Principi universali o ideologia?' in Mario Dogliani and Stefano Sicardi (eds), *Diritti Umani e Uso della Forza: Profili di diritto costituzionale interno e internazionale* (Turin, Giappichelli, 1999) 45

Dogliani, Mario and Sicardi, Stefano (eds), *Diritti Umani e Uso della Forza: Profili di diritto costituzionale interno e internazionale* (Turin, Giappichelli, 1999)

Doherty, Fiona and Mageean, Paul, *Investigating Lethal Force Deaths in Northern Ireland* (Belfast, Northern Ireland Human Rights Commission, 2006)

du Bois-Pedain, Antje, Ulväng, Magnus and Asp, Petter (eds), *Criminal Law and the Authority of the State* (Oxford, Hart, 2017)

Dubnick, Melvin J, 'Accountability as a Cultural Keyword' in Mark Bovens, Robert E Goodin and Thomas Schillemans (eds), *The Oxford Handbook of Public Accountability* (Oxford, Oxford University Press, 2014) 23

Dugard, John, 'International Law and the South African Constitution' (1997) *European Journal of International Law* 77

Duncan, G, *Democratic Theory and Practice* (Cambridge, Cambridge University Press, 1983)

Dupré, Catherine, *The Age of Dignity: Human Rights and Constitutionalism in Europe* (Oxford, Hart, 2015)

Duranti, Marco, *The Conservative Human Rights Revolution: European Identity, Transnational Politics, and the Origins of the European Convention* (Oxford, Oxford University Press, 2017)

Duxbury, Alison, *The Participation of States in International Organisations: The Role of Human Rights and Democracy* (Cambridge, Cambridge University Press, 2011)

Dworkin, Ronald, *Taking Rights Seriously* (London, Bloomsbury, 2011 [1977])

—— *Law's Empire* (London, Fontana, 1986)

Dyson, Kenneth HF, *The State Tradition in Western Europe: A Study of an Idea and Institution* (Oxford, Martin Robertson, 1980)

Dzehtsiarou, Kanstantsin, 'European Consensus and the Evolutive Interpretation of the European Convention on Human Rights' (2011) 12.10 *German Law Journal* 1730

—— 'Does Consensus Matter? Legitimacy of European Consensus in the Case Law of the European Court of Human Rights' (2011) *Public Law* 534

—— *European Consensus and the Legitimacy of the European Court of Human Rights* (Cambridge, Cambridge University Press, 2015)

Dzehtsiarou, Kanstantsin and Greene, Alan, 'Legitimacy and the Future of the European Court of Human Rights: Critical Perspectives from Academia and Practitioners' (2011) 12.10 *German Law Journal* 1707

Early, Lawrence, Austin, Anna, Ovey, Clare and Chernishova, Olga (eds), *The Right to Life under Article 2 of the European Convention on Human Rights: Twenty Years of Legal Developments since McCann v The United Kingdom* (Oisterwijk, Wolf Legal Publishers, 2016)

Ebert, Franz Christian and Sijniensky, Romina I, 'Preventing Violations of the Right to Life in the European and the Inter-American Human Rights Systems: From the *Osman* Test to a Coherent Doctrine on Risk Prevention?' (2015) 15 *Human Rights Law Review* 343

Écoiffier, Matthieu, 'À Ferguson, la 'plaie' toujours vive' *Libération* (28–29 May 2016) 2–4

Editorial, 'Holding Power to Account: Count the Value, Not the Cost' (28 April 2016) *The Guardian* 30

Editorial, 'Those Who Dared to Tell the Truth are the Antigones of Our Time' (30 April 2016) *The Guardian* 38

Eijkman, Quirine, 'A Socio-Legal Perspective on Human Rights and Policing' (2007) 25.1 *Netherlands Quarterly of Human Rights* 5

Elias, Norbert, *The Civilising Process: Volume 2 – State Formation and Civilization* (Oxford, Basil Blackwell, 1982)

Engdahl, David E, 'Soldiers, Riots and Revolution: The Law and History of Military Troops in Civil Disorders' (1971) 57.1 *Iowa Law Review* 1

Etxabe, Julen, 'The Legal Universe after Robert Cover' (2010) 4.1 *Law and Humanities* 115

—— *The Experience of Tragic Judgement* (London, Routledge, 2013)

European Commission for Democracy through Law, *Report on the Rule of Law*, adopted by the Venice Commission at its 86th plenary session (Venice, 25–26 March 2011) Study no 512/2009, CDL-AD(2011)003rev (Strasbourg, Council of Europe, 2011)

Fairgrieve, Duncan, 'État de droit and Rule of Law: Comparing Concepts – A Tribute to Roger Errera' (2015) *Public Law* 40

Farlam, IG, Hemraj, PD and Tokota, BR, *Marikana Commission of Inquiry: Report on Matters of Public, National and International Concern Arising out of the Tragic Incidents at the Lonmin Mine in Marikana, in the Northwest Province* (Pretoria, 2015)

Fawcett, JES, *The Application of the European Convention on Human Rights* (Oxford, Clarendon Press, 1987)

Ferrara, Alessandro, *The Force of the Example: Explorations in the Paradigm of Judgment* (New York, Columbia University Press, 2008)

Fitzpatrick, Peter, 'Death as the Horizon of the Law' in Desmond Manderson (ed), *Courting Death: The Law of Mortality* (London, Pluto Press, 1999) 19

Fletcher, George P, 'The Right to Life' (1979) 13 *Georgia Law Review* 1371

—— *Basic Concepts of Criminal Law* (Oxford, Oxford University Press, 1998)

Flikschuh, Katrin, 'Human Rights in Kantian Mode: A Sketch' in Rowan Cruft, S Matthew Liao and Massimo Renzo (eds), *Philosophical Foundations of Human Rights* (Oxford, Oxford University Press, 2015) 653

Flogaitis, Spyridon, Zwart, Tom and Fraser, Julie (eds), *The European Court of Human Rights and its Discontents: Turning Criticism into Strength* (Cheltenham, Edward Elgar, 2013)

Follesdal, Andreas, 'Why the European Court of Human Rights might be Democratically Legitimate – A Modest Defence' (2009) 27.2 *Nordisk Tidsskrift for Menneskerettigheter* 289

Forowicz, Magdalena, *The Reception of International Law in the European Court of Human Rights* (Oxford, Oxford University Press, 2010)

Forst, Rainer (Jeffrey Flynn, trans), *The Right to Justification* (New York, Columbia University Press, 2007)

—— (Ciaran Cronin, trans), *Justification and Critique: Towards a Critical Theory of Politics* (Cambridge, Polity Press, 2014)

Franck, Thomas, *The Power of Legitimacy among Nations* (Oxford, Oxford University Press, 1990)

Frankenberg, Günter, 'The Learning Sovereign' in András Sajó (ed), *Militant Democracy* (Utrecht, Eleven International Publishing, 2004) 113

—— *Comparative Law as Critique* (Cheltenham, Edward Elgar, 2016)

Fraser, David, *Law after Auschwitz: Towards a Jurisprudence of the Holocaust* (Durham, NC, Carolina Academic Press, 2005)

Fredman, Sandra, 'Emerging from the Shadows: Substantive Equality and Article 14 of the European Convention on Human Rights' (2016) 16 *Human Rights Law Review* 273

Freeman, Michael, *Human Rights: An Interdisciplinary Approach* (Cambridge, Polity Press, 2011)

Gallie, WB, 'Essentially Contested Concepts' (1956) 56 *Proceedings of the Aristotelian Society* 167

Gearty, Conor, 'Democracy and Human Rights in the European Court of Human Rights: A Critical Appraisal' (2000) 51.3 *Northern Ireland Legal Quarterly* 381

—— *Liberty and Security* (Cambridge, Polity Press, 2013)

—— 'Is the Human Rights Era Drawing to a Close?' (2017) 5 *European Human Rights Law Review* 425

Geertz, Clifford, *The Interpretation of Cultures* (London, Fontana Press, 1993)

Genette, Gérard (Jane E Lewin, trans), *Narrative Discourse Revisited* (Ithaca, NY, Cornell University Press, 1988)

Genoa Social Forum, *Genova: Il Libro Bianco* (Milan, Nuova Iniziativa Editoriale, 2002)

Gerards, Janneke, 'Margin of Appreciation and Incrementalism in the Case Law of the European Court of Human Rights' (2018) 18 *Human Rights Law Review* 495

Gerards, Janneke and Brems, Eva, 'Introduction' in Eva Brems and Janneke Gerards (eds), *Shaping Rights in the ECHR: The Role of the European Court of Human Rights in Determining the Scope of Human Rights* (Cambridge, Cambridge University Press, 2013) 1

Gerards, Janneke and Senden, Hanneke, 'The Structure of Fundamental Rights and the European Court of Human Rights' (2009) 7.4 *International Journal of Constitutional Law* 619

Gerth, HH and Mills, C Wright (eds), *From Max Weber: Essays in Sociology* (London, Routledge, 1991)

Glas, Lize R, *The Theory, Potential and Practice of Procedural Dialogue in the European Convention on Human Rights System* (Cambridge, Intersentia, 2016)

Glendon, Mary Ann, *The Forum and the Tower: How Scholars and Politicians have Imagined the World, from Plato to Eleanor Roosevelt* (New York, Oxford University Press, 2011)

Goodhart, Michael, 'Democracy as Human Rights' in Thomas Cushman (ed), *Handbook of Human Rights* (Abingdon, Routledge, 2014) 68

Goodrich, Peter, *Legal Discourse: Studies in Linguistics, Rhetoric and Legal Analysis* (Basingstoke, Macmillan, 1987)

Goold, Benjamin J and Lazarus, Liora (eds), *Security and Human Rights* (Oxford, Hart, 2007)

Gordon, Jane, 'A Developing Human Rights Culture in the UK? Case Studies of Policing' (2010) 6 *European Human Rights Law Review* 609

Government of Greece and the Council of Europe, *Democracy and Human Rights*, Proceedings of the Colloquy organised by the, 24–26 September 1987 (Kehl, NP Engel, 1990)

Graver, Hans Petter, 'Sense and Sensibility: Classic Rhetoric as a Model for Modern Legal Thinking' (2008) 53 *Scandinavian Studies in Law* 231

Greer, Steven, *The European Convention on Human Rights: Achievements, Problems and Prospects* (Cambridge, Cambridge University Press, 2006)

—— 'The Interpretation of the European Convention on Human Rights: Universal Principle or Margin of Appreciation?' (2010) 3 *UCL Human Rights Review* 1

Greer, Steven and Wildhaber, Luzius, 'Revisiting the Debate about 'Constitutionalising' the European Court of Human Rights' (2013) 12.4 *Human Rights Law Review* 655

Griffin, James, *On Human Rights* (Oxford, Oxford University Press, 2008)

Gross, Emanuel, 'Legal Aspects of Tackling Terrorism: The Balance between the Right of a Democracy to Defend Itself and the Protection of Human Rights' (2001) 6 *UCLA Journal of International Law and Foreign Affairs* 89

Gundle, Stephen and Rinaldi, Lucia (eds), *Assassinations and Murder in Modern Italy: Transformations in Society and Culture* (Basingstoke, Palgrave Macmillan, 2007)

Günther, Klaus, 'The Legacies of Injustice and Fear: A European Approach to Human Rights and their Effects on Political Culture' in Philip Alston (ed), *The EU and Human Rights* (Oxford, Oxford University Press, 1999) 117

Haas, Michael, *International Human Rights: A Comprehensive Introduction* (London, Routledge, 2014)

Habermas, Jürgen (William Rehg, trans), *Between Facts and Norms: Contributions to a Discourse Theory of Law and Democracy* (Cambridge, Polity Press, 1996)

Hale, Baroness of Richmond, 'Human Rights in the Age of Terrorism: The Democratic Dialogue in Action' (2008) 39 *Georgetown Journal of International Law* 383

Hallam, Elizabeth, Hockey, Jenny and Howarth, Glennys, *Beyond the Body: Death and Social Identity* (London, Routledge, 1999)

Hamilton, Michael and Buyse, Antoine, 'Human Rights Courts as Norm Brokers' (2018) 18 *Human Rights Law Review* 205

Hanne, Michael and Weisberg, Robert (eds), *Narrative and Metaphor in the Law* (Cambridge, Cambridge University Press, 2018)

—— 'Introduction: Narrative and Metaphor in the Law' in Michael Hanne and Robert Weisberg (eds), *Narrative and Metaphor in the Law* (Cambridge, Cambridge University Press, 2018) 1

Harlow, Carol, 'Accountability and Constitutional Law' in Mark Bovens, Robert E Goodin and Thomas Schillemans (eds), *The Oxford Handbook of Public Accountability* (Oxford, Oxford University Press, 2014) 195

Harper, Robert Berkley, 'Accountability of Law Enforcement Officers in the Use of Deadly Force' (1983) 26 *Howard Law Journal* 119

Harris, David, 'The Right to Life under the European Convention on Human Rights' (1994) 1 *Maastricht Journal of European and Comparative Law* 122

Harvey, Paul, 'Militant Democracy and the European Convention on Human Rights' (2004) 29.3 *European Law Review* 407

Heidegger, Martin (John MacQuarrie and Edward Robinson, trans), *Being and Time* (Oxford, Blackwell, 1962)

Heinze, Eric and Freedman, Rosa, 'Public Awareness of Human Rights: Distortions in the Mass Media' (2010) 14.4 *International Journal of Human Rights* 491

Held, David, 'Central Perspectives on the Modern State' in Gregor McLennan, David Held and Stuart Hall (eds), *The Idea of the Modern State* (Milton Keynes, Open University Press, 1984) 29

—— *Models of Democracy* (Stanford, Stanford University Press, 2006)

Hendin, Stuart E, QC, 'The Evolution of the Right to Life by the European Court of Human Rights' (2004) 4.1 *Baltic Yearbook of International Law* 75

Henkin, Louis, *The International Bill of Rights: The Covenant on Civil and Political Rights* (New York, Columbia University Press, 1981)

—— *The Age of Rights* (New York, Columbia University Press, 1990)

Hessbruegge, Jan Arno, *Human Rights and Personal Self-Defense in International Law* (Oxford, Oxford University Press, 2017)

Heyns, Christof, Report of the Special Rapporteur on Extra-judicial, Summary or Arbitrary Executions (1 April 2014), United Nations Human Rights Council A/HRC/26/36

Hirschfield, Paul J and Simon, Daniella, 'Legitimating Police Violence: Newspaper Narratives of Deadly Force' (2010) 14.2 *Theoretical Criminology* 155

Honderich, Ted (ed), *The Oxford Companion to Philosophy*, 2nd edn (Oxford, Oxford University Press, 2005)

Howarth, David, *Discourse* (Buckingham, Open University Press, 2000)

Howarth, Glennys, *Death and Dying: A Sociological Introduction* (Cambridge, Polity, 2007)

Hughes, Cheryl L, 'Reconstructing the Subject of Human Rights' (1999) 25.2 *Philosophy and Social Criticism* 47

Hunt, Lynn (ed and trans), *The French Revolution and Human Rights: A Brief Documentary History* (Boston, Bedford/St Martin's, 1996)

—— 'Introduction: The Revolutionary Origins of Human Rights' in Hunt, Lynn (ed and trans), *The French Revolution and Human Rights: A Brief Documentary History* (Boston, Bedford/St Martin's, 1996) 1

Huscroft, Grant, Miller, Bradley W and Webber, Grégoire (eds), *Proportionality and the Rule of Law: Rights, Justification, Reasoning* (Cambridge, Cambridge University Press, 2014)

Hutchinson, Michael R, 'The Margin of Appreciation Doctrine in the European Court of Human Rights' (1999) 48.3 *International and Comparative Law Quarterly* 638

Ishay, Micheline R, *The History of Human Rights: From Ancient Times to the Globalization Era* (Berkeley, University of California Press, 2004)

Jackson, Bernard, *Law, Fact and Narrative Coherence* (Liverpool, Deborah Charles Publications, 1988)

Jackson, Jonathan, Hough, Mike, Bradford, Ben and Kuha, Jouni, 'Empirical Legitimacy as Two Connected Psychological States' in Gorazd Meško and Justice Tankebe (eds), *Trust and Legitimacy in Criminal Justice: European Perspectives* (Cham, Springer, 2015) 137

Jacot-Guillarmod, O, 'The Relationship Between Democracy and Human Rights' in *Democracy and Human Rights*, Proceedings of the Colloquy organised by the Government of Greece and the Council of Europe, 24–26 September 1987 (Kehl, NP Engel, 1990) 43

Jagland, Thorbjorn, 'Don't Reject Europe Court as Caricature' (13 December 2016) *New York Times* 1

Jobard, F, 'Comprendre l'Habilitation à l'Usage de la Force Policière' (2001) 25.3 *Déviance et Société* 325

Joerges, Christian and Singh Ghaleigh, Navraj (eds), *Darker Legacies of Law in Europe: the Shadow of National Socialism and Fascism over Europe and its Legal Traditions* (Oxford, Hart, 2003)

Jones, Trevor, Newburn, Tim and Smith, David J, *Democracy and Policing* (London, Policy Studies Institute, 1994)

Joseph, Sarah, 'Denouement of the Deaths on the Rock: the Right to Life of Terrorists' (1996) 14.1 *Netherlands Quarterly of Human Rights* 5

Jowell, Jeffrey and Cooper, Jonathan (eds), *Understanding Human Rights Principles* (Oxford, Hart, 2001)

Joy, Morny (ed), *Paul Ricoeur and Narrative: Context and Contestation* (Alberta, University of Calgary Press, 1997)

Kahn, Paul W, *The Cultural Study of Law: Reconstructing Legal Scholarship* (Chicago, The University of Chicago Press, 1999)

—— 'Freedom, Autonomy, and the Cultural Study of Law' (2001) 13 *Yale Journal of Law and the Humanities* 141

Kant, Immanuel (M Gregor, ed and trans), *Groundwork of the Metaphysics of Morals* (Cambridge, Cambridge University Press, 1991)

Kearney, Richard (ed), *Paul Ricoeur: The Hermeneutics of Action* (London, Sage Publications, 1996)

Kellner, Hans, '"As Real as it Gets" – Ricoeur and Narrativity' in David E Klemm and William Schweiker (eds), *Meanings in Texts and Actions: Questioning Paul Ricoeur* (Charlottesville, University Press of Virginia, 1993) 49

Kennedy, David, 'The International Human Rights Movement: Part of the Problem?' (2001) 3 *European Human Rights Law Review* 245

Kitchin, Hilary, *The Gibraltar Report: Inquest into the Deaths of Mairead Farrell, Daniel McCann & Sean Savage, Gibraltar, September 1988* (London, National Council for Civil Liberties, 1989)

Klemm, David E and Schweiker, William (eds), *Meanings in Texts and Actions: Questioning Paul Ricoeur* (Charlottesville, University Press of Virginia, 1993)

Kuipers, Sanneke and 'T Hart, Paul, 'Accounting for Crises' in Mark Bovens, Robert E Goodin, and Thomas Schillemans (eds), *The Oxford Handbook of Public Accountability* (Oxford, Oxford University Press, 2014) 589

Kuttab, Jonathan, 'Overt Forms of State Violence' in Kathleen E Mahoney and Paul Mahoney (eds), *Human Rights in the Twenty-First Century: A Global Challenge* (Dordrecht, Martinus Nijhoff Publishers, 1993) 241

Ladd, John, 'Ideological Components of the Concepts of Collective Violence, Human Rights, and Solidarity' in Kathleen E Mahoney and Paul Mahoney (eds), *Human Rights in the Twenty-First Century: A Global Challenge* (Dordrecht, Martinus Nijhoff Publishers, 1993) 223

Landman, Todd, *Human Rights and Democracy: The Precarious Triumph of Ideals* (London, Bloomsbury, 2013)

Larkin, John F, 'Dialogue at Cross Purposes? The Northern Ireland Inquest and Article 2 of the European Convention on Human Rights' in Lawrence Early, Anna Austin, Clare Ovey and Olga Chernishova (eds), *The Right to Life under Article 2 of the European Convention on Human Rights: Twenty Years of Legal Developments since McCann v The United Kingdom* (Oisterwijk, Wolf Legal Publishers, 2016) 161

Lautenbach, Geranne, *The Concept of the Rule of Law and the European Court of Human Rights* (Oxford, Oxford University Press, 2013)

Lavender, Nicholas, 'The Problem of the Margin of Appreciation' (1997) 4 *European Human Rights Law Review* 380

Leach, Philip, Paraskeva, Costas and Uzelac, Gordana, *International Human Rights and Fact Finding: An Analysis of the Fact-Finding Missions Conducted by the European Commission and Court of Human Rights*, Report by the Human Rights and Social Justice Research Institute at London Metropolitan University (2009)

—— 'Human Rights Fact-Finding. The European Court of Human Rights at a Crossroads' (2010) 28.1 *Netherlands Quarterly of Human Rights* 41

Leben, Charles, 'Is there a European Approach to Human Rights?' in Philip Alston (ed), *The EU and Human Rights* (Oxford, Oxford University Press, 1999) 69

Leino, Päivi, 'A European Approach to Human Rights? Universality Explored' (2002) 71 *Nordic Journal of International Law* 455

Leishman, Frank, Loveday, Barry and Savage, Stephen P (eds), *Core Issues in Policing* (London, Longman, 1996)

Lessa, Francesca and Payne, Leigh A (eds), *Amnesty in the Age of Human Rights Accountability* (Cambridge, Cambridge University Press, 2012)

Letsas, George, 'Two Concepts of the Margin of Appreciation' (2006) 26.4 *Oxford Journal of Legal Studies* 705

—— *A Theory of Interpretation of the European Convention on Human Rights* (Oxford, Oxford University Press, 2007)

Leverick, Fiona, *Killing in Self-Defence* (Oxford, Oxford University Press, 2006)

Linden-Retek, Paul P, 'Cosmopolitan Law and Time: Toward a Theory of Constitutionalism and Solidarity in Transition' (2015) 4.2 *Global Constitutionalism* 157

Littlejohn, Edward J, Smitherman, Geneva and Quick, Alida, 'Deadly Force and its Effects on Police-Community Relations' (1984) 27 *Howard Law Journal* 1131

Loader, Ian, 'The Cultural Lives of Security and Rights' in Benjamin J Goold and Liora Lazarus (eds), *Security and Human Rights* (Oxford, Hart, 2007) 27

—— 'In Search of Civic Policing: Recasting the "Peelian" Principles' (2016) 10 *Criminal Law and Philosophy* 427

Loader, Ian and Walker, Neil, *Civilizing Security* (Cambridge, Cambridge University Press, 2007)

Locke, John (Peter Laslett (ed)), *Two Treatises of Government* (Cambridge, Cambridge University Press, 1988)

Loewenstein, Karl, 'Militant Democracy and Fundamental Rights, I' (1937) 31.3 *The American Political Science Review* 417

—— 'Militant Democracy and Fundamental Rights, II' (1937) 31.4 *The American Political Science Review* 638

Loughlin, Martin, 'Rights, Democracy, and Law' in Tom Campbell, KD Ewing and Adam Tomkins (eds), *Sceptical Essays on Human Rights* (Oxford, Oxford University Press, 2001) 41

Loughlin, Martin and Meierhenrich, Jens (eds), *The Cambridge Companion to the Rule of Law* (Cambridge, Cambridge University Press, forthcoming)

MacCormick, Neil, *Rhetoric and the Rule of Law* (Oxford, Oxford University Press, 2005)
Macdonald, R St J, Matscher, F and Petzold, H (eds), *The European System for the Protection of Human Rights* (Dordrecht, Martinus Nijhoff Publishers, 1993)
Macklem, Patrick, 'Militant Democracy, Legal Pluralism, and the Paradox of Self-Determination' (2006) 4.3 *International Journal of Constitutional Law* 488
Macpherson, CB, *The Life and Times of Liberal Democracy* (Oxford, Oxford University Press, 1977)
Madsen, Mikael Rask and Verschraegen, Gert (eds), *Making Human Rights Intelligible: Towards a Sociology of Human Rights* (Oxford, Hart, 2013)
—— 'Making Human Rights Intelligible: An Introduction to a Sociology of Human Rights' in Mikael Rask Madsen and Gert Verschraegen (eds), *Making Human Rights Intelligible: Towards a Sociology of Human Rights* (Oxford, Hart, 2013) 1
Mahoney, Kathleen E and Mahoney, Paul (eds), *Human Rights in the Twenty-First Century: A Global Challenge* (Dordrecht, Martinus Nijhoff Publishers, 1993)
Mahoney, Paul, 'The Relationship between the Strasbourg Court and the National Courts' (2014) 130 *Law Quarterly Review* 568
Mahoney, Paul and Sundberg, Fredrik, 'The European Convention on Human Rights: A Case Study of the International Law Response to Violence' in Kathleen E Mahoney and Paul Mahoney (eds), *Human Rights in the Twenty-First Century – A Global Challenge* (Dordrecht, Martinus Nijhoff Publishers, 1993) 361
Manderson, Desmond, (ed) *Courting Death: The Law of Mortality* (London, Pluto Press, 1999)
—— 'Introduction: Tales from the Crypt – A Metaphor, An Image, A Story' in Desmond Manderson (ed), *Courting Death: The Law of Mortality* (London, Pluto Press, 1999) 1
Marks, Susan, 'The European Convention on Human Rights and its "Democratic Society"' (1996) 66 *British Yearbook of International Law* 209
—— 'False Contingency' (2009) 62.1 *Current Legal Problems* 1
—— 'Human Rights and Root Causes' (2011) 74.1 *Modern Law Review* 57
Mathieu, Bertrand, *Le droit à la vie dans les jurisprudences constitutionnelles et conventionnelles européennes* (Strasbourg, Editions du Conseil de l'Europe, 2005)
Mavronicola, Natasa, 'Taking Life and Liberty Seriously: Reconsidering Criminal Liability Under Article 2 of the ECHR' (2017) 80.6 *Modern Law Review* 1026
McBride, Jeremy, 'Protecting Life: A Positive Obligation to Help' (1999) 24 *European Law Review – Supplement: Human Rights Survey* 43
McClintock, Michael, 'Establishing Accountability for State Violence' in Kathleen E Mahoney and Paul Mahoney (eds), *Human Rights in the Twenty-First Century – A Global Challenge* (Dordrecht, Martinus Nijhoff Publishers, 1993) 247
McCorquodale, Robert, 'Defining the International Rule of Law: Defying Gravity?' (2016) 65.2 *International and Comparative Law Quarterly* 277
McDonnell, Duncan, 'The Genoa G8 and the Death of Carlo Giuliani' in Stephen Gundle and Lucia Rinaldi (eds), *Assassinations and Murder in Modern Italy: Transformations in Society and Culture* (Basingstoke, Palgrave Macmillan, 2007) 73
McHarg, Aileen, 'Reconciling Human Rights and the Public Interest: Conceptual Problems and Doctrinal Uncertainty in the Jurisprudence of the European Court of Human Rights' (1999) 62.5 *Modern Law Review* 671
McIntosh, Sam, 'Taken Lives Matter: Open Justice and Recognition in Inquests into Deaths at the Hands of the State' (2016) 12.2 *International Journal of Law in Context* 141
McLennan, Gregor, Held, David and Hall, Stuart (eds), *The Idea of the Modern State* (Milton Keynes, Open University Press, 1984)
Melzer, Nils, *Targeted Killing in International Law* (Oxford, Oxford University Press, 2009)
Meško, Gorazd and Tankebe, Justice (eds), *Trust and Legitimacy in Criminal Justice: European Perspectives* (Cham, Springer, 2015)
Meyer-Ladewig, Jens, 'The Rule of Law in the Case Law of the Strasbourg Court' in Hermann-Josef Blanke and Stelio Mangiameli (eds), *The European Union After Lisbon: Constitutional Basis, Economic Order and External Action* (Berlin, Springer, 2012) 233

Minow, Martha, Ryan, Michael and Sarat, Austin (eds), *Narrative, Violence and the Law: The Essays of Robert Cover* (Ann Arbor, The University of Michigan Press, 1995)

Mirandola, Sofia, 'The Involvement of the Deceased Victim's Next of Kin in Criminal Investigations: An Analysis of the Standards under Article 2 of the Convention and of Directive 2012/29/EU on the Rights of Victims of Crime' in Lawrence Early, Anna Austin, Clare Ovey and Olga Chernishova (eds), *The Right to Life under Article 2 of the European Convention on Human Rights: Twenty Years of Legal Developments since McCann v The United Kingdom* (Oisterwijk, Wolf Legal Publishers, 2016) 179

Moeckli, Daniel, Shah, Sangeeta and Sivakumaran, Sandesh (eds), *International Human Rights Law*, 2nd edn (Oxford, Oxford University Press, 2014)

Moeckli, Daniel, 'Human Rights Strategies in an Age of Counter-Terrorism' in Reza Banakar (ed), *Rights in Context: Law and Justice in Late Modern Society* (Farnham, Ashgate, 2012) 215

Moore, Mark H, 'Accountability, Legitimacy and the Court of Public Opinion' in Mark Bovens, Robert E Goodin and Thomas Schillemans (eds), *The Oxford Handbook of Public Accountability* (Oxford, Oxford University Press, 2014) 632

Moravcsik, Andrew, 'The Origins of Human Rights Regimes: Democratic Delegation in Postwar Europe' (2000) 54.2 *International Organization* 217

Morsink, Johannes, *The Universal Declaration of Human Rights: Origins, Drafting and Intent* (Philadelphia, University of Pennsylvania Press, 1999)

Mowbray, Alastair R, 'A New European Court of Human Rights' (1994) *Public Law* 540

—— 'The Composition and Operation of the New European Court of Human Rights' (1999) *Public Law* 219

—— 'The Role of the European Court of Human Rights in the Promotion of Democracy' (1999) *Public Law* 703

—— 'Duties of Investigation under the European Convention on Human Rights' (2002) 51 *International and Comparative Law Quarterly* 437

—— *The Development of Positive Obligations under the European Convention on Human Rights by the European Court of Human Rights* (Oxford, Hart, 2004)

—— 'The Creativity of the European Court of Human Rights' (2005) 5.1 *Human Rights Law Review* 57

—— 'An Examination of the European Court of Human Rights Approach to Overruling its Previous Case Law' (2009) 9 *Human Rights Law Review* 179

—— 'A Study of the Principle of Fair Balance in the Jurisprudence of the European Court of Human Rights' (2010) 10.2 *Human Rights Law Review* 289

—— 'Contemporary Aspects of the Promotion of Democracy by the European Court of Human Rights' (2014) 20.3 *European Public Law* 469

—— 'Subsidiarity and the European Convention on Human Rights' (2015) 15 *Human Rights Law Review* 313

Moyn, Samuel, *The Last Utopia: Human Rights in History* (Cambridge, Mass, Harvard University Press, 2010)

Mulgan, Richard, '"Accountability": An Ever-Expanding Concept?' (2000) 78.3 *Public Administration* 555

—— *Holding Power to Account: Accountability in Modern Democracies* (Basingstoke, Palgrave Macmillan, 2003)

Munslow, Alun, *Narrative and History* (Basingstoke, Palgrave Macmillan, 2007)

Murdoch, Jim and Roche, Ralph, *The European Convention on Human Rights and Policing: A Handbook for Police Officers and Other Law Enforcement Officials* (Strasbourg, Council of Europe Publishing, 2013)

Myjer, Egbert, 'Investigation into the Use of Lethal Force: Standards of Independence and Impartiality' in Lawrence Early, Anna Austin, Clare Ovey and Olga Chernishova (eds), *The Right to Life under Article 2 of the European Convention on Human Rights: Twenty Years of Legal Developments since McCann v the United Kingdom* (Oisterwijk, Wolf Legal Publishers, 2016) 115

Narveson, Jan, 'Force, Violence and Law' in James B Brady and Newton Garver (eds), *Justice, Law and Violence* (Philadelphia, Temple University Press, 1991) 149

Neier, Aryeh, *The International Human Rights Movement: A History* (Princeton, Princeton University Press, 2012)
Neocleous, Mark, *War Power, Police Power* (Edinburgh, Edinburgh University Press, 2014)
Newman, Zach, '"Hands Up, Don't Shoot": Policing, Fatal Force, and Equal Protection in the Age of Colorblindness' (2015) 43.1 *Hastings Constitutional Law Quarterly* 117
Ní Aoláin, Fionnuala, *The Politics of Force: Conflict Management and State Violence in Northern Ireland* (Belfast, The Blackstaff Press, 2000)
—— 'The Evolving Jurisprudence of the European Convention Concerning the Right to Life' (2001) 19.1 *Netherlands Quarterly of Human Rights* 21
—— 'Truth Telling, Accountability and the Right to Life in Northern Ireland' (2002) 5 *European Human Rights Law Review* 572
Nickel, James W, *Making Sense of Human Rights*, 2nd edn (Oxford, Blackwell Publishing, 2007 [1987])
Nicol, Danny, 'Original Intent and the European Convention on Human Rights' (2005) *Public Law* 152
Niwot, Melody, 'Narrating Genoa: Documentaries of the Italian G8 Protests of 2001 and the Persistence and Politics of Memory' (2011) 23.2 *History and Memory* 66
Norrie, Alan, 'The Problem of Mistaken Self-Defense: Citizenship, Chiasmus and Legal Form' (2010) 13.2 *New Criminal Law Review* 357
Northern Ireland Human Rights Commission, *Dealing with Northern Ireland's Past: Towards a Transitional Justice Approach* (Belfast, NIHRC, 2013)
Nsereko, Daniel D, 'Arbitrary Deprivation of Life: Controls on Permissible Deprivations' in BG Ramcharan (ed), *The Right to Life in International Law* (Dordrecht, Martinus Nijhoff, 1985) 245
O'Boyle, Michael, 'The Use of Lethal Force under Article 2 of the European Convention on Human Rights', DH-ED-COLL (90) 9, Council of Europe, 23 October 1990
O'Boyle, Michael and Brady, Natalia, 'Investigatory Powers of the European Court of Human Rights' (2013) 4 *European Human Rights Law Review* 378
O'Connell, Mary Ellen, 'The Law on Lethal Force Begins with the Right to Life' (2016) 3.2 *Journal on the Use of Force and International Law* 205
Olson, Greta, 'On Narrating and Troping the Law: The Conjoined Use of Narrative and Metaphor in Legal Discourse' in Michael Hanne and Robert Weisberg (eds), *Narrative and Metaphor in the Law* (Cambridge, Cambridge University Press, 2018) 19–36
Opsahl, Torkel, 'The Right to Life' in R St J Macdonald, F Matscher and H Petzold (eds), *The European System for the Protection of Human Rights* (Dordrecht, Martinus Nijhoff Publishers, 1993) 207
Osse, Anneke and Cano, Ignacio, 'Police Deadly Use of Firearms: An International Comparison' (2017) 21.5 *The International Journal of Human Rights* 629
Ost, François, 'The Original Canons of Interpretation of the European Court of Human Rights' in Mireille Delmas-Marty (Christine Chodkiewicz, trans), *The European Convention for the Protection of Human Rights: International Protection versus National Restrictions* (Dordrecht, Martinus Nijhoff Publishers, 1992) 283
Paine, Thomas, *Common Sense* (Philadelphia, Robert Bell, 1776)
Palmer, Stephanie, 'Death on the Rock and the European Convention on Human Rights' (1996) 55.1 *The Cambridge Law Journal* 1
Pavel, Nicolae, 'The Right to Life as a Supreme Value and Guaranteeing the Right to Life' (2012) 4.2 *Contemporary Readings in Law and Social Justice* 970
Pellauer, David, 'Foreword: Recounting Narrative' in Morny Joy (ed), *Paul Ricoeur and Narrative: Context and Contestation* (Alberta, University of Calgary Press, 1997) ix
Pettiti, Louis-Edmond, Decaux, Emmanuel and Imbert, Pierre-Henri (eds), *La Convention Européenne des Droits de l'Homme* (Paris, Economica, 1999)
Philp, Mark, 'Delimiting Democratic Accountability' (2009) 57 *Political Studies* 28
Picard, E, 'Commentaire de l'article 12 de la Déclaration des droits de l'homme et du citoyen' (1991) 5 *Les Cahiers de la sécurité intérieure* 201
Pieniążek, Marcin, 'The Application of Paul Ricoeur's Theory in Interpretation of Legal Texts and Legally Relevant Human Action' (2015) 28 *International Journal for the Semiotics of Law* 627
Pintore, Anna, *I diritti della democrazia* (Bari, Laterza, 2003)

Pitkänen, Maija, 'Fair and Balanced Positive Obligations: Do They Exist?' (2012) 5 *European Human Rights Law Review* 538
Polkinghorne, Donald E, *Narrative Knowing and the Human Sciences* (Albany, State University of New York Press, 1988)
Ponsaers, Paul, 'Is Legitimacy Police Property?' in Gorazd Meško and Justice Tankebe (eds), *Trust and Legitimacy in Criminal Justice: European Perspectives* (Cham, Springer, 2015) 93–110
Přibáň, Jiří, *Legal Symbolism: On Law, Time and European Identity* (Aldershot, Ashgate, 2007)
Primus, Richard, 'A Brooding Omnipresence: Totalitarianism in Postwar Constitutional Thought' (1996–97) 106 *Yale Law Journal* 423
'Protesters March on Fifth Anniversary of Death of Mark Duggan' (6 August 2016) *The Guardian*
Przetacznik, Franciszek, 'The Right to Life as a Basic Human Right' (1976) 9 *Revue des Droits de l'Homme: Revue de Droit International et Comparé* 585
Punch, Maurice, *Shoot to Kill: Police Accountability, Firearms and Fatal Force* (Bristol, The Policy Press, 2011)
Punch, Maurice, Crawshaw, Ralph and Markham, Geoffrey, 'Democratic Principles and Police Fatal Force: Avoidance of Debate, Unresolved Accountability and Human Rights' (2016) 46 *International Journal of Law, Crime and Justice* 2
Pustorino, Pietro, *L'Interpretazione della Convenzione Europea dei Diritti dell'Uomo nella Prassi della Commissione e della Corte di Strasburgo* (Naples, Editoriale Scientifica, 1998)
Rainey, Bernadette, Wicks, Elizabeth and Ovey, Clare (eds), *Jacobs, White & Ovey The European Convention on Human Rights*, 7th edn (Oxford, Oxford University Press, 2017)
Rainwater, Mara, 'Refiguring Ricoeur: Narrative Force and Communicative Ethics' in Richard Kearney (ed), *Paul Ricoeur: The Hermeneutics of Action* (London, Sage Publications, 1996) 99
Ramcharan, BG, (ed), *The Right to Life in International Law* (Dordrecht, Martinus Nijhoff, 1985)
—— 'The Concept and Dimensions of the Right to Life' in BG Ramcharan (ed), *The Right to Life in International Law* (Dordrecht, Martinus Nijhoff, 1985) 1
—— 'The Drafting History of Article 6 of the International Covenant on Civil and Political Rights' in BG Ramcharan (ed), *The Right to Life in International Law* (Dordrecht, Martinus Nijhoff, 1985) 42
—— 'The Drafting History of Article 2 of the European Convention on Human Rights' in BG Ramcharan (ed), *The Right to Life in International Law* (Dordrecht, Martinus Nijhoff, 1985) 57
Raymond, Margaret, 'Rejecting Totalitarianism: Translating the Guarantees of Constitutional Criminal Procedure' (1998) 76 *North Carolina Law Review* 1193
Reidy, Aisling, Hampson, Françoise and Boyle, Kevin, 'Gross Violations of Human Rights: Invoking the European Convention on Human Rights in the Case of Turkey' (1997) 15.2 *Netherlands Quarterly of Human Rights* 161
Reiter-Korkmaz, Axelle, 'Droit à la vie et répression du terrorisme' (1996) 26 *Revue Trimestrielle des Droits de l'Homme* 252
—— 'Usage de la force meutrière lors d'une opération de sauvetage d'une jeune fille kidnappée' (1999) 39 *Revue trimestrielle des droits de l'homme* 555
Requa, Marny and Anthony, Gordon, 'Coroners, Controversial Deaths and Northern Ireland's Past Conflict' (2008) *Public Law* 443
Ricoeur, Paul, *Temps et Récit* (Paris, Editions du Seuil, 1983)
—— (Kathleen McLaughlin and David Pellauer, trans), *Time and Narrative, Volume 1* (Chicago, University of Chicago Press, 1984)
—— (Kathleen Blamey and David Pellauer, trans), *Time and Narrative, Volume 3* (Chicago, University of Chicago Press, 1988)
—— 'L'identité narrative' (1988) 140–141 *Esprit* 295
—— 'Between Hermeneutics and Semiotics' (1990) 3.8 *International Journal for the Semiotics of Law* 115–32
—— 'L'identité narrative' (1991) 95.221 *Revue des Sciences Humaines* 35
—— (Kathleen Blamey, trans), *Oneself as Another* (Chicago, University of Chicago Press, 1992)
—— 'A Response by Paul Ricoeur' (David Pellauer, trans) in Morny Joy (ed), *Paul Ricoeur and Narrative: Context and Contestation* (Alberta, University of Calgary Press, 1997) xxxix

—— 'Who Is the Subject of Rights?' in Paul Ricoeur (David Pellauer, trans), *The Just* (Chicago, University of Chicago Press, 2000) 1

—— 'The Act of Judging' in Paul Ricoeur (David Pellauer, trans), *The Just* (Chicago, University of Chicago Press, 2000) 127

(David Pellauer, trans), *The Just* (Chicago, University of Chicago Press, 2000)

Rivers, Julian, 'Proportionality and Variable Intensity of Review' (2006) 65.1 *Cambridge Law Journal* 174

Rocco, Alfredo, 'The Political Doctrine of Fascism' (1926–27) 11 *International Conciliation* 393

Rosanvallon, Pierre (Arthur Goldhammer, trans), *Democratic Legitimacy: Impartiality, Reflexivity, Proximity* (Princeton, Princeton University Press, 2011)

Rosas, Allan, 'Democracy and Human Rights' in Allan Rosas, Jan Helgesen and Donna Gomien (eds), *Human Rights in a Changing East-West Perspective* (London, Pinter, 1990) 17

Rosas, Allan, Helgesen, Jan and Gomien, Donna (eds) *Human Rights in a Changing East-West Perspective* (London, Pinter, 1990)

Rousseau, Jean-Jacques, (Donald A Cress, ed and trans), *On the Social Contract* (Indianapolis, Hackett, 1987)

Rudrum, David, 'From Narrative Representation to Narrative Use: Towards the Limits of Definition' (2005) 13.2 *Narrative* 195

Russell, Hannah, 'Understanding "Quelling a Riot or Insurrection" under Article 2 of the ECHR' (2015) 5 *European Human Rights Law Review* 495

—— *The Use of Force and Article 2 of the ECHR in Light of European Conflicts* (Oxford, Hart, 2017)

Ryan, Michael, 'Meaning and Alternity' in Martha Minow, Michael Ryan and Austin Sarat (eds), *Narrative, Violence and the Law: The Essays of Robert Cover* (Ann Arbor, The University of Michigan Press, 1995) 267

Sajó, András (ed), *Militant Democracy* (Utrecht, Eleven International Publishing, 2004)

—— *Constitutional Sentiments* (New Haven, Yale University Press, 2011)

Samuels, Alec, 'The Police Officer Shoots and Kills: the Strasbourg Jurisprudence' (2006) 1 *Archbold News* 7

Sarat, Austin (ed), *Pain, Death and the Law* (Ann Arbor, University of Michigan Press, 2001)

—— 'Introduction: On Pain and Death as Facts of Legal Life' in Austin Sarat (ed), *Pain, Death and the Law* (Ann Arbor, University of Michigan Press, 2001) 1

—— (ed) *Law, Violence and the Possibility of Justice* (Princeton, Princeton University Press, 2001)

—— 'Situating Law Between the Realities of Violence and the Claims of Justice: An Introduction' in Austin Sarat (ed) *Law, Violence and the Possibility of Justice* (Princeton, Princeton University Press, 2001) 3

Scarry, Elaine, *The Body in Pain. The Making and Unmaking of the World* (New York, Oxford University Press, 1985)

Scheinin, Martin, Krunke, Helle and Aksenova, Marina (eds), *Judges as Guardians of Constitutionalism and Human Rights* (Cheltenham, Edward Elgar, 2016)

Scott, John and Marshall, Gordon, *The Oxford Dictionary of Sociology* (Oxford, Oxford University Press, 2009)

Seibert-Fohr, Anja, *Prosecuting Serious Human Rights Violations* (Oxford, Oxford University Press, 2009)

Sen, Amartya, 'Human Rights and the Limits of Law' (2006) 27.6 *Cardozo Law Review* 2913

Shapiro, Ian and Hacker-Cordón, Casiano (eds), *Democracy's Edges* (Cambridge, Cambridge University Press, 1999)

Shelton, Dinah (ed), *The Oxford Handbook of International Human Rights Law* (Oxford, Oxford University Press, 2013)

Shue, Henry, *Basic Rights: Subsistence, Affluence and US Foreign Policy* (Princeton, Princeton University Press, 1996)

Sicilianos, Linos-Alexander, 'Preventing Violations of the Right to Life: Positive Obligations under Article 2 of the ECHR' (2014) 3.2 *Cyprus Human Rights Law Review* 117

—— 'Out of Harm's Way: Positive Obligations under Article 2 of the European Convention on Human Rights' in Lawrence Early, Anna Austin, Clare Ovey and Olga Chernishova (eds), *The Right to Life under Article 2 of the European Convention on Human Rights: Twenty Years of Legal Developments since McCann v The United Kingdom* (Oisterwijk, Wolf Legal Publishers, 2016) 29

—— 'The European Court of Human Rights at a Time of Crisis in Europe' (2016) 2 *European Human Rights Law Review* 121

Sikkink, Kathryn, 'The Age of Accountability: The Global Rise of Individual Criminal Accountability' in Francesca Lessa and Leigh A Payne (eds), *Amnesty in the Age of Human Rights Accountability* (Cambridge, Cambridge University Press, 2012) 19

Simpson, AW Brian, *Human Rights and the End of Empire: Britain and the Genesis of the European Convention* (Oxford, Oxford University Press, 2001)

Simpson, Kirk, *Truth Recovery in Northern Ireland: Critically Interpreting the Past* (Manchester, Manchester University Press, 2009)

Singh, Rabinder, 'The Place of the Human Rights Act in a Democratic Society' in Jeffrey Jowell and Jonathan Cooper (eds), *Understanding Human Rights Principles* (Oxford, Hart, 2001) 179

Sivakumaran, Sandesh, 'International Humanitarian Law' in Daniel Moeckli, Sangeeta Shah and Sandesh Sivakumaran (eds), *International Human Rights Law* (Oxford, Oxford University Press, 2014) 479

Skinner, Stephen, 'Citizens in Uniform: Public Defence, Reasonableness and Human Rights' (2000) *Public Law* 266

—— 'Death in Genoa: the G8 Summit Shooting and the Right to Life' (2003) 11.3 *European Journal of Crime, Criminal Law and Criminal Justice* 233

—— 'Stories of Pain and the Pursuit of Justice: Law, Violence, Experience and Jurisprudence' (2009) 5 *Law, Culture and the Humanities* 131

—— '*Giuliani and Gaggio v Italy*: the Context of Violence, the Right to Life and Democratic Values' (2010) *European Human Rights Law Review* 85

—— 'The Right to Life, Democracy and State Responsibility in "Urban Guerilla" Conflict: the European Court of Human Rights Grand Chamber Judgment in *Giuliani and Gaggio v Italy*' (2011) 11.3 *Human Rights Law Review* 567

—— 'Tainted Law? The Italian Penal Code, Fascism and Democracy' (2011) 7.4 *International Journal of Law in Context* 423

—— 'Violence in Fascist Criminal Law Discourse: War, Repression and Anti-Democracy' (2013) 26.2 *International Journal for the Semiotics of Law* 439

—— 'Deference, Proportionality and the Margin of Appreciation in Lethal Force Case Law under Article 2 ECHR' (2014) 1 *European Human Rights Law Review* 32

—— 'The Core of McCann: Lethal Force and Democracy under the European Convention on Human Rights' in Lawrence Early, Anna Austin, Clare Ovey and Olga Chernishova (eds), *The Right to Life under Article 2 of the European Convention on Human Rights: Twenty Years of Legal Developments since McCann v The United Kingdom* (Oisterwijk, Wolf Legal Publishers, 2016) 67

—— 'Crimes Against the State and the Intersection of Fascism and Democracy in the 1920s–30s: Vilification, Seditious Libel and the Limits of Legality' (2016) 36.3 *Oxford Journal of Legal Studies* 482

—— 'Criminal Law and the Use of Force: Ideology and State Power in Fascist Italy and England in the Interwar Period' in Stephen Skinner (ed), *Ideology and Criminal Law: Fascist, National Socialist and Authoritarian Regimes* (Oxford, Hart, forthcoming) Ch 14

—— (ed), *Ideology and Criminal Law: Fascist, National Socialist and Authoritarian Regimes* (Oxford, Hart, forthcoming)

Slaughter, Joseph, 'A Question of Narration: The Voice in International Human Rights Law' (1997) 19 *Human Rights Quarterly* 406

Smith, John, 'The Right to Life and the Right to Kill in Law Enforcement' (1994) *New Law Journal* 354

Smith, Matthew, 'The Adjudicatory Fact-Finding Tools of the European Court of Human Rights' (2009) 2 *European Human Rights Law Review* 206

Smyth, Marie and Fay, Marie-Therese (eds), *Personal Accounts from Northern Ireland's Troubles: Public Conflict, Private Loss* (London, Pluto Press, 2000)
Soifer, Aviam, 'Covered Bridges' (2005) 17.1 *Yale Journal of Law and the Humanities* 55
Souvignet, Xavier, *La prééminence du droit dans le droit de la Convention européenne des droits de l'homme* (Brussels, Bruylant, 2012)
Spielmann, Dean, 'Allowing the Right Margin: The European Court of Human Rights and the National Margin of Appreciation Doctrine: Waiver or Subsidiarity of European Review?' (2012) 14 *Cambridge Year Book of European Legal Studies* 381
Squire, Corinne, Davis, Mark, Esin, Cigdem, Andrews, Molly, Harrison, Barbara, Hydén, Lars-Christer and Hydén, Margareta, *What is Narrative Research?* (London, Bloomsbury, 2014)
Squires, Peter and Kennison, Peter, *Shooting to Kill? Policing, Firearms and Armed Response* (Chichester, Wiley-Blackwell, 2010)
Stammers, Neil, 'A Critique of Social Approaches to Human Rights' (1995) 17 *Human Rights Quarterly* 488
Starmer, Keir, *European Human Rights Law: The Human Rights Act 1998 and the European Convention on Human Rights* (London, Legal Action Group, 1999)
Swaine, Jon, Laughland, Oliver and Lartey, Jamiles, 'Shoot to Kill: A US Horror Story' *The Guardian* (2 June 2015) 1
Sweeney, James, 'The Elusive Right to Truth in Transitional Human Rights Jurisprudence' (2018) 67 *International and Comparative Law Quarterly* 353
Tabucchi, Antonio (JC Patrick, trans), *The Missing Head of Damasceno Monteiro* (New York, New Directions Publishing, 1999)
Tait, Allison and Norris, Luke, 'Narrative and the Origins of Law' (2011) 5.1 *Law and Humanities* 11
Tamanaha, Brian, *On the Rule of Law: History, Politics, Theory* (Cambridge, Cambridge University Press, 2004)
Tavernier, Paul, 'Le recours à la force par la police' in Christian Tomuschat, Evelyne Lagrange and Stefan Oeter (eds), *The Right to Life* (Leiden, Martinus Nijhoff Publishers, 2010) 41
'The Observer Files – This week in 1988' (11 March 2018) *The Observer* 60
Thiel, Markus (ed), *The 'Militant Democracy' Principle in Modern Democracies* (Farnham, Ashgate, 2009)
—— 'Introduction' in Thiel, Markus (ed), *The 'Militant Democracy' Principle in Modern Democracies* (Farnham, Ashgate, 2009) 1
—— 'Comparative Aspects' in Thiel, Markus (ed), *The 'Militant Democracy' Principle in Modern Democracies* (Farnham, Ashgate, 2009) 379
Thomson, Judith Jarvis, 'Self-Defense' (1991) 20.4 *Philosophy and Public Affairs* 283
Tilly, Charles, *Democracy* (Cambridge, Cambridge University Press, 2007)
Tomuschat, Christian, 'The Right to Life – Legal and Political Foundations' in Christian Tomuschat, Evelyne Lagrange and Stefan Oeter (eds), *The Right to Life* (Leiden, Martinus Nijhoff, 2010) 3
—— 'Democracy and the Rule of Law' in Dinah Shelton (ed), *The Oxford Handbook of International Human Rights Law* (Oxford, Oxford University Press, 2013) 469
Tomuschat, Christian, Lagrange, Evelyne and Oeter, Stefan (eds), *The Right to Life* (Leiden, Martinus Nijhoff, 2010)
Trechsel, Stefan, 'Spotlights on Article 2 ECHR, The Right to Life' in Wolfgang Benedek, Hubert Isak and Renate Kicker (eds), *Development and Developing International and European Law* (Frankfurt am Main, Peter Lang, 1999) 671
Tsakyrakis, Stavros, 'Proportionality: An Assault on Human Rights?' (2009) 7.3 *International Journal of Constitutional Law* 468
Tushnet, Mark, 'Critical Legal Studies and the Rule of Law' in Martin Loughlin and Jens Meierhenrich (eds), *The Cambridge Companion to the Rule of Law* (Cambridge, Cambridge University Press, forthcoming) Harvard Public Law Working Paper No 18-14.
Tyulkina, Svetlana, *Militant Democracy: Undemocratic Political Parties and Beyond* (Abingdon, Routledge, 2015)

Uniacke, Suzanne, *Permissible Killing: The Self-Defence Justification of Homicide* (Cambridge, Cambridge University Press, 1994)
United Nations Manual on the Effective Prevention and Investigation of Extra-Legal, Arbitrary and Summary Executions, Model Protocol for a legal investigation of extra-legal, arbitrary and summary executions, UN Doc E/ST/CSDHA/.12 (1991)
United Nations Office of the High Commissioner for Human Rights, Human Rights Committee, Draft 'General Comment No 36 on Article 6 of the International Covenant on Civil and Political Rights, on the Right to Life' (120th session, July 2017)
Valdés, Mario J, *A Ricoeur Reader: Reflection and Imagination* (Toronto, University of Toronto Press, 1991)
Van Boven, Théo, 'Convention des droits de l'homme et des libertés fondamentales' in Louis-Edmond Pettiti, Emmanuel Decaux and Pierre-Henri Imbert (eds), *La Convention Européenne des Droits de l'Homme* (Paris, Economica, 1999) 125
Van Dijk, Pieter, Van Hoof, Fried, Van Rijn, Arjen and Zwaak, Leo, *Theory and Practice of the European Convention on Human Rights*, 5th edn (Antwerp, Intersentia, 2018)
Van Hoecke, Mark, *Law as Communication* (Oxford, Hart, 2002)
Van Kley, Dale (ed), *The French Idea of Freedom: The Old Regime and the Declaration of Rights of 1789* (Stanford, Stanford University Press, 1994)
—— 'Introduction' in Dale Van Kley (ed), *The French Idea of Freedom: The Old Regime and the Declaration of Rights of 1789* (Stanford, Stanford University Press, 1994) 6
Vegleris, Phédon Th, 'Valeur et Signification de la Clause "Dans une Société Démocratique" dans la Convention Européenne des Droits de l'Homme' (1968) 1.2 *Les Droits de l'Homme: Revue de Droit International et Comparé* 219
Veitch, Scott, *Law and Irresponsibility: On the Legitimation of Human Suffering* (Oxford, Routledge-Cavendish, 2007)
Voeten, Erik, 'Domestic Implementation of Human Rights Judgments in Europe: Legal Infrastructure and Government Effectiveness Matter: A Reply to Dia Anagnostou and Alina Mungiu-Pippidi' (2014) 25.1 *European Journal of International Law* 229
Vogel, Howard J, 'In the Cause of Justice: Reflections on Robert Cover's Turn Toward Narrative' (1989) 7 *Journal of Law & Religion* 173
Voland, Thomas and Schiebel, Britta, 'Advisory Opinions of the European Court of Human Rights: Unbalancing the System of Human Rights Protection in Europe?' (2017) 17 *Human Rights Law Review* 73
Waddington, PAJ, '"Overkill" or "Minimum Force"?' [1990] *Criminal Law Review* 695
—— *Policing Citizens: Authority and Rights* (London, UCL Press, 1999)
—— 'Public Order Policing: Citizenship and Moral Ambiguity' in Frank Leishman, Barry Loveday and Stephen P Savage (eds), *Core Issues in Policing* (London, Longman 1996) 114
Waldron, Jeremy, 'Security and Liberty: The Image of Balance' (2003) 11.2 *The Journal of Political Philosophy* 191
Warren, Mark E, 'Accountability and Democracy' in Mark Bovens, Robert E Goodin, and Thomas Schillemans (eds), *The Oxford Handbook of Public Accountability* (Oxford, Oxford University Press, 2014) 39
Wasserman, David, 'Justifying Self-Defense' (1987) 16.4 *Philosophy and Public Affairs* 356
Weber, Max, 'Politics as a Vocation' in HH Gerth and C Wright Mills (eds), *From Max Weber: Essays in Sociology* (London, Routledge, 1991) 77
Weil, Simone (Mary McArthy, trans), 'The Iliad, or the Poem of Force' (1965) 18.2 *Chicago Review* 5
Weisberg, Richard H, *Poethics* (New York, Columbia University Press, 1992)
West, Robin, 'Jurisprudence as Narrative: An Aesthetic Analysis of Modern Legal Theory' (1985) 60 *New York University Law Review* 145
White, Hayden, *The Content of the Form: Narrative Discourse and Historical Representation* (Baltimore, The Johns Hopkins University Press, 1987)
—— (Robert Doran, ed), *The Fiction of Narrative: Essays on History, Literature, and Theory 1957–2007* (Baltimore, The Johns Hopkins University Press, 2010)

White, James Boyd, *Heracles' Bow: Essays on the Rhetoric and Poetics of Law* (Madison, Wis., University of Wisconsin Press, 1985)
White, Morton, *The Philosophy of the American Revolution* (New York, Oxford University Press, 1978)
Wicks, Elizabeth, 'The United Kingdom Government's Perceptions of the European Convention on Human Rights at the Time of Entry' (2000) *Public Law* 438
—— *The Right to Life and Conflicting Interests* (Oxford, Oxford University Press, 2010)
Wildhaber, Luzius, 'Criticism and Case-Overload: Comments on the Future of the European Court of Human Rights' in Spyridon Flogaitis, Tom Zwart and Julie Fraser (eds), *The European Court of Human Rights and its Discontents: Turning Criticism into Strength* (Cheltenham, Edward Elgar, 2013) 9
Williams, AT, 'Human Rights and Law: Between Sufferance and Insufferability' (2007) 123.1 *Law Quarterly Review* 133
Xenos, Dimitris, *The Positive Obligations of the State under the European Convention of Human Rights* (Abingdon, Routledge, 2012)
Yorke, Jon, (ed), *The Right to Life and the Value of Life: Orientations in Law, Politics and Ethics* (Farnham, Ashgate, 2010)
—— 'Introduction: The Right to Life and the Value of Life: Orientations in Law, Politics and Ethics' in Jon Yorke (ed), *The Right to Life and the Value of Life: Orientations in Law, Politics and Ethics* (Farnham, Ashgate, 2010) 1
Zedner, Lucia, 'In Pursuit of the Vernacular: Comparing Law and Order Discourse in Britain and Germany' (1995) 4 *Social and Legal Studies* 517
Zidaru, Lorena, 'Încălcarea art. 2 din Convenţia Europeană a Drepturilor Omului prin utilizarea în mod nejustificat a armelor de foc' (2012) 2 *Revista Forumul Judecătorilor* 163
Zielonka, Sarabeth M, 'The Universality of the Right to Life: Article 2 and the Margin of Appreciation in the Jurisprudence of the European Court of Human Rights' (2014) 47 *NYU Journal of International Law and Politics* 245
Zwaak, Leo, 'Council of Europe' case comment section, (2001) 19.3 *Netherlands Quarterly of Human Rights* 317
Zysset, Alain, 'Searching for the Legitimacy of the European Court of Human Rights: The Neglected Role of 'Democratic Society'' (2016) 5.1 *Global Constitutionalism* 16
—— *The ECHR and Human Rights Theory: Reconciling the Moral and the Political Conceptions* (London, Routledge, 2017)

INDEX